Also available at all good book stores

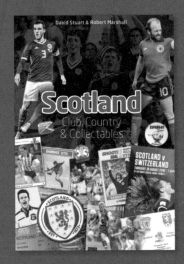

9781785315459

9781785313318

Scottish Football

Pitch Publishing Ltd
A2 Yeoman Gate
Yeoman Way
Durrington
BN13 3QZ

Email: info@pitchpublishing.co.uk
Web: www.pitchpublishing.co.uk

First published by Pitch Publishing 2021
Text © 2021 Robert Marshall and David Stuart

1

A CIP catalogue record for this book is available from the British Library.

13-digit ISBN: 9781785318641
Design and typesetting by Olner Pro Sport Media. Visit www.olnerpsm.co.uk
Printed in India by Replika Press

Scottish Football

Souvenirs from the Golden Years

1946 to 1986

Robert Marshall & David Stuart

Foreword

Born in 1959 and 1963 respectively, Robert Marshall and David Stuart lived and spectated through much of the Golden Years of Scottish Football. They just didn't realise at the time that it was such a special era, and mistakenly thought it was the norm which would last forever – with perhaps a World Cup success for Scotland being thrown in at some stage.

Robert's first senior club game attended was Partick Thistle against Rangers in a league encounter in September 1969. His first cup final was the Celtic against Partick Thistle 1971 League Cup Final while his introduction to European football came about at Ibrox Stadium in October 1973 when Rangers played the Turkish side Ankaragücü in the first round of the European Cup Winners' Cup. Although Robert also visited Parkhead and Love Street to cheer on Celtic and St Mirren in Europe, he very much regrets never making the relatively short journey from Glasgow to Dundee to savour any of United's 1970s and 1980s European exploits.

David's first cup final was also that same 1971 event while his senior club debut took place on 12 August 1970 – a League Cup tie between Partick Thistle and Queen of the South which the Jags won 4-1. David's first foray into Europe was under the Firhill floodlights in September 1972 when Partick Thistle entertained Honvéd of Hungary in the first round of the UEFA Cup. David's big regret from the Golden Years is not keeping all of his football cards voraciously collected in the first half of the 70s.

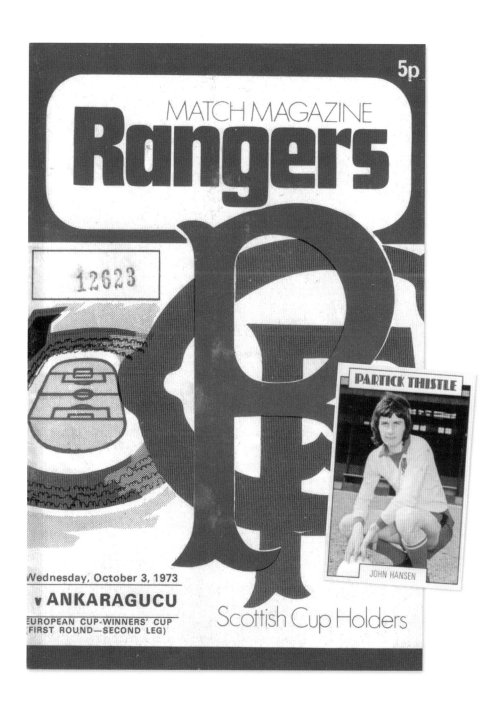

Indeed, with football comes football collectibles and these treasures not only enhanced our childhood, they steered us through the minefield and helped get us over the pain that was adolescence. Eventually we would discover girls, but the likes of football trading cards, programmes, comics, magazines and annuals were our first loves. The simple truth is these ever-faithful memorabilia never stood us up or broke our hearts, they were always there for us and that's why we *still* love them.

The men in the white coats don't frighten us so why not join us on a journey through four decades when Scottish club football was arguably at its most egalitarian (relatively speaking) and entertaining best. It wasn't a painless part of our sporting history, however; indeed for a variety of reasons there were also many dark days that should not be forgotten. But this book seeks to celebrate the good times, be they unlikely cup final victories or notable scalps and achievements in European football, as well as to cherish all the associated collectibles that go with them. We hope you enjoy it.

Robert and David

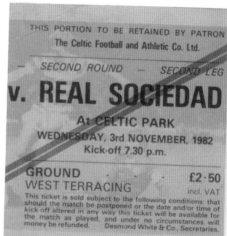

Sports Citizen

No. 33,508   SATURDAY, OCTOBER 23, 1971   PRICE 3p

FOOTBALL FINAL

Anglo star ready for Scots recall — Page 2

SIZZLING THISTLE ROAST THE CELTS

UR-GOAL
ORY DAY
R FIRHILL

ARYHILL'S a great place e in today! years of being unpredictable. Thistle came stingly good today cy hammered the

It's the goal—number 4—that sends Thistle fans into raptures of joy at Hampden this afternoon, when, from a Lawrie free kick, Bone slams the ball home in 36 minutes against Celtic.

RESULTS

SCOTTISH LEAGUE CUP
Final
CELTIC 1   PARTICK TH. 4

SCOTTISH LEAGUES

Division I	Division II
Airdrie ... 1 East Fife .. 1	Brechin ... 2 Albion R
Clyde ... 0 Dundee U. 3	Clydebank 1 Cowdenl
	E. Stirling 1 Dumbart

Dedication

This book is dedicated to those who introduced
us to Scottish football, and to those who follow
it for the pure love of the game.

Contents

Introduction

Between 1890/91 and 1903/04, the first 14 seasons of league football in Scotland produced six different champions: Dumbarton, Rangers, Celtic, Hearts, Hibernian and Third Lanark, in that order.

There then followed the first great period of duopoly when for 27 consecutive seasons only either Celtic or Rangers won the league flag before Motherwell triumphed in 1931/32. The Old Firm dominance then resumed before the axis powers said enough is enough and the Second World War brought a seven-season suspension of official tournament football (1939/40 to 1945/46 inclusive).

Fast-forward to the present, and now we are in the second great period of duopoly with 2020/21 being the THIRTY-SIXTH consecutive season where again, only either Celtic or Rangers have been crowned champions of Scotland!

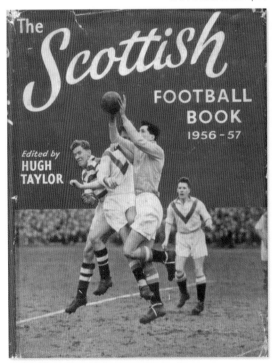

So let's hark back to the Golden Years of Scottish football; ie the 40 post-Second World War seasons from 1946/47 to 1985/86 inclusive when no fewer than eight teams were crowned champions of Scotland: Aberdeen, Celtic, Dundee, Dundee United, Hearts, Hibernian, Kilmarnock and Rangers.

During the Golden Years a total of nine clubs won the Scottish FA Cup while for the League Cup the tally was ten. Overall, 15 different clubs managed to pick up at least one of the three major trophies available.

With the introduction of the League Cup competition in 1946/47, a Treble was now up for grabs and this was first achieved by Rangers in 1948/49. The feat was repeated by Rangers in 1963/64, 1975/76 and 1977/78 and by Celtic in 1966/67 and 1968/69, so a total of six trebles were achieved during the Golden Years. Since 1986/87 seven trebles have been won (four by Celtic and three by Rangers) with the former completing a quadruple Treble across 2016/17, 2017/18, 2018/19 and 2019/20. Put another way, the Parkhead club won 12 consecutive major trophies – which is fantastic if you are a Celtic supporter but a tad boring for the rest of us. By comparison, England's Treble has been up for grabs since 1960/61 but it has only been achieved once – by Pep Guardiola's Manchester City in 2018/19.

No clubs other than Celtic and Rangers have won the Scottish Treble but the first non-Old Firm outcome (of sorts) was clinched in 1951/52 when Hibernian won the league, Motherwell lifted the Scottish Cup and Dundee collected the League Cup. This 'alternative treble' (or extremely rare, barren season for both Celtic and Rangers) occurred just once more – in 1954/55 when Aberdeen, Clyde and Hearts took the honours. Another rarity was the 1964/65 league championship when Rangers and Celtic finished fifth and eighth respectively. Perhaps symbolically, The Beatles released their *Help!* album on 6 August 1965.

Between 1981/82 and 1985/86 Aberdeen enjoyed no less than five consecutive seasons when they won at least one trophy. Hearts managed three in a row (1957/58–1959/60) while Dundee, Dundee United, Hibs and Motherwell all managed to achieve success in two consecutive seasons. No clubs outside of the Old Firm have won trophies in consecutive seasons since the aforementioned Aberdeen 1980s Golden Age.

The Golden Years also bore witness to all three of Scotland's European successes at club level (four if you include the European Super Cup) with Celtic bringing back the European Cup and Rangers and Aberdeen the European Cup Winners' Cup. During the first three decades of European club competitions, Scottish sides recorded a whole string of impressive results. Hibernian, Dundee and Dundee

United all came close to reaching Paris, Wembley and Rome for the finals of the European Cup but fell at the semi-final stage. Similarly, Dunfermline Athletic and Kilmarnock made it to the last four of the Cup Winners' Cup and Inter-Cities Fairs Cup respectively. St Mirren, meanwhile, lifted the Anglo-Scottish Cup.

At international level, Scotland arguably underperformed during the 1960s but either side of The Beatles, psychedelia and a moon landing, the national team appeared at the finals of six World Cups and returned home from one undefeated, but somehow without the trophy. By way of compensation, Scotland were crowned outright British champions on seven occasions in addition to sharing several titles.

The period 1946 to 1986 also represented Golden Years for football collectibles – paper rationing in the 1940s and 1950s notwithstanding, although sometimes less is more. Recent, big, bloated cup final programmes usually costing £5 or £6 and consisting of 84 A4-sized pages are a perfect reminder that it's quality not quantity that counts. Besides, these would-be 'bookazines' are also a bit of a bugger when it comes to storage. Much more collectable are the pragmatic, austerity issues of those 1940s and '50s – with pen pic wording such as 'his sagacity, artistry and artifice are virtues that delight the connoisseur' being used to describe Clyde's Archie Robertson in the 2.5p, 12-page 1958 Scottish Cup Final programme. Commercial awakening in the mid-1960s followed and the widespread use of full colour continued to evolve throughout the '70s and '80s. By the 1986 Scottish Cup Final the programme cover price was £1 and Hearts skipper Walter Kidd was described as 'uncelebrated and efficient rather than spectacular'.

Special mentions and praise are due for Clyde and Aberdeen, who over the years have seen their souvenir programmes regularly pick up awards from publications such as the well-respected *Programme Monthly* and *Football Collectable*. Quite often, the quality of the historical content of

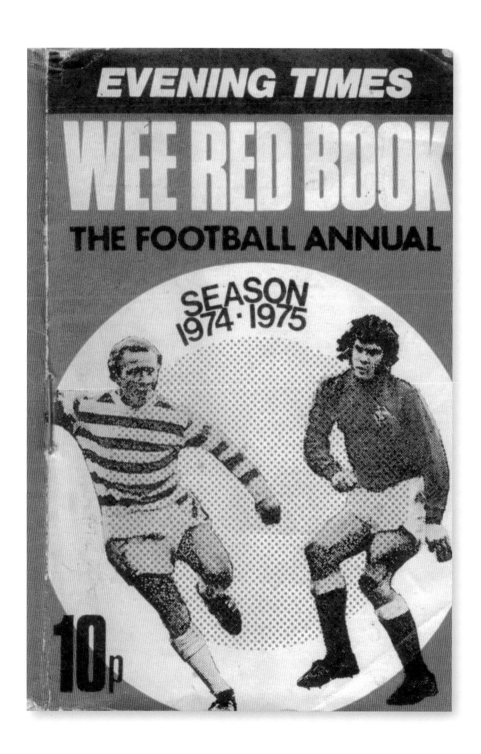

EVENING TIMES

WEE RED BOOK

THE FOOTBALL ANNUAL

SEASON 1974·1975

10p

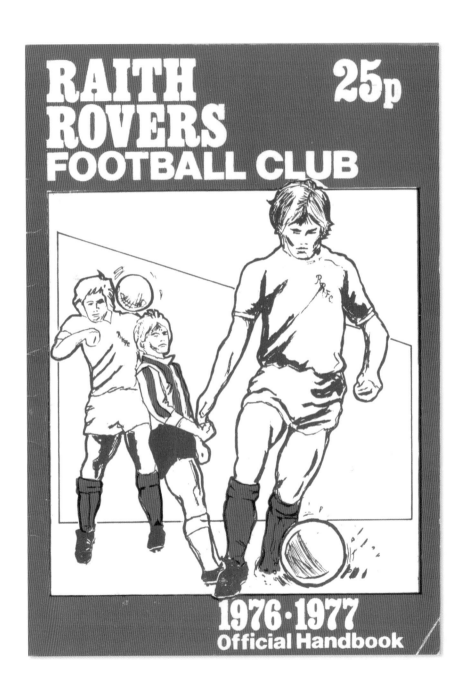

RAITH ROVERS FOOTBALL CLUB

25p

1976·1977
Official Handbook

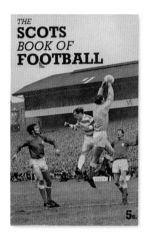

their matchday mags are pure Herodotus.

For trading cards, the possible heyday was the 1960s and '70s when AandBC ruled the roost (with Anglo Confectionery and Barratt's in strong support) until the arrival of FKS and Panini took the hobby to even higher levels, especially in the 1980s.

With regard to magazines, the early 70s would see a run of titles that follow on from each other with *Football Scot*, *Scottish Football Monthly* and finally *Scottish Football Weekly* – edited by a young Chick Young – all very colourful and giving in-depth insight into Scottish football from schoolboys, juniors and women's football to the professional game. The newspapers would do their bit too with many great items of memorabilia given away over the years as souvenir supplements.

For annuals, the season would often start with the *Glasgow Evening Times*'s *Wee Red Book* which was eagerly snapped up for those all-important fixtures lists. If you were really lucky, your team had a handbook produced at the start of the season too. However, it was Christmas and the *Scottish Book of Football* edited by Hugh Taylor that we all looked forward to unless you were hoping for *Playing for Rangers* or *Playing for Celtic* from Santa instead.

Let's not look back in anger, nor merely wallow in nostalgia, but instead let's pay heed to the words of wisdom of those sages of song, Kool and the Gang, when in 1980 they encouraged everyone to 'Celebrate good times, come on!'. And, by Jove (or John Hansen), they really were good times.

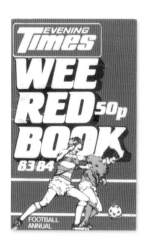

Part One

one

Major Scottish Competition Winners

Summary of the Golden Years

Season	League Champions	Scottish Cup Winners	League Cup Winners
1946/47	Rangers	Aberdeen	Rangers
1947/48	Hibernian	Rangers	East Fife
1948/49	Rangers	Rangers	Rangers
1949/50	Rangers	Rangers	East Fife
1950/51	Hibernian	Celtic	Motherwell
1951/52	Hibernian	Motherwell	Dundee
1952/53	Rangers	Rangers	Dundee
1953/54	Celtic	Celtic	East Fife
1954/55	Aberdeen	Clyde	Hearts
1955/56	Rangers	Hearts	Aberdeen
1956/57	Rangers	Falkirk	Celtic
1957/58	Hearts	Clyde	Celtic
1958/59	Rangers	St. Mirren	Hearts
1959/60	Hearts	Rangers	Hearts
1960/61	Rangers	Dunfermline Athletic	Rangers
1961/62	Dundee	Rangers	Rangers
1962/63	Rangers	Rangers	Hearts
1963/64	Rangers	Rangers	Rangers
1964/65	Kilmarnock	Celtic	Rangers
1965/66	Celtic	Rangers	Celtic
1966/67	Celtic	Celtic	Celtic
1967/68	Celtic	Dunfermline Athletic	Celtic
1968/69	Celtic	Celtic	Celtic
1969/70	Celtic	Aberdeen	Celtic
1970/71	Celtic	Celtic	Rangers
1971/72	Celtic	Celtic	Partick Thistle
1972/73	Celtic	Rangers	Hibernian
1973/74	Celtic	Celtic	Dundee
1974/75	Rangers	Celtic	Celtic
1975/76	Rangers	Rangers	Rangers
1976/77	Celtic	Celtic	Aberdeen
1977/78	Rangers	Rangers	Rangers
1978/79	Celtic	Rangers	Rangers
1979/80	Aberdeen	Celtic	Dundee United
1980/81	Celtic	Rangers	Dundee United
1981/82	Celtic	Aberdeen	Rangers
1982/83	Dundee United	Aberdeen	Celtic
1983/84	Aberdeen	Aberdeen	Rangers
1984/85	Aberdeen	Celtic	Rangers
1985/86	Celtic	Aberdeen	Aberdeen

[League Championships, Scottish FA Cup and Scottish League Cup]

Summary of Trophy Wins

Club	League	Scottish Cup	League Cup	Total
1 Rangers	13	14	13	40
2 Celtic	15	12	9	36
3 Aberdeen	4	6	3	13
4 Hearts	2	1	4	7
5 Hibernian	3	-	1	4
6 Dundee	1	-	3	4
7 Dundee United	1	-	2	3
8 East Fife	-	-	3	3
9 Clyde	-	2	-	2
10 Dunfermline Athletic	-	2	-	2
11 Motherwell	-	1	1	2
12 Kilmarnock	1	-	-	1
13 Falkirk	-	1	-	1
14 St.Mirren	-	1	-	1
15 Partick Thistle	-	-	1	1
Totals	**40**	**40**	**40**	**120**

1946/47 ▸ 1949/50

The 1939/40 Scottish season had ended after only five games with Rangers at the top of a two-tier league system, but it would re-emerge after the Second World War as a three-tier framework no longer with Divisions One and Two but Divisions A, B and C.

During the war there had not been a lot of *esprit de corps* among the clubs. Initially there was a regionalised set up but Hearts, Hibs and Aberdeen were not overjoyed at that, with no matches against the Old Firm and the money they generated. Kilmarnock were out on a limb with Rugby Park being requisitioned as a fuel dump, plus Dundee and St Johnstone would not commit to much football if any during this period either.

When the dust settled, two names were gone from the pantheon of Scottish football. Edinburgh side St Bernard's had been in at the start of football north of the border and in 1895 they lifted the Scottish Cup. However, Hearts and Hibernian were the dominant forces in the capital and the Auld Reekie Saints always struggled to get crowds. The war years would see them mothballed by 1942 and due to spiralling debts, they were lost to Scottish football.

Stirling-based King's Park FC also became defunct. Only two bombs fell on the town of Stirling during the war and one of them destroyed the stand of the club's Forthbank Stadium. Due to the hostilities and ongoing financial issues the club would fold before the end of the war. However, one of their directors, Tom Fergusson, along with others, established Stirling Albion within the town.

As the leagues resumed, Rangers were still under the rule of the legendary Bill Struth, who remained in charge until 1954, and during this period they would capture four league titles, three Scottish Cups and two League Cups. That success was built on a rock-solid defence generally known as the 'Iron Curtain'. The typical line-up of this collective was goalkeeper Bobby Brown, full-backs George Young and Jock Shaw, centre-half Willie Woodburn and wing-backs Ian McColl and Sammy Cox among others.

Shaw (Rangers)

Rangers' main rivals at this point would be the more flamboyant Hibernian side, initially under the guidance of Willie McCartney who sadly died before the fruits of his labour brought major honours to the club. His successor was team trainer Hugh Shaw who had worked alongside McCartney since 1936. Shaw would oversee Hibs winning three championships and it was under Shaw that the 'Famous Five' would first play all together, on 21 April 1949. The five consisted of Eddie Turnbull, Lawrie Reilly, Willie Ormond, Bobby Johnstone and arguably one of the all-time greats of Scottish football, Gordon Smith. Not only would Gordon win championships with Hibernian but there was also one each with Hearts and Dundee.

Season by Season: the Winners and Losers

1946/47
Rangers topped the league in the first season back with 46 points out of 60 in the 16-team Division A. Hibernian lost out by two points, and Rangers' victory over Hamilton in April would see them as champions. The top goalscorer was Bobby Mitchell of Third Lanark with 22 goals, while his team only achieved 11th place. Bobby moved to Newcastle United in 1949 and won three FA Cups with the club (scoring in the 1955 final) as well as two Scotland caps.

Kilmarnock and Hamilton Academical were relegated to Division B with champions Dundee and Airdrieonians promoted from the 14-team second tier. Division C had only ten sides including the reserves of Dundee, St Johnstone and Dundee United. Newly formed Stirling Albion were crowned champions but with Dundee 'A' as runners-up it was Leith Athletic who were to be promoted.

The Scottish League Cup was introduced that season due to the popularity of the wartime Southern League Cup. It is seen as the least venerated of the major Scottish trophies but in many ways, it was harder to win than the Scottish Cup. It would, of course, all depend on the make-up of your initial League Cup section as each comprised teams from your own division. Generally, each group was made up of four teams playing each other home and away. Rangers won their section by taking all 12 points from St Mirren, Morton and Queen's Park. Hibernian topped their group, which also included Celtic. The semi-finals saw Aberdeen triumph over Hearts 6-2 and Rangers beat Hibernian 3-1 in front of a crowd of over 123,000 at Hampden. In April 1947 'only' 82,700 watched the final, as Rangers ran out comfortable winners 4-0 thanks to a Jimmy Duncanson brace and a goal each from Torry Gillick and Billy Williamson.

Two weeks later and Aberdeen returned to Hampden and victory in the Scottish Cup Final. The semi-finals would see Hibernian beat Motherwell in a marathon of a game that would last two hours and 22 minutes with Hugh Howie hitting the winner in the 141st minute. Aberdeen also had beaten Dundee 2-1 in the quarter-finals with a goal scored in the 130th minute. Arbroath from Division B were the Dons' surprise opponents in the other semi-final having dispatched Hearts at the last-eight stage. Aberdeen won 2-0 at Dens Park, Dundee, in front of 22,000 spectators. As great as the Hibernian side of this era was, Hampden glory would evade them in both cup tournaments with Aberdeen winning the final 2-0 in front of 82,140. Goalscorers for the Dons were George Hamilton and South Africa-born Stan Williams.

1947/48

Hibernian won the championship with 48 points from 60, with Rangers two points behind them. Rangers lost their final league match of the season at home to Hearts, but Hibernian's superior goal count meant that even had Rangers won that day they would still have finished runners-up.

Top scorer was Falkirk's Archie Aikman with 20 goals as his side finished seventh. Archie moved to Manchester City in 1949 but was involved in a car crash in pre-season and never made an appearance for the Maine Road side. He went on to play for Stenhousemuir, Falkirk briefly once more, and Dundee United.

G. HAMILTON SCOTLAND

Autograph
ARCHIE AIKMAN
(Falkirk F.C.)

Airdrie only lasted a season in Division A and dropped down alongside Queen's Park. Celtic were among relegation candidates at one point but a final-day hat-trick from Jock Weir against Dundee saw them safe and by the season's end they were four points clear of relegation.

Promoted that year as champions of Division B were East Fife who netted 103 goals in 30 games – no relegation the previous season had bolstered the division to 16 teams. Albion Rovers, with Jock Stein in their side, were also promoted. Leith Athletic were relegated to Division C, which was won by East Stirlingshire, with four more reserve sides added.

The League Cup was a more compact tournament this time with the group games in the main opening the season and the final coming in October. The first section saw Rangers and Celtic joined by Hearts and Hibs in the one group. The semi-finals saw Aberdeen play East Fife and Rangers face Falkirk, and perhaps surprisingly Falkirk and East Fife would both prevail, each winning their games 1-0. The final saw 53,785 turn up to witness a 0-0 draw. A week later only 31,000 were there to see East Fife demolish Falkirk 4-1 in the replay. Davie Duncan scored a hat-trick and was to win three Scotland caps at the end of that season, scoring in a 2-0 victory over Belgium. Aikman netted for Falkirk, as he had done in the semi against Rangers.

The Scottish Cup that year saw some big scores early on as Arbroath beat Babcock and Wilcox 9-1 and St Mirren thrashed Shawfield Amateurs 8-0 in the first round, while Queen's Park inflicted an 8-2 crushing over Highland outfit Deveronvale in the next. A post-war record crowd of 142,070 attended the Rangers v Hibernian semi-final at Hampden that year. Rangers grabbed victory through a Willie Thornton goal as Hibs' Hampden hoodoo continued. This was the only match that season in which Hibs failed to score. Ironically, over at Ibrox, former Hibernian player Eddie Murphy netted an extra-time winner for Morton against Celtic in the other semi. The crowd at Ibrox was a mere 80,000, meaning

Autograph.........
JOHN STEIN   *(Albion Rovers F.C.)*
7

that a staggering 212,070 watched football in Glasgow that day. The final itself also went to extra time and a replay, with the first match ending 1-1 in front of a crowd of 129,176. A few days later, over 4,500 more fans flocked to Hampden to see Rangers defeat Morton 1-0 through a Billy Williamson goal.

1948/49

Rangers captain Jock Shaw would be the first player to lift the Scottish Treble of league and both cups. His brother Davie had been the captain of the Hibs side that won the title in 1947/48. Hibernian had a comparatively poor season and finished third, seven points behind Rangers. However, Rangers were not to get it all their own way and the championship was lost by Dundee and won by the Gers on the final day of the season. With one match remaining Dundee were a point ahead and victory over Falkirk at Brockville would see them become champions, but it was not to be. Dundee's Alex Stott was the season's top goalscorer with 30 and in a nervy first half Dundee were awarded a penalty, which keeper Nicol saved from Stott. After half-time, Falkirk quickly went 2-0 up and although Stott was to grab one back, Falkirk eventually ran out 4-1 winners. Rangers, meanwhile, travelled to Cliftonhill, the home of Albion Rovers. The Wee Rovers were to concede 105 goals that season including four that day as they went down 4-1. Stott only ever played 23 league games for Dundee, netting 30 goals as he moved to Partick Thistle the following season.

Having conceded those 105 goals, Rovers were relegated. Morton, with the great Jimmy Cowan between the sticks, also went down but with a goal difference of minus 12. The Ton conceded 51 times overall, which was one fewer than third-placed Hibernian. Cowan played at Wembley that year as the Scots defeated England 3-1.

Raith Rovers won Division B on goal average from Stirling Albion with East Stirlingshire dropping down again. Forfar Athletic were to win Division C, which now had second teams from Airdrie and Queen's Park, among others.

BILLY CAMPBELL

The League Cup threw up a section with Rangers, Hibernian, Celtic and Clyde with Rangers winning by one point over Hibernian. The semi-finals saw Raith Rovers beat Hamilton Accies 2-0 at Celtic Park and Rangers crush Dundee 4-1. The final itself was played in March. A crowd of only 57,450 turned up to see Rangers win 2-0 over Raith. Gillick and Willie Paton netted the goals.

Rangers romped through their passage to Scottish Cup glory and indeed the treble. In the league they lost 2-1 away to Third Lanark in mid-January but did not suffer another defeat that season and drew only twice thereafter. The Scottish Cup run started with a 6-1 home victory over Elgin City, followed by a 3-0 away win at Motherwell. They then beat Partick Thistle 4-0 in the quarter-finals and swept past East Fife 3-0 in the semi-final in front of a crowd of 104,958. The other semi saw Clyde win 2-1 over luckless Dundee after a replay. The final itself saw Rangers continue their imperious form and win 4-1 with two penalties from George Young and one each from Williamson and Jimmy Duncanson with Peter Galletly netting for Clyde.

1949/50

Once again, it was between Rangers and Hibernian for the championship and it came down to the final games. On 29 April 1950 Hibernian travelled to Ibrox knowing a win would give them the title. However, in front of a post-war league record crowd of 101,000 Rangers' Iron Curtain defence stood firm and the match ended in a goalless draw. A couple of days later Rangers travelled a few miles across the city to Cathkin Park, the home of Third Lanark. Rangers were 2-0 up after 20 minutes but a sturdy Hi Hi side brought it back to 2-1 and just before half-time, a penalty was awarded to the home side. Henderson missed it but shortly after half-time an equaliser was scored. Despite the efforts of Thirds the Rangers defence stood resolute and once more the championship headed back to Ibrox.

Hearts finished third in the league and began to challenge the Rangers/Hibernian dominance,

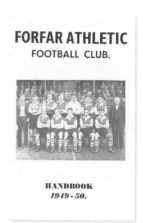

Morris (East Fife)

but their efforts would not come to full fruition until the latter half of the 1950s. Hearts legend Tommy Walker returned to the club in 1948 from Chelsea, initially in a player-assistant manager role, but with the death of manager Davie McLean in February 1951 he took over. He went on to become Hearts' most successful manager by winning two championships, one Scottish Cup and four League Cups. Ironically, as a player, Walker never won any major honours with the Edinburgh club. The spearhead of his Hearts side were known as the 'Terrible Trio': Willie Bauld, Jimmy Wardhaugh and Alfie Conn, who scored over 500 league goals for the club between them. Bauld was to top the scoring charts for 1949/50 with 30, but he won a mere three caps for Scotland, netting twice.

Stirling Albion dropped straight back down after one season in Division A alongside Queen of the South. Morton were champions of Division B, three points clear of Airdrieonians. There was to be no relegation as Division C had changed in format and was now split into two leagues made up of mainly reserve sides. Edinburgh City would quit the league and switch to the juniors but folded by 1955. The name lives on with the current club, which has been part of the SPFL since 2016.

The League Cup once again paired Rangers and Celtic in the same section along with Aberdeen and St Mirren. Cowdenbeath nearly pulled off a major shock, leaving Ibrox with a 3-2 win in the first leg of their quarter-final, but they lost 3-1 to Rangers in the return match.

The semi-finals saw Hibernian play Dunfermline of Division B and Rangers meet East Fife. Surprisingly, the teams from Fife were to gain a place in the final with both winning 2-1. East Fife ran out 3-0 winners in the final in front of a smallish crowd of 39,744 at Hampden with goals from Davie Duncan, Charlie 'Cannonball' Fleming and Henry Morris, all coming in the first 20 minutes.

GREAT GOALKEEPERS

Niven (East Fife)   Cowan (Morton)

Brown (Rangers)   Henderson (Queen of the South)

MORE WINGERS

Andrews (Dundee)   Collins (Celtic)

Ormond (Hibs)   Gunn (Dundee)

Rangers retained the Scottish Cup but not without a couple of replays on their way to the final. In the quarter-finals Raith Rovers held them to a 1-1 draw at Stark's Park before losing 2-0 at Ibrox. In the semi-finals it was Division B-bound Queen of the South who were to hold Rangers to another 1-1 draw before succumbing to a 3-0 loss in the replay. The other semi saw East Fife beat Partick Thistle 2-1 at Ibrox. In the final a goal by Willie Findlay in the first minute put Rangers ahead and despite the Fifers creating several chances, two second-half goals by Willie Thornton saw Rangers win the cup for the third year in a row.

Findlay (Rangers)

1950/51 ▸ 1959/60

The 1950s started with Hibernian in dominance and ended with Hearts at the top. Rangers, though, won more championships than any other side in the era but both cups had several provincial clubs being triumphant. In reading through reports of finals and other big matches, two things become evident – first that Hampden may have had massive crowds of 100,000-plus but due to the West and East terraces being wide open spaces the wind whipped through the arena, not making for great football; secondly, like FA Cup finals of the 50s, many big games in the latter half of the decade seem to have players limping on the outside-left position unable to take any real active part in the action.

In this era, players expected to be clouted by an opponent and were expected to give it back. Sending-offs were still very rare. Willie Woodburn of Rangers, however, would be made an example of in the mid-50s and after a series of violent outbursts on the field he was given a life ban from football. Although it was to be rescinded three years later, Woodburn never returned to the sport.

1950/51

The preceding seasons had seen close finishes to the title race but this campaign saw Hibernian romp home a full ten points ahead of Rangers. They finished in style by defeating Rangers 4-1 and Celtic 3-0, both at Easter Road. Hibs' Lawrie Reilly topped the scoring charts with 22 goals, and went on to lead the way for three consecutive seasons.

It was Clyde's and Falkirk's turn for the drop from Division A to B. Unusually both teams that dropped down the season before bounced straight back up with Queen of the South being declared champions and Stirling Albion runners-up, on goal average. Queens had a goal average of 1.97 and Stirling of 1.77. If the modern system of goal difference was used then both teams would have had a difference of plus 39. Nowadays, Albion would emerge as champions with the greater goals scored; 78 against Queens 69.

SCOTTISH STARS

   The League Cup sections saw Rangers bow out
in the first round as Aberdeen won a group that also
contained Clyde and Morton. In the quarter-finals
the Dons were paired with Hibernian. Aberdeen won
the first leg 4-1 at Pittodrie but surprisingly lost by
the same score at Easter Road in the return. The first
replay was scheduled for a 4.40pm kick-off at Ibrox
Park on 2 October as with no floodlights a later start
was not an option. Both teams had played each
other 48 hours beforehand in a league match at
Pittodrie, which the Dons won 2-0, but the Monday
evening replay still did not yield up a winner as
they drew 1-1 after extra time. At Hampden a day
later, with the same kick-off time, Aberdeen finally
flagged and Hibernian emerged 5-1 winners in front
of a respectable crowd of 30,000.
   Four days later and Queen of the South of
Division B were the Edinburgh club's semi-final

opponents with Hibernian winning 3-1 at Tynecastle thanks to an Eddie Turnbull hat-trick. Motherwell, who had beaten Celtic 4-1 at Celtic Park in the quarter-finals, also faced a team from the second tier in Ayr United. Ayr were 3-2 ahead with seven minutes remaining but a late surge from Motherwell saw them run out 4-3 winners.

As to the final, a sturdy performance from the Motherwell defence in the first half would lead the way to their forwards Kelly, Forrest and Watters producing three goals in the final 16 minutes to grab the cup. Hibernian had an off day and left despondent after another poor outing at Hampden.

The surprise winners of the Scottish Cup were Celtic who had yet to make any real impact after the war. The 1950/51 league season had seen the Bhoys play 30 games, winning 12, drawing five and losing 13. They scored 48 goals and conceded 46 to finish seventh. Celtic had started the calendar year of 1951 with five straight league defeats. In the cup they had travelled to Bayview, home of East Fife, for their opening tie and had gained a 2-2 draw. They won the replay at Celtic Park 4-2. This was followed up by a 4-0 home win against Borders team Duns. Celtic were only one of four teams drawn to play in the third round with another six given byes to the quarter-finals due to the unevenness of numbers. The Celts duly dispatched Hearts at Tynecastle 2-1 and went on to defeat Aberdeen 3-0 at home in the next round.

The semi-finals would see Celtic face Raith Rovers at Hampden in front of a crowd of 84,000 and Motherwell play Hibernian at Tynecastle with 46,000 in attendance. The ties ended in 3-2 victories for Celtic and Motherwell respectively with Rovers pushing Celtic all the way. Willie Penman equalised with nine minutes remaining, but Irishman Charlie Tully netted the winner shortly after.

If there was no Hampden hoodoo for Hibernian, the gods were not kind to them in this game in Edinburgh either. They conceded an early goal to Archie Kelly and shortly afterwards lost left-back John Ogilvie to a broken leg. Playing the rest of the match with only ten men, a Lawrie Reilly double was not enough as a second goal by Kelly and one by Don McLeod saw Motherwell head for Hampden for their second final that season.

The Scottish Cup Final took place on a windswept day in front of just under 132,000 fans. It was said to be a rather dour affair that was only lit up by the winning goal from Celtic's John McPhail which was described by the *Evening Times* as a 'dandy', giving Celtic their first Scottish Cup victory since 1937.

1951/52

Hibernian won the league again, this time with a four-point advantage over Rangers. East Fife came third and any revival of Celtic's fortunes following the previous season's Scottish cup success was severely dimmed as they finished ninth. Rangers always seemed to be playing catch-up to Hibernian

HIBERNIAN (Winners of Scottish League Division A)—Standing: Combe, Paterson, Govan, Younger, H. Shaw (Manager), Buchanan, Ogilvie Souness, Gallagher. Seated: Smith, Johnstone, Reilly, Turnbull, Ormond.

in not only points but games and a poor finish consisting of one loss and three draws did not help. Once again Lawrie Reilly topped the scoring charts, this time with 27 to his name. Hibernian's goals tally of 92 was 31 ahead of Rangers' total of 61.

Stirling Albion continued their seesaw existence by dropping down again. They finished on 15 points with a loss of 99 goals in 30 games. Defeats of 8-0 to Hibs, 6-0 to Aberdeen and 7-1 to Morton heavily contributed to that total. As for Morton, despite that win, they too were relegated.

Bouncing straight back up again were the previous season's relegated sides, Clyde and Falkirk. Clyde won the division by one point. The Bully Wee had lost 2-1 to Falkirk in their final match leaving the Bairns just three points behind with two games still to play and the title within their grasp. However, Falkirk came back to earth with a thud as Cowdenbeath hammered them 5-0 the following Saturday.

The League Cup was much more straightforward this season, with no replays. The semi-finals paired Rangers with Celtic and Motherwell with Dundee. At Hampden, Rangers swept Celtic aside 3-0 and over at Ibrox on the same day Dundee overpowered Motherwell 5-1 with the controversial Bobby Flavell providing a hat-trick. Flavell had joined Millonarios FC in the early 1950s. Colombian football existed outside of the exigencies of FIFA and had attracted several players from Europe and Argentina with the promise of good wages and high living. On his return to Scotland, he was banned from playing for six months before joining Dundee.

Rangers' Willie Findlay gave his side the lead in the 21st minute of the final, which they held to half-time, but Flavell scored shortly after the restart. The 69th minute saw Dundee take the lead through Johnny Pattillo and it looked as though they would hold on until a disputed equaliser from Willie Thornton in the 88th minute. However, the day would be Dundee's as almost from the kick-off they gained a free kick inside the Rangers half. The story goes that captain Alfie Boyd ran past Steel saying he was going to the right side of the area and to try and chip the ball to him. Steel coolly told him he would place it on his head. He did, and it was 3-2 to Dundee.

Scottish Cup holders Celtic fell by the wayside, quickly losing out to Third Lanark after a replay in the first round. Likewise, Hibernian fell at the first hurdle, losing out 4-0 in a replay to Raith Rovers after two 0-0 games. The second round saw Rangers defeat Elgin City 6-0 at Ibrox and high-scoring Dundee thump Wigtown & Bladnoch 7-1 away from home. The quarter-finals saw Dundee beat Aberdeen 4-0 at home and Motherwell beat Rangers following a replay. Hearts had also progressed after a replay with Airdrie. The first tie saw them split four goals evenly and then the replay produced ten with six for the Edinburgh side.

Dundee dispatched Third Lanark 2-0 in the semi-final at Easter Road but over at Hampden, Hearts and Motherwell could not be separated in front of a crowd of 98,547. The replay produced a similar 1-1 score, but the second replay would see Motherwell run out 3-1 winners. An incredible aggregate crowd of just under 240,000 watched these matches.

Motherwell had been to the Scottish Cup Final on four previous occasions and lost each one. Manager George Stevenson had played in the three in the 1930s and was in charge for the 1951 final. The 1952 event took place in front of 136,274 which meant Motherwell's Scottish Cup run had been played in front of an amassed attendance of over 500,000. Having lost 5-1 to Dundee in the League Cup semi a few months before, Motherwell showed that one good thumping deserves another and ran out 4-0 winners. The scoreline flattered the Fir Park men and in captain Willie Kilmarnock they had the man of the match, as the defender cleared the ball off the line three times to keep the Dundee forwards at bay.

1952/53

Hibernian were denied a third straight championship as Rangers clinched a draw with 15 minutes to spare down at Palmerston, home of Queen of the South, in their final match. A moment of individual

magic from Willie Waddell would see Hibernian consigned to second place, losing out to Rangers on goal average. Had goal difference been in play then Hibs would have won it by one goal. As usual Hibs' frontline would bang in the goals, totalling 93 this time with Lawrie Reilly netting 30 of those to be joint top scorer alongside East Fife's Charlie Fleming. However, their problems were in defence. Hibs conceded 51 goals in only 30 games and only twice achieved a victory with a clean sheet. They had two large wins in their final matches, beating Third Lanark 7-1 and then Raith Rovers 4-1, but that was not enough. Rangers hit 80 goals but more importantly only conceded 39, although that too is still more than one per game.

There were goals aplenty that season elsewhere in the league; fifth-placed Clyde hit 78 and shipped 78 goals, winning 13 games and losing 13, while drawing the other four. Bottom club Third Lanark scored a remarkable 52 goals. Surprisingly, joining them in the drop were the previous season's Scottish Cup winners, Motherwell. They ended the season on 26 points with Raith, Falkirk and Airdrie all a point ahead of them. Stirling Albion continued their seesaw existence by winning Division B, one point clear of Hamilton Academical.

The League Cup saw Rangers get thumped 5-0 by Hearts on the opening day of the season. It was an inauspicious start but the Ibrox club prevailed and won their section which also included Aberdeen and Motherwell. Ayr United inflicted an 11-1 mauling over Dumbarton which stands as a record win for Ayr and joint record defeat for Dumbarton. The quarter-finals saw Hibernian beat Morton 6-0 and then 6-3 over two legs but they faced a sterner test in the semi-finals in the shape of Dundee, with Kilmarnock and Rangers paired in the other tie.

Kilmarnock had perhaps been fortuitous in their route to the semi-final, facing only clubs from Division B like themselves, but they emerged as victors against Rangers by snatching victory in the 88th minute through Willie Jack. Dundee won against Hibernian at Tynecastle, where the Hibs forward line were said to have an off day except Reilly who scored. Flavell and Steel hit a goal each for the Dens Park side to go through to the final.

The final itself was dominated by Kilmarnock but without the finishing touch, often the undoing of the underdog. Dundee took the lead through Flavell with eight minutes remaining and he added a second when a clearing punch from goalkeeper Bobby Henderson travelled, with wind assistance, three quarters of the pitch for Flavell to nip in after the bounce and score. Dundee therefore became the first side to retain the League Cup.

The Scottish Cup began with 8-1 hammerings for Stenhousemuir from Hibernian and for Leith Athletic from Airdrieonians. East Fife also won 7-1 against Vale of Leithen. Holders Motherwell lost to Aberdeen in the third round, drawing with them 5-5 at Pittodrie and going down 6-1 in the rematch.

Aberdeen would have another three replays to come, however. The quarter-finals saw them paired with Hibernian and the first tie ended 1-1 at Easter Road, quickly followed by a 2-0 victory at home. The semi-final against Third Lanark with a lowly crowd of 18,468 at Ibrox ended all square. Relegation-bound Thirds took the lead in the replay after 30 minutes through Wattie Dick but a double from Harry Yorston saw Aberdeen through to the final.

In contrast, Rangers' route to the final had been more straightforward with wins at the first attempt against Arbroath, Dundee, Morton, Celtic and then Hearts. The crowd for the semi-final against Hearts had attracted almost 100,000 more fans than the other semi. Rangers went behind early on but won through goals from Derek Grierson and John Prentice.

Prentice also scored early in the final in front of a crowd of 129,761, but Harry Yorston equalised late on and once again the Dons headed for a replay. Rangers duly won it with Northern Ireland international Billy Simpson hitting the winner late in the first half.

1953/54

Surprisingly, Celtic emerged from the doldrums and secured both the championship and Scottish Cup, and many people have pointed to the winning of the Coronation Cup as the springboard for the successful season. However, they began their championship campaign with a defeat away to Hamilton, which with League Cup fixtures as well as Glasgow Cup matches was their 11th game and they had already lost five and drawn three. Hardly the form of champions.

On 6 February Celtic lost 3-2 at Tynecastle in dubious circumstances. Deep into injury time Hearts forward Jimmy Wardhaugh charged at George Hunter and the Celtic goalkeeper tried to throw the ball out; the linesman called for a goal as the ball was over the line. The *Glasgow Herald* speculated at this point that with a seven-point advantage Hearts could afford to slip up and still win the title. Hearts did falter, losing three of their

CELTIC (Scottish League Champions and Cup Winners)—Standing: A. Dowdells (Trainer), Haughney, Meechan, Bonnar, Evans, Peacock, J. McGrory (Manager). Seated: Higgins, Fernie, Stein, Fallon, Tully, Mochan.

last five games, but Celtic had three in hand and won their last nine in a row to overtake Hearts and finish top on 43 points, five clear of the Tynecastle outfit. A remarkable turnaround.

Wardhaugh emerged as top goalscorer, this time with 27 to his name. Partick Thistle were third on 35 points having won more games than Hearts but too many losses meant they were never really challengers. Lanarkshire teams Airdrieonians and Hamilton would drop down. Hamilton's victory in the opening fixture against Celtic was to be one of only four wins for them that season.

Motherwell would score 109 goals in winning Division B, although Kilmarnock with 38 fewer goals would only lose out by three points. Remarkably, on the last day of the season Motherwell drew 6-6 with bottom club Dumbarton. Dumbarton would be the first team relegated to Division C since season 1948/49 as a non-reserve team, Brechin City, finally won the third tier.

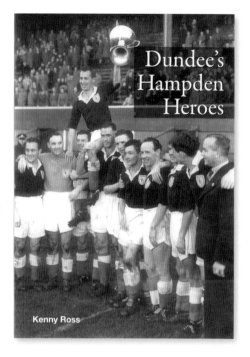

If the Scottish League Cup was like the Jules Rimet Trophy and was to be given for keeps to the first team to win it three times, it would be nestling in the trophy room of East Fife. Manager Scot Symon had led East Fife to the Second Division championship of 1948, the League Cup victories in 1948 and 1950 as well as to the Scottish Cup Final in 1950. By 1953 however, ex-Rangers goalkeeper Jerry Dawson was in charge at Methil. The Fifers won their cup section which contained both Aberdeen and Celtic and then defeated local rivals Dunfermline 9-4 on aggregate in the quarter-finals. Hibernian and Partick Thistle had also come through their last eight ties easily enough.

The semi-finals saw an all-Glasgow affair and the two east coast teams matched up. Partick Thistle, with a wind advantage in the first half, apparently developed a shoot-on-sight tactic and found themselves 2-0 up at half-time through

Wright and Howitt. Rangers failed to follow suit in the second half and Thistle headed for their first League Cup Final. Over at Tynecastle, East Fife had led in the first half but two rather suspect goals by Lawrie Reilly in the 70th and 72nd minutes saw Hibs in front. Reilly had allegedly barged into the opposition keeper for the first goal and had used a hand in the second, it was reported. However, successive blunders by defender Hugh Howie saw the award of two penalties to East Fife and the Methil side headed to their third League Cup Final.

In the final, played in front of a lowly crowd of 38,529, Thistle lost two poor goals early on to Gardiner and Fleming. Although they would fight back to 2-2 following strikes from Wright and McKenzie, a glorious winner from a Christie shot from outside the box, three minutes from time, saw the cup head back to Fife.

And so to the Scottish Cup. Previously, Leith Athletic had campaigned for a change to the Scottish Leagues asking that all non-reserve sides be promoted to Division B. This proposal had been rejected and at the start of the 1953/54 season they refused to play any more fixtures in Division C and so were expelled from the league. On 30 January 1954 they played Fraserburgh of the Highland League in the Scottish Cup with a scratch team. The 5-4 defeat was to be their final match, as they were wound up by 1955.

Celtic slogged their way to the final by winning away matches against teams from the bottom of Division A, beating Falkirk 2-1, Stirling Albion 4-3 and Hamilton 2-1 in the quarter-finals. The second round had seen some big scores involving teams from the Borders with Coldstream losing 11-0 to Raith Rovers, Duns 8-0 to Aberdeen and Tarff Rovers 9-1 to Partick Thistle, all at home. Peebles Rovers would lose a replayed game 7-2 in the Highlands to Buckie Thistle. Buckie would lose out 5-3 to Partick in the next round. Rangers found Third Lanark a harder nut to crack, drawing 0-0 at Cathkin Park before a 4-4 replay at Ibrox. However, a 3-2 victory at home saw them through to the quarter-finals.

The semi-finals saw Celtic play Motherwell of Division B and Aberdeen play Rangers. Aberdeen by this point had dispatched both Hibernian and Hearts in the previous rounds. A combined crowd of just over 200,000 saw Motherwell and Celtic draw 2-2 with the Well hitting the equaliser in the last minute in the first match and then Celtic winning 3-1 in the replay. Aberdeen forward Joe O'Neill had just recovered from a fractured skull to face Rangers at Hampden in front of a 110,939 crowd and would bag himself a hat-trick as the Dons routed their opponents 6-1.

Sadly, O'Neill missed the final but with both teams playing well at the time it was always going to be a tight match. A Fernie shot was deflected into goal by the unlucky Alec Young six minutes into the second half but Aberdeen would bounce back almost immediately as Paddy Buckley picked up on a loose clearance from Jock Stein to equalise. However, Jock's future right-hand man, Irishman Sean Fallon, netted the winner after some fine wing play by Willie Fernie. A glorious, if unexpected, double for Celtic who were skippered by Stein and managed by Jimmy McGrory.

1954/55
Although they had lost out on cup glory in 1954, Aberdeen more than made up for it by bagging the championship the following year. They won on 49 points, three ahead of challengers Celtic, who only lost three league games all season, but eight draws compared to Aberdeen's one was their downfall. A seismic change had taken place at Ibrox as long-serving manager Bill Struth had retired in 1954 and had been replaced with ex-player and former East Fife manager Scot Symon.

Rangers were third in the division, ending five points behind Celtic. Once again, Willie Bauld ended the season as top scorer with 21.

Stirling Albion avoided relegation but only by default. Their tally for the season saw them win two, draw two and lose 26 with 105 goals conceded. However, an expansion of the leagues would see no

relegation that year, with Division C being scrapped for 1955/56. All the non-reserve teams were promoted with Motherwell the other side to benefit from this.

Airdrie bounced back up as champions after only one season in Division B. Dunfermline Athletic were also promoted, returning to the top flight for the first time since 1936/37.

The League Cup again saw Celtic start their season poorly, winning only one game in their group with Hearts topping it. Holders East Fife narrowly qualified for the next round with a point to spare ahead of Aberdeen and Hibernian. The quarter-finals saw Motherwell knock out Rangers over two legs with the semi-finals pitting Motherwell against East Fife and Hearts against Airdrie.

ABERDEEN (Scottish League Champions)—Standing: Mitchell, Smith, Martin, Allister, Young, Glen. Seated: Leggatt, Hamilton, Buckley, O'Neil, Hather.

CLYDE (Scottish Cup Winners)—Standing: Murphy, Haddock, Hewkins, Granville, Anderson, Laing. Seated: Divers, Robertson, Hill, Brown, Ring

The small crowd of 18,883 that turned out at Hampden saw Motherwell beat the Fifers 2-1 in a match that was noted for both sides playing the offside trap. Christie put East Fife in front after three minutes but a goal direct from a free kick by Willie Kilmarnock shortly before half-time levelled things. Alex Bain hit the winner in the 63rd minute. The other tie at Easter Road saw Hearts win 4-1, although it was tighter than it seemed. Hearts lost a goal after ten seconds to Price. They then led 2-1 but just before half-time Hugh Baird missed a penalty for Airdrie and in the second half Hearts added two more to their advantage.

The final itself saw a crowd of 55,460 turn up. Hearts won 4-2 in a highly entertaining game with Willie Bauld hitting a hat-trick. Wardhaugh netted their other goal while Alex Bain and Willie Redpath replied for Motherwell. Jubilant Hearts fans invaded the pitch after the match to celebrate their first major trophy in 48 years.

The Scottish Cup was extended, and the senior sides gradually joined the tournament after the third round. Teams from Aberdeen, Edinburgh and Glasgow Universities all took part. Edinburgh lost 9-0 to Fraserburgh and Glasgow 5-1 to Huntly, while

Aberdeen fared a wee bit better, drawing 3-3 with Girvan Amateurs before succumbing to a 2-0 defeat in Girvan. Thus ended the University Challenge.

The fifth round saw holders Celtic join the fray and beat Alloa 4-2 away at Recreation Park. Aberdeen were given a bye to round six and disposed of Rangers after a replay. In the quarter-finals Airdrie beat Motherwell 4-1 and Celtic beat Hamilton 2-1, as they had at the same stage the previous season. Clyde thumped Falkirk 5-0 and Aberdeen defeated Hearts 2-0 after a replay.

Celtic were paired with Airdrie and Aberdeen with Clyde for the semi-finals. Both ties ended in 2-2 draws. Clyde v Aberdeen saw Buckley hit a brace for the Dons and Tommy Ring a double for Clyde, who saw a penalty missed by Archie Robertson. Clyde won the replay through a penalty taken, and scored this time, by Robertson. Celtic prevailed against Airdrie through two goals by John McPhail. Airdrie had a great season, reaching the semi-finals of both cups and winning Division B.

It was announced on the day of the match that the all-Glasgow affair would be the first Scottish Cup Final to be televised live. It didn't affect the crowd as 106,234 turned up to watch from the stands and terraces. Both the crowd at Hampden and the audience at home were served up poor fare, it seems. Jimmy Walsh gave Celtic the lead late in the first half but an Archie Robertson corner two minutes from the final whistle was misjudged by Celtic goalkeeper John Bonnar and ended up in the net to give Clyde the draw. The replay, which was not televised, took place four days later and saw Clyde take the cup home to Shawfield for only the second time in their history, with a 1-0 victory. Tommy Ring scored the winner just after half-time.

1955/56

The leagues were rebranded and expanded and were now known as Divisions One and Two. The expansion saw 18 teams in the top tier and a lopsided 19 in the lower competition, meaning a free Saturday for one team every week. Rangers

JIM WARDHAUGH
Hearts and Scotland

won their first title under Scot Symon with 52 points, six ahead of Aberdeen despite losing three of their last five matches. Hearts came third after scoring 99 goals with Jimmy Wardhaugh the division's top scorer on 28.

Stirling Albion were not so fortunate this year and dropped down to Division Two with 13 points. Scottish Cup holders Clyde were relegated too with 22 points. Berwick Rangers, Dumbarton, East Stirlingshire, Montrose and Stranraer had all been added to the Division Two roster that year. Montrose finished bottom with 11 points and conceded 133 goals. Queen's Park won the title with 54 points, returning to the top tier for the first time since 1947/48. High-scoring Ayr United were only three points behind, scoring 105 goals in the process to return to the top flight for the first time in 20 years.

The restructuring had thrown up one anomaly in that with five extra teams another new section was added to the League Cup – making nine in total, with two top-tier teams facing teams from the lower division and a supplementary round played too. Rangers had been grouped with Celtic and within four days of each other, Celtic beat them 4-1 at Ibrox but then lost 4-0 to their great rivals at Celtic Park. Rangers progressed through to the next round with a point to spare.

Holders Hearts met Aberdeen in the quarter-finals and lost 5-3 away and 4-2 at home. The Dons faced Rangers in the semi-final and St Mirren played Motherwell. Aberdeen went ahead early at Hampden through Graham Leggat and then went two up after Bobby Wishart netted just before half-time. Johnny Hubbard scored six minutes into the second half and only five minutes after this Leggat was stretchered off with a shoulder injury, leaving Aberdeen with only ten men for the remainder of the match. However, the Dons endured to reach another cup final. Motherwell and St Mirren drew 3-3 in an entertaining match at Ibrox that had gone to extra time and included a hat-trick from forward Tommy Gemmell of St Mirren. The replay saw the Saints win 2-0 with goals from Davie Laird and Jackie Brown.

The final was to be played in front of a crowd of 44,106 and neither side apparently played as well as they could. Just after half-time Leggat dived for a Hather cross and missed it but it then struck the unfortunate Jim Mallan and ended up in the St Mirren net. A fine header by Bobby Holmes in the 59th minute restored parity. In the 79th minute Graham Leggat attempted a shot from 35 yards which caught St Mirren goalkeeper Jim Lornie off his line and so the cup headed north to Aberdeen.

The Scottish Cup fourth round saw Peebles Rovers and Brechin City contest an epic tie. The first match ended 1-1, the replay 4-4, the next replay 0-0 and then finally came a resounding 6-2 victory for City. Rangers knocked Aberdeen out in the fifth round 2-1 at Ibrox but were crushed 4-0 by high-scoring Hearts in the quarter-finals.

Hearts and Raith Rovers drew a blank in the semi-final at Easter Road but in the replay, Jimmy Wardhaugh grabbed a double and Ian Crawford another as Hearts ran out 3-0 winners. The other semi was a replay of the previous year's final with Celtic facing Clyde and a crowd of 65,200 watched the Glasgow side win 2-1 with goals from Mike Haughney and Sharkey. Billy McPhail scored for Clyde.

Hearts were said to be deserved of their win in the final but Celtic had pushed them all away. Two goals from left-winger Ian Crawford put Hearts in the driving seat with the second coming just after half-time. Celtic pushed back and in the 55th minute Haughney seemingly pushed keeper Duff, who then dropped the ball for Haughney to score with no infringement seen by the referee. Such was football at the time. Hearts clung on however and a goal by Alfie Conn ten minutes from time gave them a memorable Scottish Cup win for the fifth time in their history.

1956/57

In January 1957 Rangers lost 1-0 to Ayr United at Somerset Park with the home side having gone down to ten men after 13 minutes. At this point the title looked beyond Rangers, who were sitting on 25 points from 18 games with Hearts top on 34 from 21. However, this was to be Rangers' last league defeat of the season and of their remaining 16 games they were to win 14 and draw just the two. Hearts only lost twice from this point, one of those defeats coming crucially against Rangers, and drew three times, including with Ayr the following week. Rangers won the title with 55 points to Hearts' 53, but unlike previous Ibrox sides they had a high goals scored tally of 96, with 48 conceded.

The league's top scorer was Hugh Baird who hit 31 goals for mid-table team Airdrie. Baird netted 111 goals in 134 league appearances playing at Broomfield from 1951 to '57. His 53 league goals total for 1954/55, when Airdrie were promoted, is a club record for one season. He went on to have spells at Leeds and Aberdeen.

Ayr were relegated in bottom place with 19 points. Dunfermline were also relegated on 24 points, finishing with ten defeats in their last 13 games. However, for Dunfermline it was the last minute of the season that was their undoing. Drawing 3-3 with Rangers and with Queen of the South drawing 0-0 with Celtic in Glasgow, they were safe due to a greater goal average, but Billy Simpson scored in the dying moments to doom them.

Clyde managed to retain their best players after relegation the previous season and won Division Two at a canter with 64 points, losing only the once and bagging 122 goals. Thirteen points behind them in second place were Third Lanark who hit 105 goals. The 1957/58 season was to be the last one with all six 'Glasgow' clubs in the top tier. At the bottom of the division, Forfar Athletic, Montrose, Berwick Rangers and East Stirling all conceded 100 or more goals each.

Whereas in previous seasons Celtic had started poorly in the League Cup, this year they took 11 points out of 12 in their section, which also included Rangers and holders Aberdeen. Partick Thistle emerged from their section with ten points in a group with both Hearts and Hibernian.

The semi-finals again matched Celtic with Clyde. Billy McPhail had joined the Parkhead club from Clyde in the same month his brother John had retired from football, so they never graced the Celtic side at the same time. Billy was to be the difference between the sides in the semi final as he netted a double as Celtic won 2-0. The other semi-final between Dundee and Partick Thistle took place at Ibrox and was said to be a dour match, ending 0-0. The replay was better with Thistle taking a 2-0 lead midway through the first half, only to lose two goals before half-time. However, a goal from a free kick by Jimmy Davidson in the second half gave the Jags victory.

And so it was that the 11th League Cup Final would be the first all-Glasgow affair and indeed Celtic's first final. 'Handicapped Thistle foil Thrustless

Presented by **SCOTTISH DAILY EXPRESS**

ST. JOHNSTONE F.C.   Season 1956-57

Celtic' was the headline in the *Glasgow Herald* as Thistle had two players hobbling about the pitch while Celtic failed to take advantage. For the final 30 minutes, Thistle retired George Smith from the match wholly but neither side was able to score. Celtic found their thrust in the replay but only after a scoreless first half. Three goals in six minutes early in the second half saw Celtic win the League Cup for the first time. Two goals came from Billy McPhail and the third by the 'wee barra' Bobby Collins.

In the first round of the Scottish Cup, Duns from the Borders travelled 50 miles to face Edinburgh University and deliver an 11-1 lesson. Arbroath hit ten against Rothes with two in reply, Montrose beat Borders side Chirnside United 9-1 and even Albion Rovers got among the goals with eight against Perth side Vale of Atholl. It was a bit calmer by round two but Fraserburgh did beat Gala Fairydean 9-0 and Arbroath added to their tally with a 6-1 victory over Brora Rangers. Forfar put a stop to Arbroath's advance in round three with a 3-1 home victory. Buckie Thistle thrashed Newton Stewart 9-2 in that round too. The fourth round saw a 5-5 draw between Nairn and Berwick Rangers with Rangers winning the replay 3-0. In the fifth round Rangers took revenge for the previous season's mauling by Hearts and won 4-0 at Tynecastle. Hibs lost 4-3 to Aberdeen at Easter Road. Rangers and Celtic were paired in the next round and played out a 4-4 draw at Celtic Park. The replay saw Celtic win 2-0 through at Ibrox.

The semi-finals saw Celtic drawn with Kilmarnock and Falkirk with Raith Rovers. Celtic needed a late equaliser at Hampden in front of a crowd of 109,145 to force a replay after a rather erratic tie due to the wind. In the replay, the wind factor came into the equation again, blowing in the opposite direction. Kilmarnock apparently adopted a defensive game and still managed to run out 3-1 winners with Celtic's goalkeeper Dick Beattie having a nightmare of a game. Falkirk emerged from the other tie, also after a replay. The first match ended 2-2 in an entertaining encounter at Tynecastle and then the Bairns won 2-0 in the rematch.

The final would be played in front of a crowd of 81,375 but a replay was needed to settle it. Again, the Hampden wind seemed to take over and as such neither team were able to take command of the match. John Prentice, the Falkirk captain, had scored in the 1952/53 final for Rangers and would do so again, hitting the opener from the spot. David Curlett of Kilmarnock netted just before half-time to end the scoring.

The *Glasgow Herald*'s report of the replay uses such great words as 'dilatoriness' and 'zephyr' – to describe the wind – and the apparent Scottish word 'breenge' to describe the tackling. The definition of breenge is to lunge violently. Enough said. Falkirk once again took the lead midway through the first half with George Merchant scoring. Kilmarnock replied with only 12 minutes to go through Curlett, but in extra time Doug Moran – one of only three players to score over 100 goals for Falkirk – scored the winner in the 101st minute.

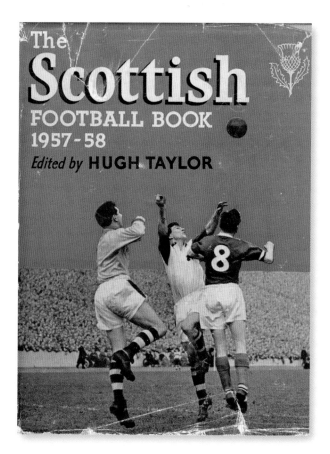

1957/58

Hearts romped home as champions, finishing a clear 13 points ahead of Rangers with 62 points. They scored an incredible 132 goals at an average of 3.88 per game. There were some high scores including a 9-0 win over East Fife, 8-0 against Queen's Park, 9-1 against Falkirk and 7-2 over Third Lanark. Incidentally, the only league match they would fail to score in was away to Thirds as they drew 0-0. However, it was not just in attack they flourished, as they only conceded 29 goals. The Jambos lost just once, to Clyde, and drew four matches.

Jimmy Wardhaugh and team-mate Jimmy Murray were the league's top goalscorers with 28 apiece. Murray would travel to Sweden with the Scotland World Cup squad and was to be the scorer of his country's first finals goal in the opening 1-1 draw with Yugoslavia. Remarkably, despite their

dominance, only one other Hearts player journeyed to Sweden: the great Dave Mackay.

Queen's Park suffered several heavy defeats throughout the season and slipped away from top-flight football for the final time as things currently stand in the 21st century. In 1957/58 they finished bottom with only nine points having conceded 114 goals. East Fife's run in the top tier would also come to an end, finishing on 23 points. Stirling Albion's 'bouncebackability' surfaced again as they won Division Two once more with 55 points. Dunfermline were second two points adrift, finishing with nine wins in ten games.

Hearts failed to win their League Cup section, with Kilmarnock coming out on top of their group. Killie lost out 4-3 on aggregate to Rangers in the quarter-finals. Brechin City had only just topped their group, gaining the same seven points as Dunfermline and Ayr United, but City's goal average saw them through to the quarter-finals where they overcame Hamilton Accies to meet Rangers at Hampden.

A flu epidemic was rife in Scotland in the winter of 1957 and there were several games called off during this period. Both Rangers and Brechin were affected by this, and several players were withdrawn on the day of the semi-final. A crowd of only 28,403 witnessed Rangers defeat Brechin 4-0. Similarly, Clyde were also to be without some first-team regulars for the other semi at Ibrox as Celtic ran out 4-2 winners.

Despite the continuing concerns, neither side had to withdraw players for the final, and a crowd of 82,293 witnessed a tantalising display of football that has become part of Celtic folklore. The devastating 7-1 victory is forever known as 'Hampden in the Sun' to the Celtic faithful and has been the subject of books, songs and poems ever since. Not only did Celtic score seven, they also hit the woodwork four times. John McPhail netted a hat-trick, Neil Mochan hit a brace with Sammy Wilson and Willie Fernie also scoring. Billy Simpson scored the consolation goal for Rangers.

The Scottish Cup Final was a much tighter affair. The format was contracted meaning that the first round proper saw several of the top sides involved and very few teams from the outlying leagues. High scores in the first round saw Clyde 5-0 winners over Dumbarton, Motherwell defeat East Stirling 7-3 and Stranraer run out 6-2 winners over Eyemouth United. Holders Falkirk defeated St Johnstone 6-3 in the second round while Rangers thumped Forfar Athletic 9-1 at Station Park. Queen of the South beat Stranraer 7-0 and Kilmarnock recorded the same scoreline against Vale of Leithen. In round three, Hearts lost 4-3 to Hibernian with Joe Baker hitting all four goals, and Clyde eliminated Celtic, winning 2-0 at Shawfield. Motherwell beat Inverness Caledonian 7-0; the Highland club had beaten Stenhousemuir 5-2 in the previous round. The quarter-finals saw Rangers squeeze through at Palmerston against Queen of the South 4-3.

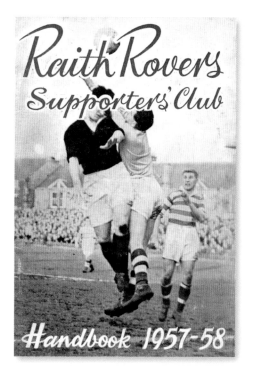

The semi-finals paired Clyde with Motherwell at Celtic Park and Rangers against Hibernian at Hampden. Bobby Ancell had taken over Motherwell in 1955 and was beginning to put together a pretty exciting young side known as the 'Ancell's Babes'. They would have three top-five finishes in the seasons that followed. Among the players at this time who would win Scotland caps were Ian St John, Willie Hunter, Andy Weir and Bert McCann. A crowd of 41,000 saw John Coyle put Clyde two up by half-time and add a third shortly after but a goal from Pat Quinn and then one from St John saw a rather frantic end to the match but no further goals.

In the other tie, Rangers striker Jimmy Millar netted after three minutes but Hibernian came back and goals by Andy Aitken and Tommy Preston put them ahead at half-time. Max Murray rescued the tie with an equaliser 12 minutes from the end. A crowd of 76,727 had turned up for the first match, but four days later a mere 75,000 travelled the Southside of Glasgow to see Rangers go down 2-1 to Hibs. Eddie Turnbull converted a penalty after 18 minutes and John Fraser added a second six minutes into the second half. Rangers scored with a penalty through Sammy Baird a few minutes later but no more goals were to follow.

The final was to be Clyde's day and although there was only one goal, it is suggested that Clyde dominated great swathes of the game and should have won by more. For Hibs, injury to Lawrie Reilly ruled him out for what would have been his final appearance. John Coyle's first-half strike would be the winner and gave Clyde their second cup success in three years. Coyle would travel to Sweden with the Scotland squad that year along with Archie Robertson and Harry Haddock. Coyle's place in international career is perhaps unique in that he travelled to a World Cup and yet never played for his country at any point.

1958/59

A photo finish in the league between Rangers and Hearts saw two points separating them on the last day. On 11 April Rangers faced Hearts at Tynecastle and lost 2-0, leaving the hosts four points behind with two matches to play and Rangers with one. Four days later Hearts beat Aberdeen 4-2 at Pittodrie to give themselves hope on the Saturday. Aberdeen needed two points to ensure safety from relegation and faced Rangers at Ibrox while Hearts met Celtic at Parkhead. Rangers slumped to a 2-1 defeat against the Dons and were booed off at Ibrox, but over at Celtic Park the home side won 2-1 to give their rivals the title. Rangers finished on 50 points and Hearts on 48 but both had identical goal averages with 92 goals scored and 51 conceded.

Motherwell finished two points below Hearts, a poor February of four league defeats and a cup exit ending their chances of success. Joe Baker was maturing into a great striker at Hibs and was the season's top scorer with 25.

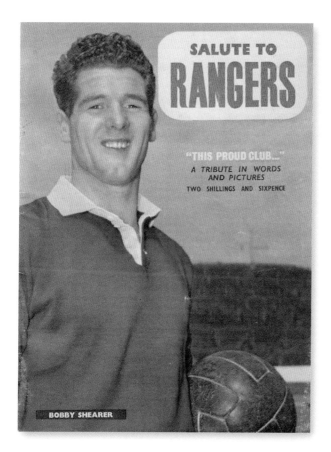

SALUTE TO
RANGERS

"THIS PROUD CLUB..."
A TRIBUTE IN WORDS
AND PICTURES
TWO SHILLINGS AND SIXPENCE

BOBBY SHEARER

Relegation came down to the last day too. Aberdeen, Raith Rovers, Dunfermline were all in the mix. Aberdeen finished on 29 points courtesy of their Ibrox win. Raith also finished on 29 following a 2-2 draw with Falkirk. Dunfermline had the poorest goal average of any of the teams going into the final day, but an 11-0 thrashing of Partick Thistle took care of that with Harry Melrose netting six of the goals. The victory took the Pars to 28 points alongside Clyde.

It would be luckless Falkirk, with 27 points, who joined the long-doomed Queen of the South, who had only garnered 18 points as well as conceding 101 goals over the season. Scotland legend John White would miss a penalty late in the draw with Raith but due to the enormity of the Dunfermline scoreline, victory would still have meant relegation.

White would play some games in Division Two at the start of the 1959/60 season before moving to Spurs in October. Like Jimmy Cowan of Morton and Harry Haddock of Clyde before him, White would be capped while a second-tier player.

Ayr United were clear winners of Division Two with 60 points, scoring 115 goals. Arbroath were runners-up with 51 points and were returning to the top flight for the first time since before the war.

Hearts topped their League Cup section, containing Rangers, and then continued in the free-scoring form that won them the championship the previous season. They defeated Ayr United 8-2 over two legs in the quarter-finals, which was matched by Celtic's thumping of Cowdenbeath 11-0 and Kilmarnock's 7-4 advantage over Dunfermline. Not so much Partick Thistle's 3-2 margin over Arbroath.

The semi-finals both attracted crowds of around 40,000. Hearts beat Kilmarnock comfortably, 3-0 at Easter Road. Over at Ibrox, Partick Thistle and Celtic played out a goalless first half and then the game looked as though it would be tipped in the favour of Celtic as Thistle's goalkeeper Tommy Ledgerwood was injured and had to leave the field for treatment with left-half Alex Wright taking over. Ledgerwood returned after extended treatment to play at outside-right. Surprisingly, Thistle then took the lead in the 72nd minute through a Davie McParland header followed shortly by a Johnny MacKenzie goal to double their advantage. Celtic netted a late consolation in the 88th minute through Jim Conway.

Unfortunately, in terms of League Cup finals, the third time was not lucky for Thistle with Hearts in blistering form. The Edinburgh side scored two through

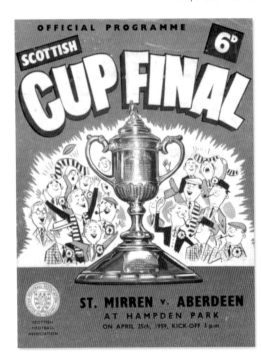

Willie Bauld and Jimmy Murray in the first ten minutes, then the pair added another one each in the 28th and 38th minutes respectively to see Hearts 4-0 up at half-time. George Smith hit a goal for the Jags a minute into the second half but a fifth and final goal from Johnny Hamilton shortly after put paid to any hopes the Firhill faithful in the 59,560 crowd had of a revival.

The Scottish Cup first round did not bring the usual flurry of eye-catching high scores. It did, however, produce one of the greatest shocks in the cup's history as Highland League team Fraserburgh beat Dundee 1-0 at Bellslea Park. A Johnny Strachan header gave Fraserburgh the victory against a side with the likes of Bill Brown, Doug Cowie and Alex Hamilton playing. The Highlanders lost out 4-3 in the next round to Stirling Albion. The second round saw St Mirren pummel Peebles Rovers 10-0, Motherwell win 7-2 at near neighbours Airdrie and Kilmarnock win 8-2 at Dumbarton. Holders Clyde bowed out to Celtic, in a seven-goal thriller of a replayed game at Shawfield. Celtic then defeated Rangers and Stirling Albion to reach the semis. Their opponents, St Mirren, had a couple of narrow victories over Motherwell and Dunfermline to face Celtic after their goal rush against Peebles.

However, the goals came flooding back in the semi-final with winger Ally Miller netting two and then Gerry Baker, the brother of Joe, adding a third before half-time. Tommy Bryceland hit the fourth in the second half as the Saints routed Celtic 4-0 in front of a crowd of 73,855 at Hampden. Aberdeen and Third Lanark were in the other semi. A smaller crowd of 33,000 turned out at Ibrox to watch the sides play out a 1-1 draw. Wattie Dick had put Thirds ahead in the first couple of minutes but Norrie Davidson replied for the Dons before half-time. Davidson scored the only goal of the replay in front of a crowd of only 16,000.

The final between St Mirren and Aberdeen had a turnout of 108,591. It was the same three scorers involved for the Saints with Bryceland giving them the lead in the 43rd minute, followed by Miller and

TOMMY BRYCELAND, St Mirren

then Baker scoring in the second half. Hugh Baird hit a late consolation goal in the 89th minute for Aberdeen, who had been contending with an injury to right-back Dave Caldwell from the 30th minute and had fielded him in the outside-left position for the remainder of the game. The Scottish Cup was therefore housed in Paisley for the first time since 1926.

1959/60

Hearts emerged as champions, their side now augmented by the legendary former Hibernian winger Gordon Smith. The Tynecastle outfit only lost three league games all season with just one coming in the latter half – to Kilmarnock, who were to be runners-up, four points behind on 50. Killie enjoyed a run of 15 consecutive wins from December to April but losing four of the first seven fixtures was their downfall.

Hearts hit 102 goals but were not the top scorers, being eclipsed by Edinburgh rivals Hibernian who notched up 106 with 42 coming from the season's top individual scorer, Joe Baker. Hibs fans enjoyed several big wins including 11-1 against Airdrie and 12-0 against Partick Thistle, both away from home. Baker went on to be capped for England that season and won five while playing for Hibs. Baker scored 102 goals in 117 league games for Hibs before moving to Torino, Arsenal, Nottingham Forest and then Sunderland before moving back to Hibernian briefly and finishing his playing days at Raith Rovers. His brother Gerry went on to play for the USA.

Jock Stein's arrival at Dunfermline as manager had seen them move away from the relegation zone in the final few weeks. Stirling Albion had reverted to type and once more dropped down with 22 points, six from safety. Down at the bottom with 15 points, Arbroath had endured a miserable season. They conceded 106 goals and at one point lost nine games in a row.

In Division Two, St Johnstone lost two in a row and found themselves only one point ahead of Dundee United but six wins and a draw in their final seven saw them home with 53 points. United lost one and drew one of their final seven, finishing three points behind. The Saints had last played in the top tier in the 1938/39 season and United in 1929/30. Cowdenbeath were rock bottom of the pile on 14 points having lost 124 goals along the way.

Given the make-up of the League Cup sections it was rare for any side to emerge with all 12 points. Motherwell, however, were to do so that year and in a group composed of Rangers, Dundee and Hibernian. Conversely, it was unusual to have no points but Hibernian did so, as did Morton. Motherwell's cup run came to a sudden halt in the quarter-finals as Hearts crushed them 7-3 over two legs. Cowdenbeath overcame local rivals East Fife 5-2, Arbroath narrowly beat Raith Rovers 4-3 and Third Lanark put out Falkirk 5-1.

In the semi-finals, a crowd of 27,500 at Easter Road saw Hearts take the lead twice only to be pegged back by a sturdy Cowdenbeath resistance. At the interval Hearts were 4-2 up but once again Cowden came back to make it 4-3, but they were then overpowered and Hearts emerged 9-3 winners. Ian Crawford netted four for the Edinburgh side. Third Lanark, with new boss George Young in charge, took their time in dispatching Arbroath in front of a 10,000 crowd at Ibrox. It wasn't until the second half with a tactical switch of players that they broke the deadlock through Joe McInnes, followed by goals from Bobby Craig and Ian Hilley, to win 3-0.

For Ian and his brother Dave the League Cup Final was special having grown up in the Mount Florida area. Thirds took the lead through McInnes after only two minutes, but Hearts would control most of the play throughout. However, it was not until the 57th minute that Johnny Hamilton equalised and two minutes later Alex Young hit the winner. Gordon Smith finally picked up a winner's medal at the national stadium as part of a League Cup and championship double.

Holders St Mirren started the Scottish Cup by belting Glasgow University 15-0. However, a three-match affair with Celtic in the next round saw them draw 1-1 and then 4-4 before succumbing to a 5-2 defeat. Twenty-two goals and they never even reached the third round. Kilmarnock and Hearts played each other six times in 1959/60. Hearts won the two in the League Cup section and then one in the league. The fourth meeting was a draw in the second round of the cup, followed by a 2-1 Killie victory in the replay. Killie, as mentioned above, won the sixth match too.

East of Scotland League team Eyemouth United joined the fray in the second round having been given a bye in the first, and duly beat Albion Rovers 2-1. They followed this up with a 3-0 victory over Cowdenbeath. Eyemouth then met Kilmarnock in the quarter-final and gave a good account of themselves before going down by the odd goal in three. To date this still sits as their best Scottish Cup run.

In the semis, Kilmarnock faced Clyde at Ibrox in front of a crowd of just under 44,000. Although Clyde had a sprightly start to the match it was Killie, through Andy Kerr, who took the lead after 30 minutes. This was quickly followed by Billy Muir hitting a second and that was how it finished. Over at Hampden a crowd of just under 80,000 turned up to watch Rangers play Celtic. Future Lisbon Lion Stevie Chalmers scored the opening goal after 25 minutes, heading in from a corner. However, Jimmy Millar equalised after 68 minutes and sent the tie into a replay. Davie Wilson had put Rangers in the lead in the replay but a reply by Neil Mochan in the 33rd minute saw Celtic in ascendancy. Celtic, with the 'notorious' Hampden wind behind them in the second half, were expected to go on and win, but

MOTHERWELL F.C. 1959-60

Left to right: (Back row) J. FOREST, W. McCALLUM, J. CATTENACH, H. WEIR, A. WYLIE, J. MARTIS, P. DELANEY; (Middle row) I. ST. JOHN, R. McCANN, J. STEWART, W. McSEVENY, R. McCALLUM, R. ROBERTS, J. MARTIN, C. AITKEN; (Front row) R. YOUNG, P. QUINN, W. REID, S. REID, M. STEVENSON, A. WEIR, G. LINDSAY, W. HUNTER, A. KERR

with Millar causing all sorts of problems the game slipped away from the Hoops. Two goals by Millar and a second from Wilson saw Rangers win 4-1.

As to the final in front of 108,017 fans, it seems as though Kilmarnock just did not perform on the day. They were also hampered with an injury to centre-half Willie Toner early in the match after a tackle from Jimmy Millar. It would be Millar who would net both goals, the first on 22 minutes and the second 22 minutes into the second half to give Rangers the cup.

1960/61▸1969/70

No doubt one of the most successful decades in Scottish football as teams made great strides in European competitions, culminating in Celtic's success in 1967.

Jock Stein began the decade by bringing Scottish Cup success to Dunfermline Athletic before winding up at Celtic. It is interesting that most of the great Celtic side were in place at Parkhead before he took over and initially he brought about few changes in personnel, achieving success through man-management and tactical nuance. Willie Waddell also brought great success to Kilmarnock over several years and would end the decade in charge at Ibrox. Furthermore, Dundee United's Jerry Kerr began to make his mark and develop the template for Jim McLean's success with the Tangerines in the 1970s and '80s. The likes of Willie Ormond, Eddie Turnbull and Ally MacLeod all began their managerial careers in this era too.

It was also a time of great players such as Jim Baxter, Jimmy 'Jinky' Johnstone, Alan Gilzean and Billy McNeill with many others coming to the fore. There was to be a Scandinavian influx added into the mix as well. Sadly, however, we lost Third Lanark as they folded at the end of 1966/67 but conversely Clydebank came into being.

1960/61

On 7 January 1961, Kilmarnock lost their third match in a row, 4-0 to Hibernian at Easter Road. At this point they did not look like a side that would challenge Rangers for the title. Rangers sat on 33 points after 20 games; Killie were fourth on 25 points. However, it was to prove a last league defeat of the season for the Ayrshire outfit as they won 12 of their final 14 matches. Rangers lost three times, including once to Killie, who ran out of games as the Ibrox side just needed a win on the final day to clinch the title. Although they got off to a nervous start in front of a home crowd, a goal by Alex Scott in the 25th minute settled nerves and Rangers ran out 7-3 winners against Ayr to be champions again.

Rangers finished on 51 points with Killie on 50. Third Lanark were third on 42 but were the league's top scorers with 100 goals. However, they did concede 80 times – only Dunfermline and Ayr United were to lose more with 81 each. The top scorer was a Thirds player in Alex Harley, who hit 42 goals. Alex would move to Manchester City and was to score 31 goals in all competitions but City were relegated despite that goal return. Harley then moved to Birmingham City for a season or so before heading back to Scotland for a short period with Dundee. Clyde and Ayr United were always hovering in the bottom two for the latter half of the season and dropped down on 23 and 22 points respectively.

On 14 January, Falkirk beat Stirling Albion 2-1 to top Division Two by one point. However, Albion won all their following 11 games to end up as the champions on 55 points, just one ahead of the Bairns. Morton finished rock bottom but Hal Stewart would join the board that year and rung in a great era for the Greenock club.

frank haffey

Goalkeeper   CELTIC & SCOTLAND

Holders Hearts didn't quite fall at the first hurdle in the League Cup, but they didn't reach the second one. They had finished equal top of their group with Clyde, both on seven points and the same goal average with the same record of 13 goals scored and seven conceded. A play-off took place at Celtic Park with Clyde winning 2-1 to face Kilmarnock in the quarter-final, which the Shawfield club lost 5-2 over the two legs. In the last eight, Rangers defeated Dundee 5-3, Queen of the South overcame Dumbarton 3-2, while Hamilton beat Stenhousemuir 8-5.

The Division Two sides both took a hammering in the semi-finals. First up Hamilton faced Killie at Ibrox and came away having lost 5-1. Kilmarnock headed in at half-time with only an Andy Kerr goal separating them from the Accies. Kerr doubled the lead on 58 minutes, but Divers brought Accies back into it soon after. A Jackie McInally goal in the 67th minute saw Killie creep further ahead then two goals in the final five minutes put a different reflection on the score. A week later, Rangers in front

1960/61 ▶ 1969/70

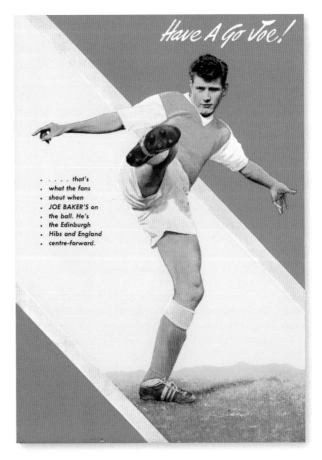

Have A Go Joe!

. . . . . that's
. what the fans
. shout when
. JOE BAKER'S on
. the ball. He's
. the Edinburgh
. Hibs and England
. centre-forward.

of a crowd of 17,000 took the lead in the second minute through Ralph Brand and never looked back. Brand hit another two with Jimmy Millar adding a brace and Alex Scott and Ian McMillan a goal apiece for a 7-0 victory over Queens.

A crowd of 82,063 attended the final. Kilmarnock were unable to get a foothold in the game and create many chances. As for Rangers, they played with great skill and effort with Millar creating the first goal for Brand who rounded keeper Jimmy Brown to score in the 37th minute. Alex Scott secured the victory with a suspected cross come shot that Brown misjudged as it was caught in the wind.

The big story of the second round of the Scottish Cup was the 15-1 hammering Hibs gave out to Peebles Rovers at Easter Road, with Joe Baker scoring nine of the goals.

In round three Motherwell drew 2-2 with Rangers at home, and St Mirren 3-3 with Third Lanark. Rangers led Motherwell 2-1 in the replay just before half-time at Ibrox but an equaliser from Delaney saw them go in all square, although the final whistle would see the Well win 5-2. After their six-goal thriller in Paisley, the Saints against Third rematch produced eight goals next time round but they were all conceded by the Glasgow side.

Motherwell lost out to Lanarkshire rivals Airdrie but St Mirren narrowly defeated Hearts in the quarter-finals. Celtic beat Hibernian after a replay and in the battle of the Athletics, Dunfermline knocked out Alloa 4-0.

The semis would see Celtic cruise to a 4-0 win over Airdrie at Hampden in front of a crowd of 72,612. Early goals from young John Hughes were followed by one apiece from Chalmers and Willie Fernie before half-time. The other tie was played at Tynecastle and proved to be a poor match with neither side able to score, even though the Pars played with ten men for the last 35 minutes due to injury to forward Charlie Dickson. A crowd of 31,390 turned up for the first match but only 16,741 souls were there for the replay. Dunfermline were the better side, but it was an own goal by St Mirren defender Stewart that sent the Pars into the final.

A crowd of 113,618 turned out at Hampden for an entertaining game in which both keepers, Eddie Connachan of Dunfermline and Frank Haffey of Celtic, excelled. The match was the first Scottish Cup Final for 31 years to finish goalless. Haffey's performance was more commendable having conceded nine goals at Wembley for Scotland the previous Saturday. However, a few days later Connachan continued to deny the Celtic forwards once more. Dunfermline's Dave Thomson headed in to give his side the lead. Two minutes from the end a mistake by Haffey saw Charlie Dickson clinch the second to give Jock Stein's side the cup. Dickson is still Dunfermline's all-time top goalscorer at the time of writing this book.

1961/62

Dundee had finished 1960/61 in tenth position with only 32 points, so it was a surprise that not only were they to be contenders for the title in 1961/62 but were to win it. Players such as Alan Gilzean, Ian Ure and Alex Hamilton would win caps for Scotland. Manager Bob Shankly merged this young talent with the experience of the likes of Bobby Cox, Bobby Seith and winger Gordon Smith. Bob's more famous brother Bill also won a championship that year: England's Second Division with Liverpool. Smith had won titles with Hibernian and Hearts.

Dundee had gotten off to a great start in the league following an early defeat to Aberdeen, going on a run of ten victories including 5-1 at Ibrox in heavy fog with Gilzean claiming four goals. However, coasting with six points in hand over Rangers in January, there followed four losses and two draws with Rangers taking a three-point advantage by mid-March. Dundee then won all their remaining games and Rangers faltered to three defeats and two draws to finish three points shy of Dundee's total of 54. Not surprisingly, Gilzean was the top goalscorer that season with 24. He would score 169 goals in 190 games for the club before moving to Spurs.

On the final day of the season five teams could all have been relegated. Yo-yo club Stirling Albion were already doomed but St Mirren were second bottom on 23 points, the same tally as Airdrie. Falkirk sat on 24 points, with St Johnstone and Raith Rovers both on 25. Four of the five clubs won on the final day so it was the Perth Saints who went down after losing to champions Dundee.

The Division Two title was close with Clyde and Queen of the South separated by one point with two games to go – both against each other. However, a well-contested match at Shawfield saw Clyde win 1-0 through captain Willie Finlay's penalty to give them the title in the first match, before Queens won the second meeting 3-0 at Palmerston. Clyde had hit 108 goals in attaining their 54 points, while at the bottom end Brechin City

conceded 123 in garnering only 12 points. They lost a further 32 goals in the cups to end up shipping a total of 155 goals overall.

Although they were to be relegated at the conclusion of 1961/62, St Johnstone topped their League Cup section which also included Celtic, Hibs and Partick Thistle. Rangers won a group that included Dundee, with Hearts and Motherwell also progressing to the last eight. St Johnstone edged out Motherwell 4-3 on aggregate in the quarter-finals with Rangers and Hearts readily overcoming East Fife and Hamilton respectively. Stirling Albion also saw off Ayr United 5-4 over two legs.

In the semis, a crowd of 41,100 was probably quite surprised to see Rangers reach the interval 2-0 down after Gardiner and Bell had scored for St Johnstone. Davie Wilson pulled one back a minute after half-time with Eric Caldow equalising from the penalty spot in the 78th minute to take the game into extra time. Wilson scored again to see Rangers into the final once more. The other tie at Easter Road, with a lower crowd of 19,000, also went to extra time and once again saw the underdog, in this

ERIC CALDOW

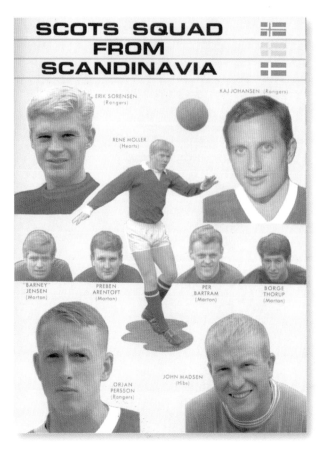

1960/61 ▸ 1969/70

case Albion, go in ahead at the interval after Dyson gave Stirling the lead on 42 minutes. Veteran striker Willie Bauld, in his final season with Hearts, hit the equaliser in the 71st minute. Willie Wallace scored the goal in extra time to see the Edinburgh side through to face Rangers in the final at Hampden.

A turnout of 88,000 saw a poor match end 1-1 with neither side showing much attacking prowess. A Jimmy Millar cross-shot from 30 yards on 18 minutes gave Rangers the lead, then a John Cumming penalty in the second half levelled the tie. As to the replay, the 47,500 were given a blitz of goals in the first 20 minutes in which Rangers took a 3-1 lead through goals by Millar, Brand and McMillan with Norrie Davidson replying for Hearts. However, due to the fog, there is the chance that few of the crowd saw the goal-laden period or the 70 minutes that followed without further scoring.

The Scottish Cup also found its way to Ibrox. Holders Dunfermline started off with a 5-1 victory over Forfar followed by a 9-0 thrashing of Wigtown & Bladnoch but fell to a 1-0 loss to St Mirren at the last-eight stage. Highland League club Inverness Caledonian knocked out East Stirlingshire and near neighbours Ross County took care of Dumbarton too. The Highlanders then both succumbed to heavy defeats in the third round, as Killie put seven past County without reply and Caley lost 6-1 to Third Lanark. Aberdeen and Clyde played out a 2-2 draw at Shawfield in the second round, but the replay ended in a 10-3 victory for Aberdeen. In round three Rangers drew 2-2 with Aberdeen before delivering a 5-1 thrashing in the replay. Celtic and Third Lanark enjoyed a 4-4 match in the quarter-finals with Celtic winning 4-0 in the replay.

The semi-finals paired Rangers with Motherwell and Celtic with St Mirren. Both ties ended 3-1 with Rangers and St Mirren making the final. At Hampden in front of a crowd of 84,321, Motherwell were deemed unlucky to lose out to Rangers with captain Bert McCann injured for most of the game. Rangers had led at half-time through a Max Murray goal before Bobby Roberts equalised for Motherwell, but the Ibrox side won due to late goals from Murray and Davie Wilson.

At Ibrox, St Mirren overwhelmed Celtic with three first-half goals. Ex-Celt Willie Fernie opened the scoring on eight minutes, Don Kerrigan added to that in the 32nd and a third came a minute later through Thor 'Tottie' Beck. Beck was an Icelandic player and among several Nordic footballers who were to turn out for Scottish clubs with innovative managers such as Hal Stewart at Morton and Jerry Kerr at Dundee United leading the way. Beck was to transfer to Rangers, who bought up several players such as Erik Sørensen and Kai Johansen from Morton and Örjan Persson from United in the '60s.

The match was disrupted with 18 minutes to go as youngsters invaded the pitch trying to avoid the mass of beer bottles thrown from the back of the terraces; a common occurrence at the time. It was held up for 16 minutes and after order was restored Alex Byrne netted for Celtic but by this time most of the crowd of 59,278 had left the stadium.

The final, played in front of a crowd of 127,940, was said to be a bit one-sided with Rangers quite dominant throughout, and with Jim Baxter in midfield and Willie Henderson on the wing playing particularly well. A goal either side of the interval by Brand and Wilson saw Rangers take the trophy for a cup double.

1962/63

Older Partick Thistle fans bemoan the winter of 1962/63 when the Jags were flying high and just one point behind league leaders Rangers. On 1 January, having won 12 of their last 13 league games and drawing the other, Thistle were due to face the Ibrox side the next day. However, heavy frost and snow would not only postpone that match, but it was to be March before any league football took place again. Rangers came out of the traps quickly after the break and won six league games in a row; Thistle stuttered and never really regained their form. Kilmarnock also overhauled Thistle to achieve second place. Rangers won the title comfortably with 57 points over Killie on 48 and then the Jags on 46. The redoubtable Jimmy Millar with 27 goals became the first Rangers player to end the season as top scorer since Alex Venters in 1938/39.

Raith Rovers were firmly bottom, only gaining nine points and conceding 118 goals along the way. Clyde were four points clear of Hibernian with three games left and Hibs with four games to go. A revival in fortune saw Hibs win three and draw one. Clyde were relegated finishing with one draw and two defeats.

St Johnstone returned to Division One at the first attempt by gaining 55 points, six clear of the runners-up. Morton looked to be sitting pretty with five games to go, a clear three points ahead of East Stirlingshire, but three defeats in a row including a pivotal one to their rivals saw Shire pip them for second place with a point to spare. Morton had hit

100 goals in the league. Brechin City remained rooted at the bottom with nine points.

Holders Rangers and previous runners-up Hearts came through their League Cup sections a point ahead of rivals. Killie, meanwhile, dominated their group with 11 points out of 12 and they would be joined in the semi-finals by Division Two club St Johnstone.

Hearts routed St Johnstone 4-0 at Easter Road in front of 23,000 spectators. Although the Saints had started well, a lovely piece of skill by the enigmatic Willie Hamilton gave Hearts the lead on 17 minutes. Willie Wallace added two more before half-time and completed his hat-trick in the second half.

The other tie at Hampden was much more competitive and the 77,000 crowd enjoyed a five-goal thriller. Killie had taken an early lead through Brian McIlroy but two goals from Brand in quick succession saw Rangers ahead. The turning point in the match was just before half-time when a John Greig shot was past keeper McLaughlin on its way to the net when Brand needlessly bundled it in with his hand. The goal was disallowed, a free kick was awarded to Kilmarnock and within a minute or so Andy Kerr grabbed an equaliser. A headed goal from Bertie Black ten minutes from the end saw Kilmarnock reach their third League Cup Final.

Although it was a tight match with chances limited for each side, a moment of magic from Hamilton saw Hearts take the cup home to Tynecastle. In the 25th minute he trapped a long ball out of defence, swerved past defender McGrory and then hit the byline to pinpoint a cross past keeper McLaughlin to give Norrie Davidson the simple task of netting for the Jambos. Willie, who also had

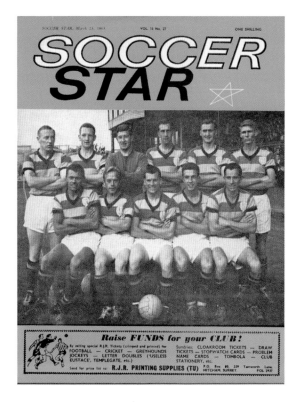

CLUB COLOURS
SCOTTISH LEAGUE DIVISION 11

1960/61 ▸ 1969/70

Cowdenbeath

Hamilton Academicals

Albion Rovers

Dumbarton

Alloa

Stenhousemuir

Montrose

Forfar Athletic

East Stirlingshire

Arbroath

spells at Hibernian and Aston Villa after leaving Hearts, was blessed with footballing talent but cursed with human frailties including alcohol misuse. He passed away due to a heart attack at the early age of 38, in Canada. But back to the game – Killie pushed for the equaliser and in the closing minutes thought they had got it only for the referee Tom 'Tiny' Wharton to disallow for the use of a hand by scorer Frank Beattie.

In the Scottish Cup, the first-round tie between Airdrie and Stranraer was apparently postponed 33 times before taking place on 11 March. Airdrie won comfortably 3-0 at home and faced holders Rangers two days later at Broomfield, suffering a 6-0 thrashing. Dundee handed out an 8-0 thumping to Montrose in that round too. Rangers then hit seven past East Stirling with the Firs Park side netting twice. Quarter-final opponents Dundee were to prove more difficult but a 1-1 draw at Dens was followed by a 3-2 victory at Ibrox. Raith put out Aberdeen, Celtic put paid to St Mirren, and Dundee United reached the semi-finals for the first time by knocking out Queen of the South after two replays.

Both semi-final ties were won 5-2 by the Old Firm. Rangers' meeting with United was played at Hampden in front of a crowd of 56,391. The match came alight between the 23rd and 37th minute when five goals were scored. Rangers took the lead through two from Millar but goals from United greats Dennis Gillespie and Ian Mitchell followed. However, Brand put Rangers ahead again in the 37th minute and Millar hit his third a minute before half-time. The second half did not match the first with only a solitary late George McLean goal to show for the teams' efforts.

Over at Ibrox, an early John Divers effort had put Celtic in the lead before a kick out from Haffey, their goalkeeper, barely got off the ground and landed at the feet of McDonald who lobbed the ball back into the net. It was 1-1 at half-time but two well-taken penalties by Duncan MacKay changed the game and although a goal from Gilfillan reduced the margin, late goals were to come from Stevie Chalmers and Frank Brogan to see Celtic through to the first Old Firm Scottish Cup Final for 35 years.

The final would go to two matches after the first game finished 1-1 with Ralph Brand and Bobby Murdoch scoring in a contest that was said to be poor. A crowd of 129,643 turned up for the first match with 120,273 present for the replay, in which Rangers outclassed Celtic to win 3-0. A double from Ralph Brand and one from Davie Wilson saw Rangers lift the Scottish Cup for the 17th time.

1963/64

Rangers dominated the Scottish season, claiming another treble and winning the league by six points from Kilmarnock. They did not have it all their own way, however, and after a home defeat to St Johnstone in late December they found themselves a point behind the Rugby Park side. Rangers retook the lead in early February and they never relented after that, finishing on 55 points. Dundee finished sixth on 45 points, scoring 94 goals with Alan Gilzean bagging 32 to end the season as the division's leading marksman.

Relegation was straightforward too, with Queen of the South and East Stirlingshire relinquishing top-flight football to which neither have since returned at the time of writing. Queens ended up with 16 points with East Stirling finishing on 12.

Morton continued to bang in a barrowful of goals, hitting an incredible 135 to top Division Two on 67 points, 14 clear of Clyde. The Greenock side won their first 20 matches, hitting eight against Brechin and Hamilton as well as seven against Brechin again and also Stenhousemuir. They only lost one league game all season. Stirling Albion, in their second season out of the top flight, had hit rock bottom with 20 points alongside Forfar who conceded 104 goals.

Holders Hearts failed to get out of their League Cup section after finishing four points behind Motherwell. Rangers topped their group, which included Celtic, beating their deadly rivals 3-0 at home and away. Hibernian and Dundee also progressed as did Morton with full points in their group. The quarter-finals saw Morton put out Motherwell, Rangers dismiss East Fife, Hibs oust Dundee and Berwick Rangers eliminate Stirling Albion over the two legs.

Berwick's reward was to meet the other Rangers at Hampden in front of a 16,000 crowd in the semi-final. Due to injury, the untried 18-year-old Tom Mealyou was between the sticks for the Borders side that night. Rangers went ahead early through Wilson but were pulled back in the 35th minute by

a goal from 25 yards by Ken Bowron. The Glasgow side, however, went ahead through a rather fortunate Brand goal just on half-time. Jim Forrest netted a third and the match ended 3-1.

Hibernian and Morton played out a 1-1 draw at Ibrox in the other semi. The Greenock side had gone into an early lead through Bobby Adamson but against the run of play were pulled back by a Neil Martin goal in the 20th minute and despite another 100 minutes of play no more goals were forthcoming. The replay was another tight affair and only a penalty scored by Allan McGraw in the 19th minute separated the teams in the end. McGraw would hit 58 goals over the season for Morton and moved to Hibernian in 1966.

1960/61 ▶ 1969/70

Both Rangers and Morton entered the final with unbeaten records in Scottish football, so something would have to give. A crowd of 105,907 turned up to Hampden with many an expectant Greenockian among the crowd and although Morton had begun on the front foot, for a lot of the first half they were defending resolutely. Early in the second half, however, a misjudgement by keeper Brown allowed Jim Forrest an easy opening for the first goal. Forrest added a second seven minutes later and his cousin, Alex Willoughby, hit a third in the 65th minute. In the closing five minutes Forrest added another two; the final score of 5-0 was harsh on the Greenock side.

The Scottish Cup generally went to form in the early rounds with large wins in round two as Rangers beat Duns 9-0 and Dundee won 9-2 at Brechin. Dunfermline bagged seven against Fraserburgh in round two, six against East Stirling in round three and then seven once more against Ayr United in the quarter-finals. Rangers beat Celtic 2-0 in the quarters with Dundee and Kilmarnock also going through to the semi-finals.

Ibrox welcomed 32,664 for the meeting of Dundee and Kilmarnock to see the Dens Park side overpower Killie 4-0. An excellent display by Gilzean who netted two, along with Andy Penman scoring one and an own goal by Jim McFadzean, added to Kilmarnock's misery. A few miles away, at Hampden Park, Rangers and Dunfermline fought out a more evenly contested tie in front of a gathering of 67,823. Keeper Jim Herriot was in fine form for the Pars but a delightful lob from Jim Baxter caught the Dunfermline defence off guard and allowed Davie Wilson to nip in and score the game's only goal just on half-time. Two days later Jock Stein was formally announced as the new manager of Hibernian, which had been in the pipeline for several weeks.

The 120,982 packed into Hampden saw Dundee defending throughout the first half of the final with keeper Bert Slater in great form. The second half saw Dundee come into it more, but a Henderson corner was nodded in by Millar to give Rangers the lead. Within 30 seconds of the restart a Gilzean cross was met by Kenny Cameron and his shot flew past Ritchie in the Rangers goal. However, another header from Millar in the final two minutes put the Gers in front and before the 90 minutes were out, Brand had added to it to ensure Rangers their 18th Scottish Cup triumph and their third in a row.

1964/65
It all came down to the last day of the season.

With five games to go Hearts had sat top of the League with 43 points, while Hibernian were second on 42. On 40 were Kilmarnock, having played 29 also. Three points adrift of Hearts but with a game in hand were Dunfermline. Hibernian, with a poor run of three losses in four games, dropped out of the reckoning. One of those defeats was to Jock Stein's Celtic. Stein had left Hibernian for Celtic in early March, and it is not hard to imagine that had he stayed on at Easter Road perhaps Hibs might have prevailed. As it was, they ended in fourth place with 46 points. Dunfermline, after a defeat to Hibs, won three games straight but a draw against St Johnstone in their penultimate fixture left them out of the equation. Their superior goal average would have won them the title but for this dropped point, and they ended up in third with 49 points.

Kilmarnock had won four matches in a row and on the final day were sitting two points behind Hearts, who had drawn away to Dundee United to have their lead reduced. Fate decreed that Killie were then to play Hearts at Tynecastle on the final day. Hearts were favourites as only a 2-0 loss or worse would see them lose out. Their Norwegian winger Roald Jensen hit the post in the first few minutes, but Killie took the lead through Davie Sneddon on 27 and Brian McIlroy quickly added another. Alan Gordon had an injury-time strike saved by keeper Bobby Ferguson to deny Hearts the championship. Both teams finished on 50 points and had it been decided on goal difference then Hearts would have won by 12 clear goals thanks to their 90 compared to Killie's 62. However, defensively

1960/61 ‣ 1969/70

Kilmarnock were quite frugal, only conceding 33 goals altogether, even more remarkable given Scottish international goalkeeper Campbell Forsyth injured an ankle with eight games left to play, although deputy Ferguson kept four clean sheets in that final run. In his time at Rugby Park, Willie Waddell, since 1957, had achieved four runners-up spots and lost in three cup finals with the club but chose to leave his position, having reached this pinnacle, to become a sports writer.

Rangers finished fifth on 44 points and although the loss of midfield maestro Jim Baxter – to a leg break in November which put him out the game for four months – could be looked upon as having a major negative impact on their form, they were

Presented with the compliments of the SCOTTISH DAILY EXPRESS

MORTON F.C.

Back row (*left to right*) : Bobby Howitt (coach), Boyd, Johanson, Reilly, Sorenson, Kiernan, Strachan, Campbell, Doug Cowie (coach)
Front row: Bertelsen, Caven, Smith, Stevenson, Adamson, McGraw, Wilson, Archie Scott (trainer)

SOUVENIR PHOTOGRAPH 1964/65

already seven points behind Hearts at that juncture. Jim Forrest ended up top goalscorer with 30 goals and was to strike 57 in all competitions. Celtic finished eighth – remarkably, Jock Stein taking over did not see a great resurgence in league form as they lost five of the nine games he was in charge of, but the Scottish Cup would be another story.

At the bottom end it was not so complicated with Third Lanark finishing last, gaining only seven points and being one goal short of joining the group of teams to have conceded 100 goals. Airdrie finished second bottom on 14 points, shipping 110 along the way.

Stirling Albion, under ex-Ranger Sammy Baird, had surged from bottom of the heap to the top in one season to bounce back up to the First Division. They had more or less led from the front and finished on 59 points, nine ahead of Hamilton Academical who were returning to the top flight for the first time since 1953/54.

A new club did appear on the roster: East Stirlingshire Clydebank, aka ES Clydebank. Brothers Jack and Charlie Steedman had taken over ownership of the Shire but felt a club based in Clydebank would be more appealing to fans so moved operations to Kilbowie Park. This development was to last for just the one season as court cases followed and East Stirling moved back to Falkirk, but the Steedmans stuck to their plan and a new club, Clydebank FC, would make their league debut in 1966/67. Brechin City had resumed their place at the bottom on 19 points, conceding 102 goals.

The League Cup saw holders Rangers win their section easily, including a 9-1 victory at Muirton Park over St Johnstone. Celtic won their group which included Hearts, Thistle and Kilmarnock and had big wins against them of 6-1, 5-1 and 4-1 respectively. The quarter-finals saw Dundee United thrash Hamilton 8-0 in the first leg, having been seven clear at half-time. Celtic lost 2-0 at Methil to East Fife but recovered the tie with a 6-0 thrashing at home. Clyde lost out to Morton and Rangers overcame Dunfermline to reach the semis.

Morton, with their recent memory of the thrashing Rangers had given them in the final the year before, were over-cautious in their tie with Celtic, where the turnout was 54,818. Their plan was to defend resolutely and perhaps get a chance on the break. It worked for 54 minutes before a bit of magic from Jinky Johnstone set up Bobby Lennox to score, and before Morton could react Charlie Gallagher had added a second to complete the scoring.

The other tie took place at Hampden with 60,000 in attendance and was a tight affair. United took the lead after 20 minutes through Doug Moran, who had scored the winner for Falkirk in the 1956/57 Scottish Cup Final, but rather than pressing home their advantage they sought to contain Rangers. Inevitably, Rangers piled on the pressure and with four minutes to go, Forrest, who had been quite ineffective until then, fired in the equaliser. He went on to score the winner in the second half of extra time to send Rangers into the final again.

A crowd of 91,423 witnessed Rangers win the final. Forrest netted twice in the second half; the first coolly slotted by Celtic keeper John Fallon in the 54th minute and eight minutes later a glorious Baxter pass found him in space to score the second. Johnstone scored in the 80th minute after a Chalmers shot rebounded off Gers keeper Ritchie's chest but the Ibrox club held fast to win the cup once more.

The Scottish Cup expanded again with two preliminary rounds. Inverness Caledonian secured a 2-1 victory over Raith Rovers in round two but lost 5-1 to Third Lanark in the first round proper. That stage also saw Partick Thistle draw 1-1 with Ayr United at

KILMARNOCK
Scottish League Div. I Champions 1964-65

Left to right — back row — Joe Mason, Campbell Forsyth, Ronnie Hamilton. *Middle —* Pat O'Connor, Eric Murray, Jackie McGrory, Bobby Ferguson, Jim McFadzean, Jack McInally, Frank Malone. *Front —* Mr Willie Waddell *(manager),* Hugh Brown, Tom McLean, Bertie Black, Matt Watson, Frank Beattie, Andy King, Dave Sneddon, Brian McIlroy, Billy Dickson, Walter McCrae *(trainer).*

Somerset and then hammer the seaside club 7-1 in the replay. The Jags lost 5-1 to Hibernian in the next round. The quarter-finals saw Celtic beat Kilmarnock 3-2, Dunfermline knocked out Stirling Albion 3-2, Hibernian put paid to Rangers 2-1 at Easter Road, and Motherwell defeated Hearts 1-0.

Celtic were paired with Motherwell for the semis and it took them two games to overcome the Lanarkshire side. In the first match, played in front of a crowd of 52,000 at Hampden, Motherwell took the lead twice through prolific scorer Joe McBride, the first in the tenth minute and the second in the 32nd. An own goal from Matt Thomson had brought Celtic back into it four minutes prior. Bertie Auld hit the second equaliser in the 60th minute from the penalty spot to set up a replay.

Celtic took the lead in the 27th minute through Chalmers who chested the ball into the goal from an Auld corner. It took until the second half for Hughes and then Lennox to net and give a proper reflection of Celtic's superiority. Unusually, the replay had a larger attendance with a crowd of 58,959. Jock Stein signed McBride the following season, when he would continue to display his scoring prowess.

The other semi was played at Tynecastle in front of a crowd of 33,000. Dunfermline won 2-0 with Hibs keeper Willie Wilson failing to collect a couple of high balls, allowing veteran Harry Melrose to net the first in the 17th minute and Alex Smith to head the other in the 52nd.

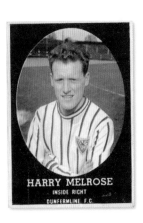

HARRY MELROSE
INSIDE RIGHT
DUNFERMLINE F.C.

Celtic had gone seven years without a trophy and there was much expectation upon them and manager Stein among the 108,800 crowd. It was Dunfermline who went ahead though in the 15th minute as Harry Melrose scored from a Jackie Sinclair pass. Against the run of play Celtic were soon back in the match as a thunderous Charlie Gallagher shot in the 31st minute rattled the bar and Auld netted the rebound. In the 43rd minute, Melrose tapped a free kick to John McLaughlin who powered a shot past Fallon to restore Dunfermline's lead. Celtic came out for the second half more determined and seven minutes later some neat play from Lennox and Auld ended with the latter hitting his second of the match. With nine minutes remaining Billy McNeill rose to powerfully head a Gallagher cross past Jim Herriot for the winning goal.

McNeill lifted his first major trophy as Celtic captain, and Stein had taken this team of underachievers and turned them into winners. As for Dunfermline, with Irishman Willie Cunningham in charge, in the space of seven days they had lost out on the league and the cup by the narrowest of margins. Four days later in a final Division One match they routed a much-changed Celtic side 5-1 at East End Park.

STILL SEEING RED
A History of Third Lanark A.C.

BERT BELL

1965/66

Celtic's first championship in 12 years was won on the last day of the season, although they had to lose 4-0 or worse to Motherwell at Fir Park to lose it. As it was, they won 1-0. Both Celtic and Rangers had led the table during the season, but a run of four games in March without a win for the Ibrox side allowed Celtic to retake the lead and they never looked back, winning six of their last seven to finish on 57 points, two more than Rangers. Champions Kilmarnock came in third, ten points behind Rangers on 45, Dunfermline fourth on 44. The Pars' Alex Ferguson hit 31 of his side's 94 goals to be the top scorer jointly with Celtic new boy Joe McBride. Celtic had netted 104 times on league business. McBride was to score 54 goals in 55 league games for Celtic but injury in December 1966 not only robbed him of a potential place in Lisbon for the European Cup Final but also curtailed his days at Celtic.

At the foot of the table, Hamilton ended up with only eight points having conceded 117 goals, including 11 to Hibernian in November. As of 12 March, having won their most recent matches, St Mirren and Morton sat on 20 points each and with six clubs below them, so they felt relatively safe. However, neither would win again that season as St Mirren

ALEX FERGUSON
RANGERS

INSIDE LEFT

grabbed two draws and Morton one, with the latter being relegated.

Queen of the South topped Division Two with 40 points in early March but were the only side to have played 30 games. Sitting fourth were Ayr United with 33 points after 25 games; a place below them were Airdrie with 32 points and the same games played. Ayr only dropped two more points to finish first on 53. Airdrie managed second with 50 with Queens on 47.

Ayr had finished the previous season second from bottom and although Tom McCreath was listed as manager, it was coach Ally MacLeod who was credited with the success of the side. Ally took over fully the following season as McCreath became a director of the club. Airdrie had scored 107 goals in total. At the bottom were Forfar Athletic on 17 points having picked the ball out of the net 120 times along the way.

Celtic and Rangers came through their League Cup sections despite losing a couple of games in doing so. The quarter-finals and semi-finals would see 62 goals scored in the ten ties and one replay. Over the two legs of the quarters Killie beat derby rivals Ayr United 4-2, Celtic crushed Raith Rovers 12-1, and Hibernian won their first leg 2-0 over Alloa followed up with a resounding 12-1 win at Easter Road with four goals each from Jim Scott and Neil Martin. Rangers dispatched of Airdrie 9-1 over the two games.

In the last four, Celtic took on Hibernian at Ibrox in front of a crowd of 50,000. In an entertaining game Joe McBride put Celtic ahead in the eighth minute but eight minutes later Hibs levelled through Jim Scott. Neil Martin put Hibs ahead just short of the hour but in the dying minutes, Wilson was unable to hold on to a Tommy Gemmell shot and Bobby Lennox pounced to net the equaliser. A similar crowd saw a vastly different second game as Celtic raced into a 2-0 lead in the first 20 minutes through McBride and Hughes. Further goals by Lennox and Murdoch added to Hibernian's misery.

The other tie over at Hampden, with 53,900 in attendance, also saw plenty of goals. By the 65th minute Rangers were rampant and leading 6-1 with a hat-trick from George 'Dandy' McLean and goals by Forrest, Willoughby and Henderson. Jackie McInally had netted Killie's reply, but Tommy McLean was to add a hat-trick late in the game as the match ended 6-4.

For the final, the *Glasgow Herald*'s headline read 'League Cup Final an Orgy of Crudeness' with five players being booked. It was a rather towsy affair, or rather a typical Old Firm game. Forrest had a couple of chances to score for Rangers early on, but the breakthrough came for Celtic in the 17th minute as defender Ronnie McKinnon handled the ball in the penalty area. John Hughes stepped up and fired the Hoops ahead. Twelve minutes later, McKinnon tackled Jinky Johnstone from behind and gave another penalty away. Hughes scored once more. Rangers kept plugging away and with seven minutes to go a John Greig shot spun off Ian Young's face and past Ronnie Simpson to score but it was too late; the day was Celtic's.

In the Scottish Cup, Gala Fairydean put six past local rivals Selkirk in the first preliminary round but lost out 5-4 to Montrose at the next stage. Dumbarton took two ties to overcome Peebles and squeezed past Glasgow Uni 2-1 in the next round. Ross County put out Forfar 4-3 in Dingwall in the second preliminary round and followed this up with a 5-3 victory at Alloa. The reward for these endeavours was a glamour tie against Rangers at Victoria Park. The fixture was postponed on several occasions due to a frozen pitch but eventually played five days before the third-round matches were due to kick off. Rangers would win 2-0 thanks to two goals in two minutes midway through the first half from George McLean and Willie Johnston.

Celtic had come through the quarters after a replay against Hearts to face Dunfermline once again, and 53,900 turned up at Ibrox to see the Celts overcome the Pars with goals from Auld in the 37th minute and Stevie Chalmers in the 66th.

Aberdeen, now managed by ex-Hibernian great Eddie Turnbull, met Rangers in the other semi-final in what turned out to be a poor 0-0 match played in front of 49,360. The replay three days later saw only 40,852 turn up to see a game that was not much better but did produce goals and a result. Forrest gave Rangers the lead in the eighth minute, but they were pegged back seven minutes before half-time as Harry Melrose shot home from a narrow angle. Rangers were the better side on the night and with 80 minutes on the clock McLean nodded home the winner.

Some 126,522 Old Firm fans turned up at Hampden fully expectant but were perhaps disappointed by a rather tense and timid affair that finished goalless. Defences were on top and it was captains Billy McNeill and John Greig who had the best chances for an opener. It would be a defender who was to net the winner in the replay; in doing so, Rangers' Danish international Kai Johansen became the first foreign player to score in a Scottish Cup Final. Celtic did produce more attacking flair but Rangers were firm in defence with Ritchie making several important saves and with veteran striker Jimmy Millar playing further back. Johansen hit the winner in the 68th minute after following up a cleared Henderson shot with a 25-yard goal worthy of taking the cup.

1966/67

This season arguably goes down as the greatest in Scottish football history. Not only would Celtic win the European Cup, but Rangers reached the final of the European Cup Winners' Cup and Kilmarnock reached the semi-finals of the Inter-Cities Fairs Cup competition in which Dundee United had earlier knocked out Barcelona. Can you imagine what the Scottish coefficient that year would have been, if such a thing existed? Of course, let us not forget that wee bit of business down at Wembley that year too, by the national side.

The league title was won by Celtic at Ibrox after a 2-2 draw with Rangers. This was a rearranged

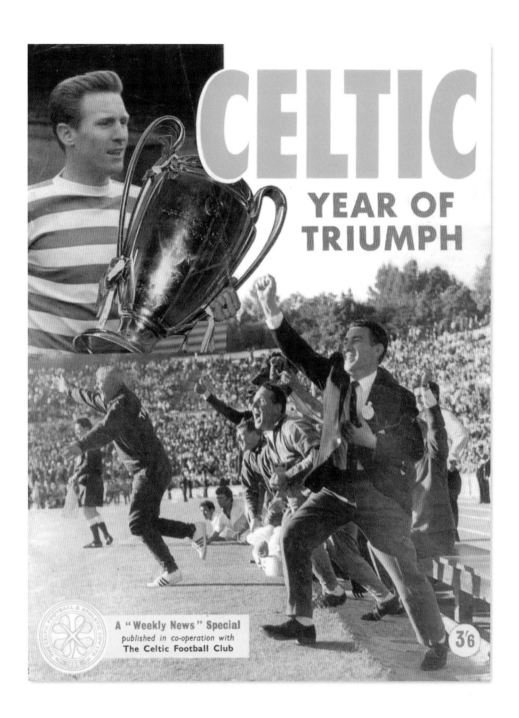

A " Weekly News " Special
published in co-operation with
The Celtic Football Club

3'6

game, cancelled due to frost at New Year. Celtic still had one match to play and were to finish on 58 points, three ahead of Rangers. Celtic only lost two league games all season, both against Dundee United. Rangers lost three times – twice to Dunfermline Athletic and once to Celtic. Clyde finished third, still their all-time highest placing, with ex-captain Davie White in charge. Celtic hit 111 goals with Stevie Chalmers as top scorer on 21. Team-mate Joe McBride had scored 18 in the league before injury in late December ended his season prematurely.

At the bottom end of the table, Ayr United had been unable to build on their progress and won one match all season, in April against St Johnstone, and gained just nine points overall. St Mirren were also relegated after finishing on 15 points.

Two major changes had come about in Division Two; firstly Clydebank were admitted into the league at the season's beginning so the roster was now made up of 20 teams. However, by the end of the season Third Lanark were wound up following liquidation. To this day, how or why this came about is still shrouded in some mystery. The blame does seem to lie with chairman Bill Hiddleston and misappropriation of funds but his death in November 1967 from a heart attack left a lot of unanswered questions.

Morton bounced straight back up, again scoring a barrowload of goals – 113 this time around including a 9-1 victory over Stenhousemuir, in which defender Jack Bolton hit four. The two Joes, Harper and Mason, also grabbed a double each. Raith Rovers finished in second place, 11 points behind Morton but pipping Arbroath for promotion by one point. At the bottom sat Brechin City once more on 23 points. However, Forfar Athletic in 16th place and Stenhousemuir in 17th conceded 106 and 104 goals respectively.

Celtic's season started with 22 consecutive wins in all competitions and they topped their League Cup section with full points. Future great Archie Gemmill was to become the Scottish game's first substitute when he replaced Jim Clunie after 23 minutes in the opening tie between St Mirren and Clyde. Morton beat Aberdeen 3-1 in their first quarter-final leg but lost 3-0 at Pittodrie. Airdrie got the better of Montrose, as did Rangers over Ayr and Celtic against Dunfermline.

Rangers met Aberdeen in a semi-final and the crowd of 38,623 saw Willie Henderson hit two goals in the first 35 minutes to put the Glasgow team ahead, but they were pulled back twice with strikes from Ally Shewan and then Jimmy Wilson. For the replay Rangers were down several players due to international duty and injuries, however, they scored through Johnston, again in the fourth minute. Alex Smith added a second in the 39th minute to end the scoring. The turnout was down to 35,000 for this one.

A crowd of 36,936 turned up at Hampden and witnessed a below-par performance from Celtic given the heights they had already hit that season but Airdrie and in particular keeper Roddy McKenzie were a 'tough nut to crack', as the cliché goes. It took until the 62nd minute before the Diamonds' goal was breached, when Bobby Murdoch latched on to a defensive clearance and shot through a crowded penalty area to score. Fourteen minutes later McBride sealed it by heading in a cross from Bertie Auld.

Some 94,532 fans were at Hampden for the final. Celtic took the lead in the 20th minute when Auld sent a cross into the area for McBride to knock down for the onrushing Lennox who smashed the ball into the net past Norrie Martin. A few minutes later, Bobby Watson had the ball in the net but Alex Smith had apparently impeded keeper Ronnie Simpson a second before the shot had been struck. The decision by referee Tiny Wharton was not welcome by the Rangers faithful and beer cans and bottles were thrown from the back of the terraces, injuring some youthful fans further down near the trackside. With no further scoring, Celtic retained the cup.

The Scottish Cup was to bring what is regarded as the biggest cup shock ever in Scotland as Berwick Rangers beat Glasgow Rangers. Berwick had come through two preliminary rounds, beating Vale of Leithen 8-1 then Forfar 2-0, before facing the Light Blues at Shielfield Park. The goal that reverberated around the football world was scored by Sammy Reid in the 32nd minute. Goalkeeper and manager Jock Wallace was the real hero of the day with a great display. Jock had only just joined the club and would go on to become a legend at Ibrox as coach and then manager. This cup upset would see the end of George McLean and Jim Forrest at Rangers

– both were immediately dropped and never played again for them.

Berwick narrowly lost 1-0 to Hibernian in the next round at Easter Road with more heroics from Wallace, including saving a penalty from Jim Scott. Aberdeen put five past Dundee and then St Johnstone as they advanced through the rounds, going on to beat Hibernian 3-0 after a replay to reach the semi-finals. Celtic had put four past Arbroath and seven past Elgin City before playing out a 5-3 goalfest with Queen's Park to also reach that stage.

At Dens Park, in front of 41,550, fans Aberdeen faced the ever-improving Dundee United who had knocked out Hearts and Dunfermline. Despite their scoring exploits earlier in the competition, the goals dried up for Aberdeen and it was to take an own goal from United defender Tommy Millar in the fourth minute to divide the sides. Winger Jim Storrie missed a few chances for Aberdeen, most notably hitting a penalty wide in the first half.

Celtic took on high-flying Clyde in front of a 56,704 crowd but it ended in a stalemate. Jock Stein commented before the replay, 'You'll see a different Celtic at Hampden tonight – a vastly different Celtic,' and indeed the crowd of 55,138 did. They blitzed the part-timers of Clyde from the start and within three minutes Lennox had them in front. Auld added a second on 22 minutes with a well-hit shot. Celtic remained in control for the rest of the game to face Aberdeen in the final.

Celtic lined up with the side that was to make history in Lisbon almost a month later and Aberdeen were reckoned to have 30,000 fans among the 127,117 crowd. Both defences played it tight and it took until the 42nd minute before the deadlock was broken. From a short corner Lennox evaded two tackles before hitting the byline to cross for Willie Wallace to score the opener past keeper Bobby Clark. Jimmy Johnstone supplied the cross for Wallace to hit a second and final goal, four minutes after the restart.

1967/68

It was close once more with Rangers falling at the last hurdle. Indeed, it had been a bit of a traumatic season for the Ibrox side. On 28 October they drew 0-0 with Dunfermline at Ibrox with a misfiring front line that included Alex Ferguson, leading to loud boos and abuse towards the players, manager and board of directors alike. Rangers were three points ahead of Celtic having played one game more at this stage but by the following Wednesday Scot Symon was unceremoniously sacked. In his time as manager, he had won six championships, the Scottish Cup five times, and four League Cups. Davie White, who had earlier moved from Clyde to Rangers as coach, stepped up to take over Symon's role.

Rangers were undefeated in the league at that point and remained so right up until the final game of the season. Celtic, meanwhile, had only lost once, to Rangers, but had drawn two matches fewer so had two points in hand. Rangers' visitors at Ibrox on that last day were Aberdeen. Rangers twice took the lead, first through Dave Smith and then Alex Ferguson but two goals by Highland League great Davy Johnston and a third from Ian Taylor in the final minute gave Aberdeen victory. Celtic's goal advantage meant that victory in their final match against Dunfermline was a mere formality. They won 2-1 and took the title with 63 points, scoring 106 goals. Bobby Lennox was to finish top goalscorer with 32 in total. Rangers finished on 61 points, scoring 93 goals.

Early February saw Motherwell third from bottom, five points ahead of Raith Rovers. A run of nine defeats in their last 12 matches, however, coupled with a revival in fortunes for Raith, saw Motherwell drop a division for the first time since the 1952/53 season. The Steelmen finished on 19 points and Rovers on 25. The string finally snapped on Stirling Albion's yo-yo and they left the top tier for the final time, amassing only 12 points and conceding 105 goals.

CLYDE FC

Back row, left to right: Pat Delaney, Jim Fraser, Harry Glasgow, Tommy McCulloch, Dave Soutar, John McHugh, Eddie Mulheron. Front: Stan Anderson, Graham McFarlane, Harry Hood, Ian Stewart, Jim Burns, Sam Hastings. (McLennan).

Division Two was won comfortably by St Mirren with 62 points having scored 100 goals in total. They were returning to the top flight after one year out. Arbroath, in second place and nine points behind, were heading back for the first time since the 1938/39 season. At the bottom were Stranraer in 18th and Stenhousemuir in 19th, both on 20 points.

Celtic took 11 points out of 12 in their League Cup section which included Rangers, Dundee United and Aberdeen, whom they beat 5-1 at Pittodrie. Morton had come through with all 12 points in the bag. Celtic defeated Ayr United 8-2 over the two legs of the quarter-finals. Dundee won 5-0 against East Fife, Morton 5-3 over Kilmarnock and St Johnstone 8-1 against Queen's Park.

In the semis, a crowd of 45,662 turned up at Hampden as Celtic tore the Greenock side apart. Within four minutes of the start, Hughes had given Celtic the lead and three minutes later he set up Wallace for number two. Danish midfielder Preben Arentoft then pulled one back for the Ton in the 12th minute. However, by the 23rd minute Morton were 5-1 down with Johnstone, Lennox and right-back Jim Craig scoring. Craig, who rarely scored, added another in the second half before Hughes finished it off with a mazy run from 50 yards and an unstoppable shot for the seventh.

A crowd of 18,000 attended the other semi as Dundee faced St Johnstone. The Saints took the lead in the first half through Gordon Whitelaw but after the interval George Miller was unfortunate enough to put the ball into his own net twice to put Dundee in front. Ex-Ranger George McLean added a third to ensure the Dens Park men went through to the final.

Some 70,000 attended the final, where there would also be eight goals, but the spread was a bit more even. Celtic were said to be great in attack but rather flat-footed in defence that day. They appeared to be on easy street after the 11th minute when Hughes netted goal number two following the opener from Chalmers five minutes earlier. However, McLean pulled one back for Dundee in the 23rd minute. Stevie Chalmers hit his second in the 71st to put Celtic two clear again but within minutes future Dundee United manager Jim McLean reduced the deficit once more. Lennox quickly restored the two-goal lead but the 85th minute saw George McLean hit his second and give Dundee hopes of an equaliser, although Wallace finished the contest at 5-3 with a final goal in the 88th minute. Celtic became the first side to win the League Cup three times in a row.

Dunfermline Athletic received acclaim for winning the 1968 Scottish Cup but perhaps plaudits should also go to Elgin City who reached the quarter-finals, putting paid to the hopes of three senior clubs along the way. Albion Rovers were first to go by the wayside as Elgin beat them 3-1 at home in the first preliminary round. Next up was a round trip of around 550 miles to Kirkcowan in Wigtownshire to defeat Tarff Rovers 3-2.

The first round proper saw Elgin despatch Forfar Athletic 3-1 at Borough Briggs and then visitors Arbroath 2-0. The quarter-finals had them travel

DUNDEE
INSIDE FORWARD
JIM McLEAN

Queen of the South

East Fife

Stranraer

Stirling Albion

Championship Cup

Queen's Park

Winners 1968-69 —
MOTHERWELL

Berwick Rangers

Falkirk

Clydebank

Brechin City

to meet Morton at Cappielow. The match ended 2-1 to the Division One club but reports suggest the gulf between the sides was much larger with poor finishing by Morton ensuring that they went in to the interval only two up thanks to goals from Joe Mason and Arentoft. Elgin's record goalscorer, Gerry Graham, netted in the 74th minute but the equaliser did not follow. Elgin were the top Highland League side at this point and from the 1959/60 season through to 1969/70 they were champions eight times.

Holders Celtic were dumped out of the competition in the first round at home to Dunfermline Athletic, losing 2-0 to goals by Hugh Robertson and

THE HALCYON DAYS OF DUNFERMLINE ATHLETIC FOOTBALL CLUB 1959-1970

BLACK & WHITE MAGIC

JIM PATERSON and DOUGLAS SCOTT   introduced by JOCK STEIN

Pat Gardner. Dundee United and Hearts played a ding-dong of a match in the second round at Tannadice with the Edinburgh side emerging 6-5 winners. The quarter-finals saw Dunfermline, now managed by George Farm, knock out Partick Thistle 1-0. Rangers lost by the same score to Hearts in a replay after a 1-1 draw. St Johnstone now under the auspices of Willie Ormond reached their second semi-final of the season by beating Airdrie 2-1. They were joined by Morton.

Hearts and Morton played out a poor game at Hampden in front of a lowly crowd of 22,569 with Roald Jensen scoring for Hearts and Stan Rankin for Morton in a three-minute spell early in the first half. The replay saw only 11,565 turn up for another lifeless affair where Willie Allan put Morton ahead in the 32nd minute with a blistering shot. George Miller nabbed the equaliser for Hearts in the 63rd so the match went to extra time. Much to the relief of many fans, they were spared a third match when Jensen converted a penalty in the 118th minute to edge Hearts through to the final.

The other tie was an equally nervy, strained affair that took two matches and extra time to sort. A crowd of 14,268 watched the first match at Tynecastle end 1-1. Kenny Wilson had put St Johnstone ahead in only the fourth minute but shortly after the interval a blunder from young Saints keeper Derek Robertson, under pressure from the Pars' Bert Paton, gifted Gardner the equaliser. The crowd dropped to 9,845 hardy souls for the replay with the pitch being cleared of four inches of snow earlier that day. Alex MacDonald put the Saints ahead in the 65th minute but eight minutes later Gardner set up Paton to level the tie. Robertson would be a hero in the 84th minute as he saved a penalty from his namesake Hugh and kept out the rebound from Paton. Pars substitute Ian Lister, though, was to win the tie with his goal in the 118th minute.

The final was played in front of 56,366 on the same day that Rangers were to lose the league at Ibrox. Hearts started the better side in the first half but were unable to really trouble the Fifers' goal. The second half saw Dunfermline come out stronger and they were soon ahead in the 56th minute when Gardner volleyed home from Jim Cruickshank's punched clearance. A second was to follow three minutes later when Cruickshank brought down Paton for a penalty. Semi-final hero Lister scored from the spot to put his side 2-0 up. Hearts swapped Norwegian Jensen for Dane René Møller in the 66th minute and within five minutes his byline cross was bundled into his own net by defender John Lunn. However, any thoughts of a Hearts revival were put to rest as Gardner sealed the cup victory with another goal three minutes later.

1968/69
Celtic won the league with a five-point margin over Rangers as well as both cups in a rather emphatic manner. The championship win itself was not won with such gusto as previous seasons, however, with Celtic losing three matches, drawing eight and scoring 89 goals. Two of their defeats were to Rangers but the Ibrox side were always playing catch-up, losing six times overall. A Rangers defeat to Dundee at Dens Park gifted Celtic the title with two games to spare but neither side finished with much flourish with several draws and defeats for both. Dundee United's Kenny Cameron was the season's top scorer, netting 26 of his team's 61 goals as they finished in fifth place.

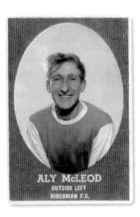

Arbroath recorded their first win in January when beating Morton and finished the season bottom on 16 points. Falkirk always seemed on the cusp of catching Raith but never managed to do so, finishing three points behind them with 18 points.

Motherwell won Division Two, 11 points ahead of Ayr United with 64 points. The Steelmen scored 112 goals with John 'Dixie' Deans hitting 32 of them. Ally MacLeod's team had taken two seasons to get back to the top tier. Stenhousemuir finished bottom for the second season in a row with 18 points. The Warriors conceded 125 goals and lost 9-1 to Forfar and 7-1 to Ayr in consecutive weeks.

The League Cup saw Celtic top with maximum points in a group that included Rangers, Partick Thistle and Morton. The Celts went on the rampage against Hamilton Accies in the quarters, crushing them 10-0 in the first leg at Parkhead with Chalmers and Lennox scoring five each – Bobby had already hit five against Partick Thistle in a group match. A much younger Celtic side won 4-2 at Douglas Park in the second leg with Kenny Dalglish making his debut as a substitute. Dundee dispatched Stranraer 10-0 over two legs, Hibernian beat East Fife 6-2 and Clyde eliminated Ayr United with a more modest 3-0 aggregate.

1960/61 ▸ 1969/70

Celtic were expected to easily overcome Clyde in their semi-final in front of 34,676 fans at Hampden but found them surprisingly formidable opposition. Indeed, Clyde had the better of the chances in the first half and defended well. However, John Hughes was once again the inspiration for Celtic, finding space in the 75th minute to pass inside for George Connelly to score the game's only goal.

The other semi at Tynecastle was quite evenly matched with Dundee opening the scoring through George McLean in the sixth minute and Colin Stein replying for Hibs a minute later. The winning goal was to come from former Morton striker Allan McGraw, who had been stretchered off with 15 minutes remaining but had returned to the fray with only five minutes left on the clock to score, ironically, in injury time.

A crowd of 74,240 turned up to witness Celtic in full flight in the final, overpowering a very decent Hibernian side. Hibs, managed by Bob Shankly, at this point had the likes of Pat Stanton, John Blackley and the two Peters, Cormack and Marinello, in their ranks but were no match for the rampant Celts. Hibernian had a couple of early chances but Wallace put Celtic ahead in the 20th minute and they didn't look back. Chalmers scored ten minutes later, followed by three from Lennox in the 44th, 58th and 73rd minutes. Right-back Jim Craig got in on the act to make it 6-0. Celtic then took their foot off the pedal and Hibs managed to grab a couple of consolation goals in the last ten minutes through Jimmy O'Rourke and Eric Stevenson. Celtic lifted the League Cup for a fourth successive time and in doing so scored 41 goals in the tournament which is more than four clubs managed in Division One for the entire season.

Forfar Athletic once more fell to Highland League opposition in the Scottish Cup as Nairn County beat them 2-1 at home in the first preliminary round. Nairn lost out to Berwick in the next round. The first round proper saw Partick Thistle and Celtic play out a 3-3 draw with Jimmy Bone snatching an equaliser in the dying moments at Firhill. Four days later Jags fans wished he hadn't bothered as Thistle lost 8-1 in the replay.

In the next round Celtic drew 0-0 with Clyde but came through the replay 3-0. In the meantime, Rangers had knocked out both Hibs and Hearts on their way to the quarters. Aberdeen won through to the semis after a replay against Kilmarnock. Morton got the better of Dundee United in a five-goal thriller in which Dane Per Bartram had four goals disallowed for offside. Rangers struggled to overcome Airdrie at Ibrox, winning through a John Greig penalty, while Celtic came through a close match with St Johnstone winning by 3-2 at home to reach the last four.

Morton got off to the best of starts at Hampden against Celtic, scoring inside two minutes through Willie Allan, but after that Celtic were in full flow and it was no surprise when Wallace headed in the equaliser in the 13th minute. The Morton fans in the 49,934 crowd would have hoped to get to the interval level but Billy McNeill forced a shot home with two minutes of the first half to go. The second half saw Chalmers and Johnstone add to Celtic's tally and Celtic headed to the final.

Over at Celtic Park on the same day, a crowd of 66,197 saw Rangers romp through their semi-final with a 6-1 thrashing against Aberdeen. Rangers had gone in front through Andy Penman in the 15th minute and Willie Henderson added to this in the 38th, but Aberdeen pulled one back through ex-Ranger Jim Forrest before the break. However, within six minutes of the restart Willie Johnston hit his first in the 47th minute followed by another Penman goal in the 51st. Johnston added goals in the 72nd and 84th minutes to complete his hat-trick and the rout was complete.

A record crowd of 132,870 for an Old Firm match jammed into Hampden for the final. Billy McNeill was given a free header in the second minute from a Lennox corner to put Celtic in front. Poor defending allowed Lennox to finish past keeper Norrie Martin and then Connelly benefited from a short kick out from Martin that went astray just before half-time. Chalmers finished off the scoring with a fourth in the 76th minute, meaning Rangers lost a Scottish Cup Final for the first time in 40 years and Celtic were on course for the treble once more.

1969/70

Celtic came so close to matching their terrific season of 1966/67 but the Scottish Cup was ultimately to elude them, as would the European Cup. The league, though, was won comfortably in the end with 12 points between them and Rangers. By December Rangers had Willie Waddell in charge following the sacking of Davie White but ended the season poorly with five losses and two draws in their last eight games. Celtic finished on 57 points and Rangers on 45, although their striker Colin Stein finished the season as top scorer with 24 goals.

Partick Thistle, managed by former Rangers boss Scot Symon, were to finish bottom and never really looked like escaping that fate at any point. The Jags won only five games and ended up with just 17 points, so after a stay of almost 70 years they exited the top flight of Scottish football. Raith Rovers had also hovered around the bottom of the league since the season's start and were relegated with 21 points.

Cowdenbeath led the charge in Division Two and defeated second-placed Falkirk on 28 March to head the table by five points with three games remaining. The Bairns, though, had six games in hand and had been picking up the points. They also defeated Cowdenbeath to ultimately finish top by one point on 56, with Cowden on 55. Hamilton would finish bottom with 20 points.

Celtic won the League Cup for the fifth successive season, overcoming in the final a St Johnstone side who netted 35 goals in the competition. Celtic topped their group with ten points, one ahead of Rangers. St Johnstone won all six matches in their section including an 8-1 crushing of Partick Thistle at Firhill, in which Henry Hall hit a hat-trick.

The quarter-finals saw Aberdeen run Celtic close as they drew 0-0 at Pittodrie and then took the lead in the second leg through Jim Forrest. However, goals in quick succession from Johnstone and Wallace saw Celtic win through to the semis. Morton beat Motherwell 3-0 at Cappielow and then lost 3-0 at Fir Park in the return and succumbed

COWDENBEATH

John Dickson
INSIDE RIGHT

HIBERNIAN Standing—Shevlane, Jones, Marshall, Stanton, Black, Blackley. Sitting—Manager W. McFarlane, Cormack, Marinello, McBride, Hamilton, Stevenson. Trainer T. McNiven.

to a Jim Muir winner in the play-off at Ibrox. St Johnstone stuffed Falkirk 13-1 over the two legs with Hall hitting a brace in both legs. Ayr United triumphed 5-1 over Dumbarton.

On-form Saints dispatched of Motherwell at Hampden in front of a semi-final crowd of 19,970 with goals in each half from Buck McCarry and Fred Aitken. At the same venue two days later, 35,100 saw an enthralling match as Ayr and Celtic drew 3-3 after extra time. Bobby Rough started it by putting Ayr ahead in the 33rd minute with Hughes equalising four minutes before the break. An unstoppable Gemmell penalty early in the second half saw Celtic go ahead but it was quickly followed with David McCulloch netting for Ayr. Rough scored once more in the 95th minute but Auld restored parity three minutes later and a replay was needed to separate the sides.

An increased crowd of 47,500 took in the second match. Ayr's Alex 'Dixie' Ingram put his side in front with a header in the 14th minute, but Harry Hood evened it up eight minutes later. The deciding goal came early in the second half as Chalmers pounced

on a mistake by Ayr captain Stan Quinn. An injury to keeper Ronnie Simpson saw Gemmell take over in goal for the last 12 minutes, but Celtic held on.

A crowd of 73,067 attended the final. It was to be a close match with the only goal coming from Celtic in the first two minutes as Auld pounced, after a Hood header glanced off the crossbar. St Johnstone found themselves up against keeper John Fallon, who held steady against anything the Perth side could produce.

The Scottish Cup started off with Gala Fairydean knocking out Stenhousemuir 1-0 in the first preliminary round. Following that, Gala lost out to Dumbarton, and Inverness Caledonian hammered Ross County 5-0. Stranraer were visited by fellow South of Scotland side St Cuthbert Wanderers and drew 1-1 before winning 5-0 in the replay. The first round proper saw Caley travel to Stranraer and win 5-2 but they then lost 3-1 to Motherwell in the next round. Tarff Rovers defeated Alloa Athletic 1-0 before losing out to Falkirk in the first round.

The quarter-finals saw the arrival of Derek McKay onto the scene. Aberdeen manager Eddie Turnbull decided only minutes before kick-off to give McKay his first start since signing for the club on a free transfer from Dundee at the beginning of the season. McKay repaid his boss by scoring the only goal against Falkirk at Brockville. Elsewhere, Kilmarnock won 1-0 away to Motherwell and Dundee likewise won at East Fife. Celtic faced Rangers in a bad-tempered affair perhaps not helped when early in the match Jim Craig headed past his own keeper only to be 'mockingly' congratulated by Willie Johnston and Colin Stein. Celtic equalised just before half-time through Lennox. Alex MacDonald was sent off for a lunge on keeper Evan Williams and as Rangers tried to wind the clock down, David Hay scored from 25 yards with four minutes remaining to give Celtic the lead. Jimmy Johnstone finished the tie off two minutes later.

Celtic took on Dundee at a Hampden semi-final in front of a 64,546 crowd in what was a tight match. Celtic managed to get the breakthrough in the 58th minute when Lou Macari scored following a short corner. Dundee hit back within six minutes with Gordon Wallace slotting home. With eight minutes remaining, however, keeper Ally Donaldson, who had made several fine saves, dropped a Gemmell cross at Bobby Lennox's feet and the tie was lost. Dundee were to suffer five Scottish Cup semi-final defeats to Celtic in the 1970s but victory did await them in a League Cup Final within a few years.

The other semi-final was played at Muirton Park, Perth, with 25,812 in attendance witnessing Aberdeen win through against Kilmarnock. In a rather tense match with few chances created by either side, McKay's 22nd-minute goal sealed the Dons' final place.

The final, with 108,334 spectators, was not without controversy around some of the decisions by referee Bobby Davidson. The first was a penalty in the 27th minute, given for handball which most saw as accidental as the ball hit the upper arm of a Celtic player. Up stepped Joe Harper to net past Williams. Bobby Lennox was then to be denied what was reported to be a perfectly good goal. Bobby Clark had thrown the ball up into the air prior to intending to punt it up the park. Lennox, however, got close enough to cause the keeper to drop it. The Celtic player took advantage and put the ball into the net but Davidson blew for an infringement.

It would, however, be unfair to dismiss Aberdeen as lucky given that they performed well with Martin Buchan, aged only 21, captaining the side and Arthur Graham at only 17 playing out on the wing. The other goals came from McKay in the 83rd minute, latching on to a rebound as Williams saved from Jim Forrest, and although Lennox netted in the 89th minute, almost immediately McKay scored again to give Aberdeen the cup.

Celtic returned to Hampden four days later to beat Leeds United in a memorable European Cup semi-final and as for 'Cup-Tie' McKay, he quit Aberdeen over a row about the cup final bonuses and slipped into football obscurity.

1970/71 ▸ 1979/80

The 1970s was initially dominated by Jock Stein's Celtic with Rangers grabbing a couple of Trebles too, but by the end of it we began to see the rise of the so-called 'New Firm', Alex Ferguson's Aberdeen and Jim McLean's Dundee United.

KENNY DALGLISH

The decade started with the tragedy of the 1971 Ibrox disaster where 66 supporters lost their lives, and ended as we slid into the '80s and the disgraceful scenes at the conclusion of the 1980 Scottish Cup Final – with the latter resulting in the introduction of legislation designed to combat the issue of hooliganism.

League reconstruction would see the introduction of the Premier Division and a third tier once again in Scottish football. The debates on its merits, numbers and format have been wrangling on ever since.

As always there were some memorable players in this period with the likes of Kenny Dalglish, Dixie Deans, Davie Cooper, Andy Ritchie, Joe Harper, Turnbull's Tornadoes and even George Best got involved.

Aberdeen	⚽
Joe Harper	

International Appearances	3
International Goals	2
League Appearances	103
League Goals	44
Height	5'6"

1970/71
The race for the league championship went right to the wire. Aberdeen, following their Scottish Cup success in 1970, competed with Celtic for the title in 1970/71, just missing out in their last two games. In early October they tasted defeat to Morton at Cappielow and then went on a 15-match run of victories. During this period, keeper Bobby Clark went 1,155 minutes without conceding a goal, which at the time was a British record.

By then, Aberdeen led Celtic by four points but having played a game more. They faced Celtic in their penultimate match at Pittodrie, the game ending all square to leave the Dons on 54 points and Celtic on 51 but having played two fewer games. A week later the Dons slumped to a 1-0 defeat to Falkirk at Brockville and Celtic picked up five points from six to win the championship. Celtic

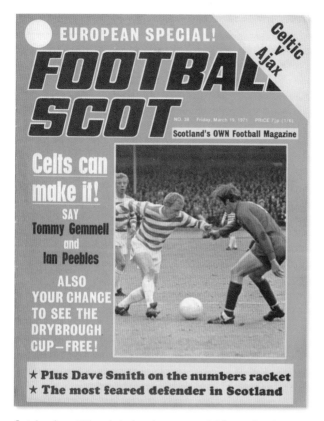

finished on 56 points having scored 89 goals along the way with Harry Hood as the division's top scorer with 22. St Johnstone continued to improve under Willie Ormond and finished the season in third place on 44 points. At the bottom, Cowdenbeath finished on 17 points, six adrift of St Mirren. This was to be their last season in the top flight. St Mirren lost out to Dunfermline on goal difference.

Partick Thistle won Division Two with 56 points, five ahead of East Fife. The Fifers had led for most of the season but Thistle always had a game or two to catch up with. Albion Rovers inflicted Thistle's last defeat – in November – and the Jags went 24 league games unbeaten after that. Teenage goalkeeper Alan Rough only conceded 26 goals in his first full season. Brechin City finished bottom with 19 points.

Having won the League Cup for five seasons in a row, Celtic were about to go on a run of four successive final defeats. They took on Dundee in the quarter-finals and began with a 2-2 draw at Dens Park before inflicting a 5-1 crushing at home. Cowdenbeath scraped through 1-0 against Falkirk in the two legs thanks to a Billy Laing goal. Rangers comprehensively beat Hibernian 3-1 in each leg to progress and Dumbarton won with the odd goal in 11 against Partick Thistle.

In the semis it took Celtic two games to dispose of Dumbarton, who matched them evenly for most of the 240 minutes of football played. The first match, in front of 40,000 fans, ended 0-0 with goalkeeper Lawrie Williams taking most of the plaudits for not only a great performance but also a double save from a Willie Wallace penalty. The replay with 32,000 in attendance witnessed Celtic take a two-goal lead through David Hay and Lennox but goals from the Sons' Charlie Gallagher, an ex-Celtic favourite, and Kenny Wilson saw this game go into extra time too. Jinky Johnstone put Celtic ahead before a controversial Lou Macari goal increased the lead and although Johnny Graham netted for Dumbarton, there was no way back for them.

Cowdenbeath put up sturdy resistance against Rangers in the other semi at Hampden in front of a 32,000 crowd but a spot-kick by Willie Johnston in the first half put the Ibrox team in front. Colin Stein added a second after the interval to complete the scoring.

The final itself was played in front of a crowd of 106,263 and was generally seen as a cracking match without much of the ugly side of football the Old Firm fixture can entail. Rangers were to win 1-0 thanks to a goal from 16-year-old Derek Johnstone, heading in from a cross by Willie Johnston in the 40th minute. Also playing that day was 18-year-old Alfie Conn, who would later join Celtic after a sojourn at Tottenham Hotspur in the mid-'70s.

Preliminary rounds were done away with in the Scottish Cup that season. Elgin knocked out Stenhousemuir and then Berwick before losing 5-0 to Aberdeen at Pittodrie. Glasgow Corporation Transport FC faced Brechin in round two and went in at half-time only one goal down. However, the wheels came off the bus in the second half as they crashed to a 4-1 defeat. Hibs put eight past Forfar in the third round and followed this with a 2-1 victory over rivals Hearts, later moving into the semis after a narrow win over Dundee. Celtic took two tries to get past Dunfermline before thrashing Raith Rovers 7-1 in the quarter-finals. Rangers knocked out in-form Aberdeen through a Colin Jackson goal to reach the last four. Airdrieonians had won through 3-2 against Kilmarnock at Rugby Park to also reach this stage.

Both semi-finals went to replays. Rangers against Hibernian served mediocre fare for the 69,429 spectators in a 0-0 draw with little goalmouth action. A week later 54,435 turned up and saw a much better match. Rangers clinched the victory with goals from Willie Henderson and Alfie Conn, Jimmy O'Rourke netting for Hibs.

The other tie was a six-goal thriller for the 39,404 crowd. Celtic had eased into the lead through Hood and then a header from Johnstone going into the interval. Derek Whiteford pulled one back for Airdrie just after the restart before Hood once more put Celtic two ahead and seemingly on their way to the final. However, in the 55th minute Billy Wilson brought Airdrie back into it. The two Drews, Jarvie and Busby, then combined for the latter to equalise. You rarely seem to get a second bite of the Old Firm cherry and so it proved as Celtic won through with yet another Johnstone header and a goal from Harry Hood. The replay was attended by almost 8,000 more fans, totalling 47,186.

The final itself saw 120,092 Old Firm supporters turn up. Bobby Lennox put Celtic ahead just before half-time but the now 17-year-old substitute Derek Johnstone earned a replay with a goal three minutes from time. In the replay a 103,000 crowd saw Celtic score two in two minutes midway through the first half from Macari and a Hood penalty. Johnstone's shot in the 58th minute rebounded off Jim Craig into his own net to make it 2-1 but that was the end of the scoring.

1971/72

The story of 1971/72 looks as though Celtic romped it, winning the title with 60 points and finishing ten clear of nearest rivals Aberdeen, but it had been close until March before the Dons' challenge began to peter out with defeats and draws. Celtic only lost two games all season, scoring 96 goals, but Aberdeen's Joe Harper topped the scoring charts with 33 for the runners-up. Rangers were third and Hibernian, now managed by Eddie Turnbull, were fourth with 44 points each.

Dunfermline won their opening-day fixture against East Fife but only one other victory was achieved by the beginning of 1972 and they were continually languishing at the bottom of the table. Also dropping down one point ahead of them on 24 were Clyde.

Dumbarton clinched the Division Two title with a run of ten wins in their final 11 games, eclipsing Arbroath on a goal difference of eight. Both finished on 52 points with Arbroath winning seven straight before a final-day draw with Queen of the South. Hamilton finished bottom with 16 points.

Celtic progressed through their League Cup section by winning their group, which included Rangers, with ten points. Partick Thistle headed into

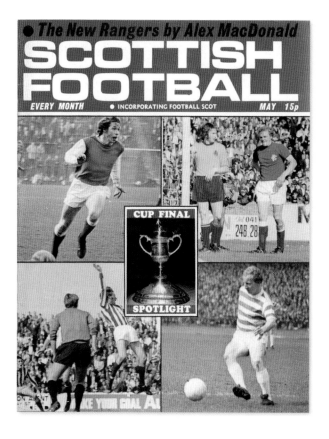

the supplementary round to face Alloa, winning 6-2 over both legs to set up a quarter-final against St Johnstone. Clydebank welcomed Celtic to Kilbowie with a programme proclaiming 'Jinky is Here'. Sadly, Mr Johnstone never made the game and the Bankies shipped five goals in the first leg of the quarter-final. The academic second leg saw the Celts run out 6-2 winners. Falkirk ousted Hibernian, winning 2-0 at Brockville before holding out to a 1-0 defeat at Easter Road. St Mirren, with Gordon McQueen in their ranks, beat Stirling Albion 5-0 over two legs. Due to the supplementary round, St Johnstone and Thistle met over a 48-hour period. The Jags came away from Perth with a 2-0 deficit but three goals in as many minutes on the half-hour mark had Thistle in front at home. A John Connolly penalty in the second half saw things all square but two more goals gave the Jags a 5-1 win on a memorable night at Firhill.

Thistle then faced Falkirk at Hampden in front of a crowd of 20,286 for a place in the final. Two goals from legendary winger Denis McQuade saw them emerge as winners and become the first side to compete in the supplementary round then go on to reach the final. Some 29,488 spectators saw Celtic take on St Mirren in the other semi-final. The dismissal of Hugh McLaughlin in the 35th minute meant the Saints were always up against it. Early in the second half, Celtic hit three goals in four minutes through Hay, Hood and Lennox to win the tie.

'In Scotland, it's League Cup Final day at Hampden Park, where Celtic meet Partick Thistle, who have no chance,' said Sam Leitch on the BBC's *Grandstand* broadcast. This pretty much summed up most people's feeling about the match, including many a Jags fan. Celtic's Lou Macari in

the tunnel before the match reportedly told Thistle players, 'At least you'll get a medal.' He was right but it wouldn't be a runners-up version as expected. By the 37th minute Thistle had been scoring for fun, leading 4-0 through goals from Rae, Lawrie, McQuade and Bone. Everyone expected a Celtic comeback in the second half, but a Kenny Dalglish goal was all they had to show in the end.

Elgin City advanced to the fourth round of the Scottish Cup with victories over Stenhousemuir, Burntisland Shipyard FC and Inverness Caley before losing out 4-1 to Kilmarnock. Otherwise, the cup pretty much went to form that year. The quarter-finals saw Celtic advance 1-0 against Hearts after a replay and Rangers also progressed after a second match, winning 4-2 at Ibrox against Motherwell. Hibernian overcame Aberdeen 2-0 at home and Killie won 3-1 away to Raith.

A semi-final crowd of 48,398 turned up to see Celtic play Kilmarnock. Dixie Deans opened the scoring late in the first half but Jim Cook produced an equaliser shortly after the interval. Deans added to his tally, but it was not until late in the game that a Macari goal secured the victory for Celtic.

A crowd of 75,884 saw Rangers pitched against the side that would later become known as Turnbull's Tornadoes with players such as Pat Stanton, John Blackley, John Brownlie and Alex Cropley all playing key roles. The first match ended in a draw with Alex MacDonald putting Rangers ahead just before half-time and Jimmy O'Rourke hitting back two minutes after the interval. There was a turnout of 67,547 for the replay in which the Hibs team was more in command and an early goal from Pat Stanton was followed up by a second from Alex Edwards in the second half.

A close encounter was predicted for this final and it seemed that way for quite a while. Billy McNeill put Celtic in front in the second minute but Alan Gordon equalised ten minutes later. Deans restored Celtic's lead not long after and 2-1 it was at half-time. Deans then increased the lead in the 54th minute and completed his hat-trick 20 minutes later. Macari added a double in the final ten minutes to end it 6-1 to Celtic.

PAT STANTON
HIBS and SCOTLAND   SCOTCARD No. 22
SCOTTISH DAILY EXPRESS TOP FOR SPORT

1972/73

It is hard to pinpoint the exact moment when Rangers lost the league. They fought Celtic all the way for the title, losing out by one point. Perhaps, in the final equation, two defeats in Ayrshire – an opening-day 2-1 loss at Somerset Park and a later reverse to Kilmarnock – were crucial. Celtic finished top with 57 points, ending the season in fine style with eight straight wins including a 3-0 final-day victory over Hibernian at Easter Road. Hibs were third on 45 points. They had topped the table after defeating city rivals Hearts 7-0 at Tynecastle on New Year's Day. Five days later, though, full-back John Brownlie broke his leg playing against East Fife. He was such a big loss, both in defence and

attack, and who knows what might have happened
had he been available. As it was, Hibernian forward
Alan Gordon was the season's top scorer with 27.

Airdrie finished bottom with 16 points. Killie only
lost once in their last seven games, but Dumbarton
finished with two wins, enough to give them a tally
of 23 points, one more than Kilmarnock.

Clyde had been leading the charge for the title
in the lower tier since early on and only two losses
in their last 22 matches saw them clinch the title
on 56 points, four ahead of Dunfermline. Brechin
finished bottom with 14 points, conceding 99 goals
in the process.

The League Cup once again saw Celtic
defeated in the final. The sections, however, were
reorganised with, in the main, two teams from each
league competing in the groups with the top two
progressing. Sixteen teams went through to the
two-legged second round with Aberdeen notably
beating Falkirk 8-0 in the first leg. Rangers lost 2-1
at Ibrox to Stenhousemuir but having been five up
from the first leg maybe the 3,000 crowd were not
that upset. Holders Partick Thistle lost 1-0 to East
Fife. The quarter-finals saw Hibs progress with a
10-3 aggregate demolition of Airdrie, Aberdeen 7-1
over East Fife and Rangers 3-1 over St Johnstone.
Celtic comfortably came through a third match with
Dundee at Hampden winning 4-1.

In the semis, 46,513 saw Hibernian emerge
victorious from a tough match with Rangers which
produced five bookings. Full-back John Brownlie
evaded a few 'hefty' tackles to shoot low past
keeper McCloy for the only goal of the game. The
39,682 who turned up for the other tie saw much
better fare. Aberdeen took the lead twice, but each
time Celtic clawed them back. Joe Harper and
Davie Robb provided the goals for the Dons with
Hood from the penalty spot and Johnstone for
Celtic before Tommy Callaghan netted the winner in
the 80th minute.

Hibernian had already defeated Celtic at
Hampden in the Drybrough Cup in early August, so
they did not go into this one fearing the worst.

1970/71 ▸ 1979/80

A 71,696 crowd saw Pat Stanton open the scoring on the hour mark after the deftest of lobs from Alex Edwards. Stanton still had a bit of work to do, moving away from goal before planting his shot past Evan Williams. Six minutes later Stanton opted for a short cross to Jim O'Rourke at the front post to head Hibs further in front. Kenny Dalglish scored in the 77th minute but Hibs held out to lift the League Cup for the first time.

Works side, Ferranti Thistle, made their first appearance in the Scottish Cup, defeating Duns in the first round before losing in a replay to Elgin City in the next. Inverness Thistle knocked out Queen's Park before losing to Ayr United in the third round. Rangers took two games to defeat Hibernian in the fourth round. Celtic won a replay at Pittodrie to eliminate Aberdeen in the quarter-finals. Partick

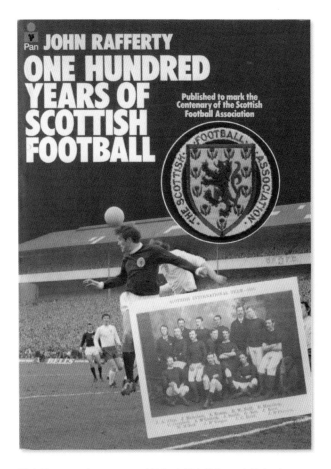

Thistle were hammered 5-1 at Firhill by a blistering Ayr performance in the last eight too.

It took Celtic two matches to overcome Dundee in the semi-final. The first game saw 55,428 leave non-plussed as the sides played out a rather drab goalless draw, then 100 minutes into the replay the 47,384 crowd were not much happier at the football on display. However, Johnstone put Celtic ahead a minute later and further goals from Dalglish and Johnstone again put the tie beyond doubt. In the other tie, a crowd of 51,815 saw Ayr have a goal from Ingram chalked off for offside within the first minute but after that they were rarely at the races as Rangers eased through 2-0 with both goals from Derek Parlane.

The 1972/73 final was a classic in many ways and was the last of the 100,000-plus crowds with

122,714 in attendance. Kenny Dalglish opened the scoring after an instinctive pass from Deans put him through in the 24th minute. A Derek Parlane header restored the balance before half-time but a minute into the second half Alfie Conn outpaced Billy McNeill to give Rangers the lead. However, that was only held for four minutes when George Connelly coolly slotted away a penalty after Greig used a hand to save a Deans shot. The winning goal would famously come from an unlikely source in Rangers defender Tom Forsyth in the 59th minute. Derek Johnstone had headed the ball past Ally Hunter against the post and it then bobbled to the other post before Forsyth 'foot-fumbled' the ball over the line, giving Rangers their first Scottish Cup win since 1966.

1973/74

Celtic coasted to the championship, winning with 53 points and finishing four clear of Hibernian for their ninth championship in a row. Their finish to the season was poor by their standards as they drew the last four matches, although the first – against Falkirk at Brockville – was enough to ensure the title. Dixie Deans netted 26 of Celtic's 82 goals to top the goalscoring charts. Hibernian, with 49 points, pipped Rangers in third by a point.

Falkirk finished bottom on 22 points (14 coming from draws) and scoring only 33 goals. Their season started with a straight 16 losses and six draws in all competitions before they crushed Dumbarton 5-1 at Boghead on the second day of 1974. East Fife also dropped down on 24 points, losing out to Dunfermline by three goals to fall out of the top flight for the final time.

In Division Two, Kilmarnock had finished with ten wins and two draws but a poor start to the season was their downfall in terms of the title. Airdrie could afford to lose a couple of games in their run-in and still finish on 60 points, two ahead of Kilmarnock. Airdrie hit 102 league goals and included an 8-0 thrashing of Brechin among their tally. Brechin finished bottom with 14 points, conceding 99 goals.

CELTIC

DIXIE DEANS

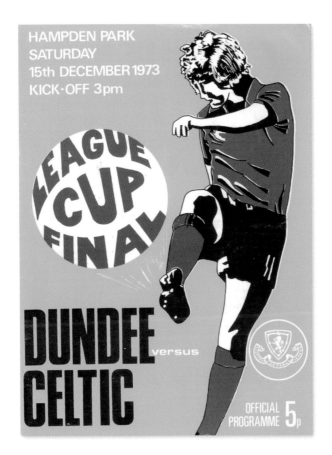

The League Cup reverted to the previous drawing procedure with teams in the same divisions forming sections and the top two progressing. Rangers topped their group with Celtic coming in second. Holders Hibernian came through as first in their section. The second round saw Celtic taken to a replay after Motherwell beat them 1-0 at Celtic Park to even the tie. The replay was won with almost the final kick of the ball as Jimmy Johnstone netted to give his side a 3-2 victory. In the quarter-finals Albion Rovers took a 2-0 lead to Rugby Park, but Kilmarnock emerged 5-2 winners of the second leg to progress. Rangers beat Hibernian while Celtic ousted Aberdeen and Dundee eliminated Clyde.

The semis saw Dundee paired with Kilmarnock in a lowly attended match at Hampden. Only 4,682 ventured out on a December evening to see former Lisbon Lion Tommy Gemmell hit his first Dundee

goal from 30 yards to win the tie in the 60th minute. A crowd of 54,864 turned up to see Celtic defeat Rangers for the third time that season. Striker Harry Hood netted a hat-trick with a goal from Alex MacDonald being Rangers' only reply.

The final itself came in the middle of the 1970s fuel crisis and with no floodlighting available it kicked off at 1.30pm after a pitch inspection of the frozen surface. A very hardy crowd of only 27,974 made it to the final with many trains not running either. Dundee, captained by Gemmell, dominated and striker Gordon Wallace produced the only goal with a great finish in the 75th minute to give his team the cup for the first time since 1952.

The second round of the Scottish Cup saw Clydebank take two games to dispose of Highland side Inverness Clachnacuddin. They were rewarded for this with a 6-1 thrashing at Celtic Park in round three. Partick Thistle won the battle of the Thistles, defeating Ferranti by the same score, and Rangers put eight past Queen's Park. Stranraer took three matches to defeat St Mirren but were thumped 7-1 by Ayr in round four. Celtic continued apace with another 6-1 win, over Stirling Albion this time. The biggest surprise was the 3-0 defeat of Rangers by Dundee at Ibrox though.

All four quarter-finals went to replays and as the dust settled, once more Celtic were paired with Dundee in the semis. A crowd of 58,250 saw an entertaining match with Jinky Johnstone coming back to his mesmeric best and providing the only goal of the game just before half-time. In the other tie 22,725 saw Hearts take the lead through veteran defender Alan Anderson but Pat Gardner equalised for Dundee United to take the tie to a replay. In the second match, seen by 12,860 fans, Hearts again took the lead in the first half, through Donald Ford, but a comeback after the interval saw United advance to their first final with a 4-2 victory. Doug Smith scored from the spot to equalise before Graeme Payne put United in front. Sub Willie Gibson netted for Hearts to restore parity before goals from teenager Andy Gray and Archie Knox sealed the win.

The final itself in front of 75,959 spectators was not a classic with Celtic winning 3-0, goals from Hood, Stevie Murray and Dixie Deans. United never seemed to exert any pressure on Celtic. The game was interrupted by two pitch invasions, not from supporters but from two dogs, both of which can be seen in the match highlights!

1974/75
All change. Not only would Rangers win the title to deny Celtic the elusive ten in a row but come the end of the season reconstruction meant that eight teams would be relegated. Joined by the top six sides from the existing second tier, they formed a new second tier (to be known as the First Division). The final 13

teams, with the addition of Meadowbank Thistle (a renamed Ferranti), then formed a new third level (the Second Division).

The season was pretty much neck and neck between Celtic and Rangers from the start, but after the turn of the year Celtic's form dipped badly. Starting with a 3-0 defeat to their rivals, they managed to lose eight of their final 14 games. In contrast Rangers lost once, in their final fixture against Airdrie, and finished on 56 points, seven clear of Hibs with Celtic languishing a further four behind.

The top scorers were Andy Gray of Dundee United and Willie Pettigrew of Motherwell with 20 goals each. Gray would move on to Aston Villa the following season. Pettigrew would hit 80 goals in 166 games for the Well before joining Dundee United. Despite Pettigrew's goals, Motherwell avoided the drop by just two points from the unlucky Airdrie, who defeated Rangers twice as well as Celtic and reached the Scottish Cup Final. Kilmarnock and Partick Thistle were also in the mix until the season's end, but they were joined in the second tier with Dumbarton, Dunfermline, Morton and, dropping out of the top flight for the final time, Clyde and Arbroath.

MOTHERWELL

WILLIE PETTIGREW

Falkirk avoided the previous season's fascination with draws and only had two stalemates. They lost ten times, but the 26 wins saw them eclipse both Queen of the South and Montrose by one point with 54. The Bairns would be joined in the new 14-team second tier with Hamilton, East Fife and St Mirren. At the bottom of the heap were Forfar who picked up nine points and conceded 102 goals altogether.

Celtic may have loosened their grip on the league but both cup competitions were won by them.

In the League Cup, holders Dundee fell at the first hurdle after finishing third in their section behind Hibernian and Rangers, who lost out due to the second round being dropped from that year's format. Celtic topped their group. Second Division Falkirk knocked out Hearts and met Hibernian in the semi-finals. The tie at Tynecastle saw 22,000 fans in attendance as Hibs won courtesy of a Joe Harper

goal in the 69th minute. Over at Hampden on the same night, Airdrie also made more of a game of it than expected against Celtic. The crowd of 19,332 had to wait until the 61st minute for Stevie Murray to net the winner for the Bhoys.

Hibs had shipped five goals the week before to Celtic at Easter Road with Dixie Deans hitting a hat-trick that day, and he was to do so in the final too. It earned him a belated Scotland call-up. The match saw Celtic play the free-flowing, attacking football they were revered for and they recorded a 6-3 victory. Jimmy Johnstone, Murray and Paul Wilson netted the other three Celtic goals. Cruelly for Joe Harper, he hit a hat-trick in a cup final and ended up on the losing side.

Montrose hit the ground running in the Scottish Cup, beating Selkirk 5-1 and then recording their record victory with a 12-1 thrashing of Vale of

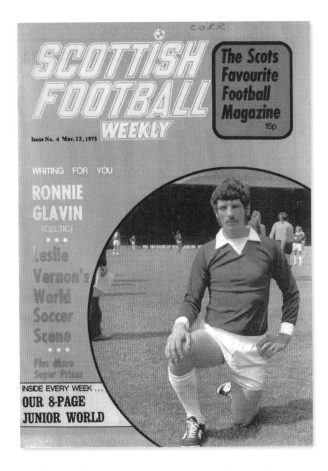

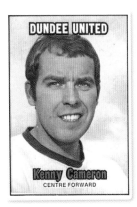

Leithen with veteran Kenny Cameron hitting four goals. In the third round they played Hamilton and after a 0-0 draw they went out with a 3-0 loss. Clachnacuddin also started well, crushing Gala Fairydean 8-1 and then beating Stirling Albion 4-3 before a narrow defeat to Dumbarton.

The third round also saw Rangers exit to Aberdeen after a replay, Celtic defeated Hibernian away and Dundee United took two games to overcome Berwick Rangers. Airdrie took two games to beat Morton in the third round and they also needed two attempts to overcome Arbroath in the quarter-finals. The last eight also saw Celtic put paid to Dumbarton, Motherwell quash Aberdeen's hopes and Dundee eliminate Hearts after a replay.

The semis paired Dundee with Celtic once more and a crowd of 40,702 took in another close match between the pair. A Tommy Gemmell mistake gifted Celtic the only goal as he ran across his area with the ball only for Ronnie Glavin to dispossess him and score.

Airdrie and Motherwell played out a poor, nervy first match – perhaps a typical semi-final – in front of a 20,574 crowd, drawing 1-1. Airdrie equalised through a Stewart McLaren own goal after Willie Pettigrew had put Motherwell ahead. The 13,173 replay crowd witnessed Motherwell's keeper Stuart Rennie be both the hero and unwitting villain. In the 39th minute he saved a penalty and the rebound shot from Paul Jonquin but late in the match fell afoul of the four-step goalkeeper rule. From the resultant indirect free kick John Lapsley hammered the ball through a throng of players to score the winner.

The final itself was played in the bright Hampden sunshine in front of a crowd of 75,457. Celtic took an early lead when a McGrain cross found an unmarked Paul Wilson. Walter McCann first hit the post and a little while later drew Airdrie level just before half-time. Moments later, Airdrie again left Wilson unmarked from a Lennox corner and went into the interval 2-1 down. The only goal of the second half was scored from the spot by Pat McCluskey after Lennox had been bundled over by Jonquin. Celtic won their 24th Scottish Cup, and fittingly, retiring captain Billy McNeill lifted the trophy to end his playing career on a high.

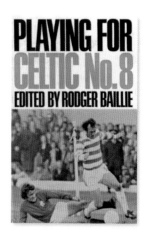

1975/76
Celtic were disadvantaged from the start of the inaugural Premier Division season with Jock Stein involved in a near-fatal car crash during the summer. Sean Fallon, his assistant, would manage Celtic for the duration. Rangers, however, were relentless – they started the season well, had a wee dip in October and November, then didn't lose again. They finished on 54 points with Celtic six behind on 48. Rangers' goal tally was a lowly 60 with Celtic hitting 71 overall. Kenny Dalglish was the top scorer with 24.

St Johnstone ended rock bottom with 11 points, 21 adrift of second bottom. Dundee were edged out of the top division on goal difference with Aberdeen and Dundee United also both on 32 points. Given the rise of both these clubs in the coming years, it is interesting to think that neither might have achieved what they did had relegation come calling.

Not much thought had been put into the new First Division so the 14 sides only played 26 games with the short-lived Spring Cup competition tagged on to the end of the season. Partick Thistle under Bertie Auld won it with 41 points, six clear of Kilmarnock. Clyde finished rock bottom on 14 points with Dunfermline also dropping down with 23.

Clydebank won the new Second Division on goal difference over Raith Rovers. A fraught night at Recreation Park, Alloa, saw them grab a 0-0 draw to claim the championship. Under the club's owners, the Steedman brothers, Bill Munro had started to put together a Bankies side that included keeper Jim Gallacher, Jim Fallon, Mike Larnach and the great Davie Cooper. Meadowbank Thistle finished bottom of the pile.

Partick Thistle achieved that rarity for any club of full points from their League Cup section which included Premier Division sides Dundee United and St Johnstone and First Division rivals Kilmarnock. Montrose provided the shock in the quarter-finals by defeating Hibs 3-2 over the two legs to face Rangers in the semi-final. Celtic and Partick Thistle were to meet in the other.

A crowd of 31,421 turned up to see Thistle play the tight defensive game they became synonymous with under Bertie Auld. The breakthrough was made in the 28th minute when Icelandic midfielder Jóhannes Eðvaldsson scored a scorcher from 30 yards. There were very little chances after this although Peter Latchford saved well from Doug Somner in the dying minutes to secure Celtic's place in the final.

Rangers beat Montrose 5-1 but surprisingly the Gable Endies went in at half-time a goal up thanks to a Les Barr penalty. Early in the second half it was nearly two as Stuart Markland hit the post, but Rangers soon equalised through Parlane and the

1970/71 ▶ 1979/80

rest is history. Goals by Jardine, Miller, Ally Scott and Johnstone put the Rangers supporters at ease in the 20,319 crowd.

Due to fears of crowd trouble, there was an early kick-off of 1pm with only 58,806 in attendance. Rangers won thanks to a headed goal from Alex MacDonald in the 66th minute. Chances were few and far in between, although Tommy Callaghan hit the bar for Celtic at one point. It was a rough game and Celtic criticised the referee's performance afterwards, particularly in his lenience towards Tom Forsyth's 'marking' of Dalglish.

In the Scottish Cup, Albion Rovers made a hard slog of things, drawing 0-0 with Hawick Royal Albert at home before winning a replay 3-0. They then faced Glasgow University and drew 1-1 at home before winning by the solitary goal in the following game. They were knocked out in the next round, losing 2-1 to Partick Thistle at Cliftonhill. Holders Celtic fell at the first hurdle as they lost out to Motherwell 3-2 at Fir Park. In the quarter-finals, Hearts took two games to dispose of Montrose and Motherwell likewise with Hibernian.

A crowd of 50,000 turned up for the Rangers v Motherwell semi-final and after a dull start they saw Well head into the interval two goals in front through McLaren and Pettigrew. Rangers hit their first goal in the 70th minute courtesy of a dubious penalty awarded by referee John Gordon. Miller scored from the spot and with some inevitability Johnstone netted a brace to send Rangers into the final.

The other tie, between Hearts and Dumbarton, drew a smaller crowd of 16,087 and saw another semi-final caught up in the stage fright and nervousness of the players. The Sons proved to be the better side but did not carve out any real chances and neither did Hearts as the match ended in a stalemate. In the replay, attended by 11,723 souls, Hearts were gifted the lead when Walter Smith attempted to clear a header for a corner and hit the back of his own net. Further goals from Rab Prentice and Drew Busby saw Hearts through to the final.

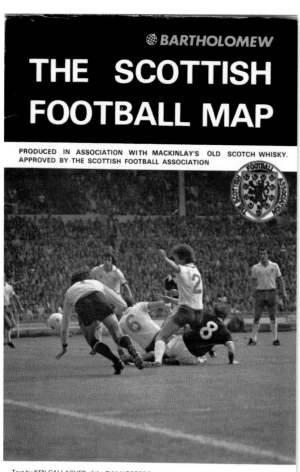

A week before the final, it took Derek Johnstone 22 seconds to hit the winner against Dundee United at Tannadice. It took him 19 seconds longer to hit the opener against Hearts at Hampden. After that the destination of the cup was no real surprise. MacDonald would send Rangers 2-0 up at the interval and Johnstone added a third in the 81st minute. Graham Shaw scored a consolation goal shortly after and Rangers won their third Treble.

1976/77

The previous season was looked upon as one of transition for Celtic but the signing of Pat Stanton from Hibs seemed to galvanise the side, as did the return of Jock Stein to the fore. Rangers, following their Treble, were expected to consolidate their position but no trophies were to head that way. After eight games they sat with eight points having already lost twice and drawn four times. Dundee United were top with 12 points from 16 and Celtic one point behind. Celtic only lost twice after this point and finished top with 55 points, 11 clear of Rangers. Aberdeen and Dundee United, having been in the relegation zone the previous season, finished third and fourth. Motherwell's Willie Pettigrew was once more the top scorer with 21 goals.

It took Killie eight games to produce a win, a relished 6-1 victory over local rivals Ayr, but that was as good as it got for them as they finished on 17. Also relegated were Hearts, for the first time in their history, with 27 points.

Alex Ferguson's young St Mirren side, featuring the likes of Billy Stark, Frank McGarvey and Tony Fitzpatrick, won the First Division championship in a division now stretched to 39 games. The Saints lost their second match but another 29 passed before they lost another, their only other defeat that season. Clydebank pushed them all the way and topped the table in October but ended four points adrift. The Bankies would become the first side to play in all three divisions. Falkirk finished bottom with 20 points with Raith Rovers demoted alongside them.

SOMERSET NEWS VOL. 7 NO. 14 10p

AYR UTD VS

KILMARNOCK

SCOTTISH PREMIER LEAGUE
SATURDAY, 1st JANUARY, 1977
Kick-off 1500 hrs.

Stirling Albion topped the third tier on 55 points, four above Alloa Athletic. Dunfermline were just pipped for the promotion spot by a point after finishing strongly. Forfar ended bottom with 24 points.

In the League Cup, Aberdeen, Celtic and Rangers all emerged unscathed from their sections. Hibernian had a notable 9-2 victory over St Johnstone but it was to no avail as they finished second to Rangers. Rangers played out an epic tie with Clydebank in the quarter-finals with Davie Cooper netting a double at Ibrox in a 3-3 draw in the first leg. Cooper netted again as the sides drew 1-1 at New Kilbowie Park a fortnight later. The first replay at Ibrox saw neither side score and so a fourth game was played. Rangers scored early through Parlane but once again Cooper was on target from a free kick to equalise. Bobby McKean hit the winner for Rangers in the second half. It was no surprise when Cooper moved to Rangers at the end of the season for £100,000. Aberdeen had also gone to a replay to overcome Stirling Albion. Hearts beat Falkirk 7-5 on aggregate with Celtic overpowering Albion Rovers 6-0.

Celtic played Hearts at Hampden in front of a crowd of 21,706 but it was the Edinburgh club who scored first through Jim Brown in the 42nd minute, although Dalglish equalised just before the break. Celtic took the initiative after the interval, hitting the post a couple of times, but the winning goal came in controversial circumstances. Referee Alexander apparently missed a foul on Shaw and within moments Dalglish was brought down and a penalty was awarded. Kenny took the kick and gave Celtic the lead. With tempers fraying, Prentice of Hearts was soon sent off for chopping down winger Johnny Doyle.

In the other semi-final, played in front of 20,990 fans, Aberdeen's play was as effervescent as manager Ally MacLeod, serving notice of their re-emergence as a force in Scottish football with a 5-1 win. A trio of old hands did the damage as Jocky Scott hit three with Drew Jarvie and Joe Harper netting one apiece. Rangers' reply was a diving header from Alex MacDonald in front of 20,990 fans.

A crowd of 69,707 attended the final, in which Celtic were the better side but lost out to the Dons in extra time. Celtic took the lead on 12 minutes when Dalglish was bundled over by Jarvie and then converted the resulting penalty. However, Aberdeen fought back and a fine worked move saw Jarvie redeem himself with a headed goal in the 25th minute. Celtic would have the bulk of the chances in the second half but poor finishing and some inspired goalkeeping by Clark took the game into extra time. Two minutes into the additional 30, Davie Robb scored the winner from close range and the cup headed north.

All three Inverness sides were involved in the first round of the Scottish Cup. Thistle defeated Clachnacuddin in the local derby while Caley got the better of the Stenhousemuir to progress.

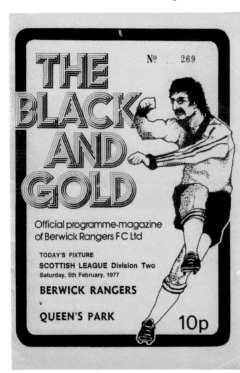

However, both teams faltered in the second round after replays to senior-level opposition. Elgin knocked out Forfar and then Stirling Albion after a replay, to face Rangers in the fourth round, exiting after a 3-0 loss. First Division high-fliers St Mirren crushed Dundee United 4-1 at Love Street but went down to Motherwell in the fourth round. Celtic needed replays to get past both Airdrie and Ayr United and reach the last eight. Hearts needed a replay to get past East Fife in the quarter-finals and Rangers beat Motherwell 2-0 with Dundee and Celtic also going through.

The semi-finals paired Rangers with Hearts and Celtic with Dundee, 23,222 watching the first tie as Rangers beat Hearts 2-0. Colin Jackson nodded home from a McLean corner deep into the second half and with nine minutes remaining McLean scored from the spot after his shot hit Dave Clunie on the arm.

Dundee had several chances to go ahead in the other encounter. Celtic fans among the 29,990 would have been relieved to see Joe Craig put their side ahead in the 79th minute. Within six minutes Craig ended the tie with a second goal.

The final was televised live and between that and the pouring rain, only 54,252 turned up to see this Old Firm encounter. Both sides set out to nullify each other's creative players and the man-marking meant that not a lot of good football was produced. The winning goal itself was surrounded in controversy as to whether Derek Johnstone handled on the line or not. Just about the whole Rangers team challenged referee Bob Valentine on this but Celtic's Andy Lynch calmly stepped up to take the penalty and score the winner. Lynch had only taken two penalties before in his career, when a Hearts player, and had missed both.

1977/78
The loss of Kenny Dalglish to Liverpool was huge for Celtic but injuries to Pat Stanton, Danny McGrain and Alfie Conn ripped the heart out of the side. After nine games they sat second from bottom having lost six times already, and their season never recovered as they finished fifth with 36 points from 36 games. Rangers also started badly, losing their first two games, but after that they began to climb the table and with free-flowing forwards in Johnstone, Gordon Smith and Cooper they began to rack up the wins and soon were leading the table. Aberdeen, with Billy McNeill in charge, chased them all the way and inflicted three of Rangers' five defeats. Rangers finished on 55 points with the Dons only two behind with two drawn matches more than the Gers. The top scorer was Derek Johnstone with 25.

Clydebank, with the loss of Davie Cooper, were always going to find it hard to compete to the same level as before and finished bottom with 19 points after scoring only 23 goals. Ayr United were also relegated and have yet to return to the top tier.

1970/71 ▸ 1979/80

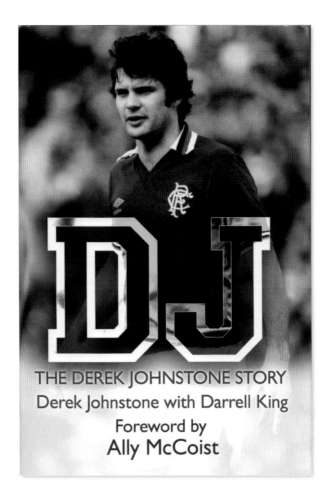

THE DEREK JOHNSTONE STORY

Derek Johnstone with Darrell King

Foreword by

Ally McCoist

The First Division had an exciting finish with three teams vying for the title and promotion. In the last few weeks Tommy Gemmell's Dundee had been leading, until a defeat to Dumbarton with three games to go gave Hearts, managed by Willie Ormond, the advantage. A few days later, a 90th-minute equaliser by Queen of the South's Peter Dickson saw Hearts drop a point and it proved costly. Morton, who were playing catch-up in terms of games and were picking up points inspired by Andy Ritchie, lost on the final day to Dundee but still won the championship. Benny Rooney's side finished on 58 points and a goal difference of plus 43 with Hearts on plus 35. Dundee were a point behind with a greater goal difference than both. At the bottom,

East Fife sat on 19 points with Alloa dropping back down on 24.

In Division Two, Craig Brown's Clyde also ended up in a dogfight with Raith Rovers for the title. Rovers finished with six straight wins including one over Clyde but it was not enough to pip them to the title. Both teams finished on 53 points with Clyde ten goals to the better. Brechin were bottom once again on 20 points.

The League Cup changed format completely to a straight knock-out tournament over two legs until the semi-final stage. Twenty-six teams were given a bye into the second round. Hibernian became the first top early scalp, losing to Queen of the South. The second round saw Queen's Park become the first side to lose a penalty shoot-out in a major Scottish Cup tournament, with Ayr United the victors. Gordon Smith grabbed a hat-trick as Rangers thumped Aberdeen 6-1 in the first leg. The Dons could only reply with a 3-1 result at Pittodrie. Forfar Athletic of the Second Division disposed of Premier Division side Ayr and then beat Queen of the South to reach the last four, where they met Rangers.

Severe weather had seen the game delayed until late February but what a fright Forfar gave the mighty Gers. With seven minutes remaining the Loons were leading 2-1 despite having gone behind to a Johnstone goal in the 24th minute. They pulled back level a minute before half-time through Ken Brown and then took the lead in the 60th minute after Brian Rankin netted to the shock of the 13,000 crowd, but Derek Parlane headed in the equaliser for Rangers. The game went to extra time but by then Forfar were a spent force and conceded three more goals. The other tie, with 18,804 in attendance, was more straightforward as two first-half goals by Joe Craig and George McCluskey gave Celtic

GREENOCK MORTON

MONTROSE

SCOTTISH LEAGUE
FIRST DIVISION

Saturday
5th November
1977

Kick-off 2.30 p.m.

No. 11 1977-78

10p

the lead over an uninspired Hearts side. That was how it remained and Celtic headed for their 14th successive League Cup Final.

Rangers, however, won 2-1 after extra time in front of a crowd of 60,168. Cooper had put Rangers ahead in the 39th minute but Eðvaldsson equalised with five minutes left. The first 90 minutes were said to have had 'more fouls than football' but the extra 30 were full of drama and excitement with chances for both sides. Gordon Smith hit the winner in the 118th minute to claim the trophy for Rangers.

In the Scottish Cup, Lowland club Vale of Leithen produced the shock of the early rounds with a 4-1 win over Forfar but then lost out to Queen's Park. Celtic hammered Dundee 7-1 in the third round. Rangers travelled to Berwick 11 years to the day after their shameful loss in 1967. John Greig was the sole survivor on the playing side but Jock Wallace, the Rangers manager, was the Berwick keeper on the day. The player-manager for Berwick was Dave Smith, who had also played for the Gers on that fateful day. There would be no reprise of the score as Rangers ran out 4-2 winners. Also in the third round, Cowdenbeath took Partick Thistle to a replay that was postponed on ten occasions before losing out to a Denis McQuade goal at Central Park. The fourth round saw Kilmarnock of the second tier knock Celtic out after a replay at Rugby Park. They would fall to Rangers in the quarter-finals, however.

Rangers met Dundee United in the first semi-final in front of a 25,619 crowd. United took control of the game but were not ruthless enough in front of goal. Rangers fans had been booing their side before a Bobby Russell cross was met by Johnstone to give them the lead in the 70th minute. Seven minutes later John Greig completed the scoring for the night to send Rangers into the final.

It is fair to say in many ways the Alan Rough backlash started in the Partick Thistle against Aberdeen semi-final. Although there were only 12,282 at the match, the TV highlights later on that evening showed Rough making two big mistakes.

For the first he missed the ball totally for Ian Fleming to have a free header at the back post, and for the second he touched a ball going past the post on to Joe Harper who passed for Fleming to score again. Fleming hit a third for his hat-trick, after Joe Harper converted a dubious penalty. Substitute Jim Melrose netted twice for the Jags but the damage had been done.

A crowd of 61,563 turned up to witness Rangers win the cup and take the Treble. Alex MacDonald once more scored a diving header in a Hampden final, from a precise Russell cross to put Rangers into the lead in the 35th minute. Derek Johnstone made it two with a header in the 57th minute before Aberdeen scored with five minutes remaining through a Steve Ritchie lob that left McCloy swinging on the bar having misjudged the flight of the ball. Billy McNeill had led Aberdeen to the runners-up spot in both the league and Scottish Cup in his only season in charge of the Dons. McNeill would take over from Jock Stein at Celtic and Alex Ferguson took over the reins at Pittodrie.

1978/79
The great seasons are those that end with the winner decided on the last day and this one certainly met that criteria. By mid-January, points had been dropping like flies for all sides as Dundee United sat top having played 19 games with only 23 points. Rangers sat second having played the same number of games and a point behind. Then came Aberdeen, Thistle, Morton, St Mirren and in seventh place Celtic on 19 points from 18 games.

In mid-March United were still top on 31 points having played 25 games but the weather had played havoc with the fixtures that winter and

Official Souvenir Programme   N°. 1085

Scottish Cup -- 3rd Round
Sponsored by
Younger's Tartan Special

VALE OF LEITHEN
v
QUEEN'S PARK
in Victoria Park, Innerleithen,
on Saturday, 28th January, 1978
Kick-off 2.45 p.m.

Admission : Adults 50p   O.A.P. & Juveniles 25p

R. SMAIL & SONS. Printers. Innerleithen.   Programme - 10p

Celtic were eight points adrift having only played 20 games. Then, on 12 April, the *Glasgow Herald* reported that 'Celtic's title hopes take a pounding' as they lost 2-1 at Tannadice and slipped ten points behind United who were also six points clear of Rangers. However, Rangers had five games on United and Celtic six. As they caught up on games and more importantly points, both sides secured wins over United.

Ultimately it came down to one night, one match and even one half. Celtic had reached the top of the table on goal difference from United on 12 May with a victory at St Mirren. United had finished their games and a win against Hearts saw Celtic go ahead further and needing victory against Rangers to secure the title. The match at Celtic Park saw Rangers take a lead in the first half and things then got worse for the Hoops as they went down to ten men with Johnny Doyle being sent off.

However, Celtic then equalised in the 67th minute through Roy Aitken and within minutes George McCluskey gave them the lead, but Rangers were not done and Bobby Russell levelled in the 76th minute. With five minutes remaining Colin Jackson headed into his own net to give Celtic the lead and then Murdo MacLeod slammed home a fourth to give them the championship and one of their most memorable victories.

In the end Celtic took the title on 48 points, three clear of Rangers who lost a final-day match to Hibernian, with Dundee United third. The top scorer was one of the great mavericks of Scottish football, Morton legend Andy Ritchie, who hit 22 goals.

Hearts and Motherwell were both relegated with the Fir Park side bottom on 17 points and Hearts six points better but 11 adrift of safety.

The second tier was also close and Dundee won it with a draw against Ayr at Dens Park. Ian Redford scored an equaliser with seven minutes left to secure the point and the league for Dundee. Kilmarnock were also promoted, a point behind on 54 and with a better goal difference than Clydebank, who were also on 54. Queen of the South were bottom on 24 points with Montrose also relegated on 25.

Berwick Rangers won the Second Division on 54 points. Lying second to Falkirk in February they then went on an undefeated run of 17 games and could afford to lose on the final day to Dunfermline who finished on 52 points. Meadowbank Thistle propped up the league on 24 points.

Rangers and Celtic came out of the hat to play in the first round of the League Cup and comfortably swatted aside Albion Rovers and Dundee respectively to progress to round two. In round three Aberdeen enjoyed a 7-1 hammering of Hamilton with Joe Harper hitting four goals at Pittodrie.

The semi-finals paired Aberdeen with Hibs and Celtic with Rangers. Both games were decided after extra time with the Dons progressing through a Stuart Kennedy goal at Dens Park in front of a 21,048 crowd, while 49,432 saw Rangers and Celtic play out a tetchy affair with Tommy Burns and Alex Miller being sent off. The 90 minutes ended 2-2 and like the league decider, this match saw an unfortunate own goal come into play. This time it was Jim Casey who was the hapless culprit as the ball cannoned off him from a Roy Baines save to end Celtic's run of 14 successive League Cup finals.

The final was played in March with 54,000 in attendance. Although Rangers had been on top it was Aberdeen who took the lead with a Duncan Davidson header that McCloy let slip through his fingers in the 58th minute. Aberdeen held out until the 77th minute when a MacDonald shot was deflected past keeper Clark. Shortly afterwards,

Doug Rougvie was dismissed for an off-the-ball incident after having already been booked. In injury time a cross from a McLean free kick was headed home by Colin Jackson to give John Greig his first trophy as manager.

In the Scottish Cup, Spartans from the East of Scotland Football League knocked out East Stirlingshire before bowing out to fellow Edinburgh side Meadowbank in the third round. Meadowbank then lost 6-0 to near neighbours Hibernian. Hibernian put out city rivals Hearts in the quarter-finals to progress. Dundee were thumped 6-3 by Rangers while Celtic lost out to Aberdeen after a replay. Partick Thistle narrowly beat Dumbarton to reach the semis.

Partick and Rangers served up an 'epic' semi-final at Hampden in front of 27,000 fans with many chances for either side but in the end there were no goals to show. Thistle fans of a certain age will tell you that Bobby Houston's disallowed goal in the final ten minutes was never offside and the lack of TV pictures has allowed the conspiracy theory around it to become part of Jags folklore. The replay saw an increased crowd of 32,300 and again it was a tight affair with Thistle having the better of the chances in the first half. In the 86th minute a Johnstone header was saved by Rough only for the Rangers player to hit home the winner from the rebound.

Just 9,387 fans turned up at Hampden to see Aberdeen play Hibs. The Dons took the lead in the 29th minute through Steve Archibald but a Gordon Rae header eight minutes later levelled the score. Two minutes before the break a Rougvie lunge on striker Ally MacLeod saw a penalty awarded. The Hibs player converted to put his team in front and into the final.

After 210 minutes of the final neither side had scored during two rather dull matches in which no one deserved to win or lose. A crowd of 50,610 turned up for the first match, followed by 33,504 for the second with 30,602 attending the third and final encounter.

The third match was fit to be a final at last with plenty of high drama and excitement. Hibernian took the lead when Tony Higgins netted in the 16th minute. Johnstone hit the equaliser in the 43rd minute and then put Rangers into the lead in the 61st but Hibs were not done. A penalty awarded in the 75th minute saw MacLeod smack home the equaliser and send the match into extra time. A soft penalty for Rangers in the 103rd minute was missed by Alex Miller, but in a season in which Colin Jackson and Jim Casey hit unfortunate own goals perhaps the winner could only be produced in the same manner with the great Arthur Duncan heading into his own net in the 119th minute of the match to give Rangers the cup.

1979/80

On 23 February 1980, Aberdeen lost 2-1 to Kilmarnock at Pittodrie for their seventh defeat of the season. They were sitting fourth in the Premier League table on 23 points, nine behind Celtic at the top, having played two fewer games. It proved to be their last defeat as they picked up 24 points from 14 games to win the championship, including two victories over Celtic. A 5-0 victory over Hibernian at Easter Road on 3 May saw them on the same points as the Glasgow side but needing to lose by ten goals or worse to Partick Thistle in their final game to slip up. The match against Thistle ended 1-1 so Aberdeen won their first title under Alex Ferguson. The Dons finished on 48 points, Celtic one behind on 47 and St Mirren third on 42. Having sold Frank McGarvey to Liverpool for £270,000, St Mirren bought strikers Frank McDougall from Clydebank

THREAVE ROVERS

SCOTTISH CUP
2nd Round

Threave Rovers
v
Keith F.C.

SATURDAY,
5th January, 1980
Meadow Park,
Castle-Douglas
Kick-off 2.15 p.m.

Official Programme 20p

for £160,000 and Doug Somner from Partick Thistle for £100,000. Somner was the top scorer that season with 25 goals. Dundee and Hibernian were relegated with Hibs bottom on 18 points and Dundee on 24. The short-lived signing of George Best had not been enough to halt the Hibees' slide.

In the First Division, Bobby Watson's Airdrie lost five league games on the trot at the end of 1979 but over their next 15 they took 26 points to top the table on goal difference from Hearts with one match to go. A veritable decider at Tynecastle awaited. With 85 minutes gone, the championship was Airdrie's, then Hearts central defender Frank Liddell latched on to a Malcolm Robertson corner to head the winner and give Bobby Moncur's side the title in dramatic fashion. Clyde finished bottom on 25 points with Arbroath also dropping down.

The Second Division ended up in a battle between the two Falkirk sides. Both clubs had topped the table at various points throughout the season but Falkirk won it with one point to spare. They finished on 50 with East Stirling on 49. Alloa Athletic finished bottom with 29 points.

Although Motherwell were a second-tier side it was still a bit of a shock to see them lose 4-3 to Queen's Park over two legs in the League Cup. The Spiders lost 5-1 on aggregate to Dundee United in the next round. Aberdeen put paid to both Rangers and Celtic to reach the semi-finals. Morton had defeated Kilmarnock on penalties to face Aberdeen in the last four. Dundee United scraped through by beating Raith 1-0 over both legs. Hamilton defeated Dundee 3-2 to reach the last semis.

Denis McQuade, who scored twice in the 1971 semi-final to give Partick Thistle victory over Falkirk, also netted a double for Hamilton in this season's semi at East End Park, Dunfermline. Unfortunately for the Accies fans in the 8,000 crowd, Dundee United scored six goals with braces for Paul Sturrock and Billy Kirkwood.

Over at Hampden with 12,000 fans in attendance, Morton started the first half nervously and by half-time were 2-0 down to Aberdeen with goals by Mark McGhee and Gordon Strachan. The second half saw the Ton have a goal disallowed

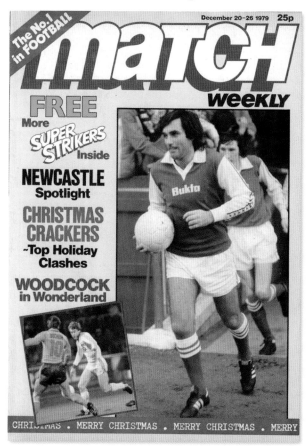

and Ritchie strike the bar. Ritchie eventually scored, from the spot in the 82nd minute, but Aberdeen saw out the game to head to the final.

The first match, played at Hampden in dreadful weather, saw both sides have chances in a thriller, with the Dons being the better side. However, there were no goals by the end of extra time for the 27,173 crowd to savour. The replay at Dens Park in front of 28,933 saw United dominate from start to finish. On the mud-soaked pitch, Pettigrew gave the Terrors an early lead on 14 minutes. He added to that in the second half, heading in a Sturrock cross. Sturrock himself finished it when his curled shot struck Willie Miller and into the net for 3-0. This was Dundee United's first major trophy success.

The shock team of the Scottish Cup early rounds was Highland club Keith. They beat Threave Rovers 3-2 in round two to face Hamilton at Douglas Park. Keith were up 3-0 at one point with Kevin Bremner, brother of former Hibs player Des, among the scorers. Two late goals by the Accies put a better slant on the score for the home side. Sadly, Keith lost out at home to Berwick Rangers in the next round. Dundee crossed the street to be thumped 5-1 by a rampant United in the third round. Remarkably, Clyde and Arbroath, who ended the season relegated from the second tier, took Rangers and Aberdeen respectively to replays in that round. Steve Archibald scored four as Aberdeen humped Airdrie 8-0 in the fourth round. Celtic needed a replay to overcome St Mirren and Rangers narrowly beat Dundee United. Hibernian needed a second game to dispose of Berwick in the quarter-finals to face Celtic in the semis.

In the semis it didn't look too bad for Hibs at half-time as they trailed to just a Bobby Lennox goal. However, early second-half goals saw Celtic race ahead and finish up as 5-0 winners. The 32,925 crowd saw George Best display some of his skills but it was not enough to stop his side's crushing defeat. The other tie at Celtic Park on the same day saw 44,000 turn up to see Rangers overcome Aberdeen through a second-half goal from Derek Johnstone.

TYNECASTLE TITLE WINNERS!

Jim Jefferies, the Hearts captain, is a very happy man! His club are back in the Scottish Premier Division and here he parades the First Division trophy in front of the Tynecastle fans.

Celtic won the final with an instinctive leg stuck out by George McCluskey to divert a wayward Danny McGrain shot past Peter McCloy in extra time. The game itself had been quite entertaining despite no goals. However, a post-match pitch invasion would escalate into a full-scale riot. The aftermath would see blame apportioned all over the place – the players, the fans, the police, the bigotry – but it was to be alcohol where the axe would fall. The introduction of the Criminal Justice (Scotland) Act 1980 banned alcohol from being allowed into football grounds in Scotland. Supporters deemed to be 'drunk' were also banned from entering stadia. Cheers.

Although Hibernian had been wearing shirts with Bukta printed across them for several seasons, it wasn't until the early 1980s that sponsorship was fully introduced so the league became the Fine Fare League and the League Cup became the Skol Cup and the local butchers could have their name printed on their local team shirts.

It was also agreed that gate receipts would no longer be split between the two competing clubs but go solely to the home side. This allowed Rangers and Celtic greater financial clout but also seemed to tie the clubs into the idea that getting the Old Firm four times a season at home was a must. To this day very few clubs are willing to give this up and we seem stuck with league set-ups that no one seems really happy with.

The '80s, however, did see a tinkering of the format as the Premier Division went from ten to 12 clubs and then back to ten. The possibility of clubs breaking away to form their own league was also mooted in this decade and would eventually happen in the late 1990s.

Although this new financial shift would not fully show itself in the early years of the '80s, particularly as Rangers ploughed money into rebuilding Ibrox at a cost to the playing side of things, it became apparent during the time Graeme Souness was at the helm of the Gers and beyond. So while the early 1980s saw Ferguson's Aberdeen and Jim McLean's Dundee United win the championship, since 1984/85 no club outside of the Old Firm has lifted the title.

JIMMY BONE — Forward. Ht.5.9.Wt.11.2. Arbroath. ▉33, ▢7. ●2, ●0 (S).

DOUG SOMNER — Forward. Ht.5.10.Wt.11.10. Partick Thistle. ▉0, ▢0.

1980/81

On 27 December, Aberdeen were sitting top of the table having just crushed Celtic 4-1 at Pittodrie. They sat three points clear with a game in hand over the Glasgow side. Celtic, however, would win 27 points out of their next 28 during a period in which Aberdeen won one, drew three and lost three in their next seven games to sit four points adrift. In the end Celtic won the title by seven clear points from the Dons, with a total of 56. Celtic hit 84 goals, a new

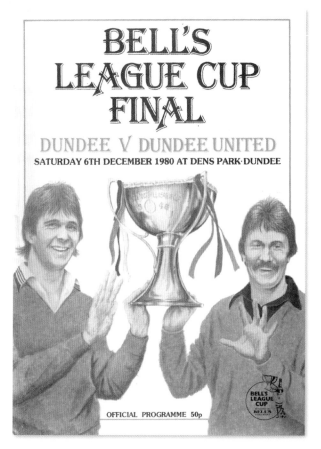

BELL'S
LEAGUE CUP
FINAL

DUNDEE V DUNDEE UNITED

SATURDAY 6TH DECEMBER 1980 AT DENS PARK·DUNDEE

OFFICIAL PROGRAMME 50p

record for the Premier League, with Charlie Nicholas, McCluskey and Frank McGarvey all contributing and the latter finishing as the season's top scorer with 23 goals. Kilmarnock and Hearts dropped out of the Premier Division on 19 and 18 points respectively.

Bertie Auld's Hibernian won the First Division with 57 points. They had started well and never really slumped at any point. Dundee looked out of the promotion race for a while but a finish of ten wins and two draws saw them pip St Johnstone on goal difference with 52 points. Berwick Rangers finished bottom with 21 points while Stirling Albion also dropped down.

Queen's Park won the Second Division, remarkably drawing more games than winning, 18 draws and 16 wins giving them a tally of 50 points. The Spiders had finished on a run of 15

IAN REDFORD   JOHN FLETCHER

games without defeat. Queen of the South finished runners-up, four points behind but one ahead of Cowdenbeath. Stranraer were bottom of the heap with 22 points.

Holders Dundee United started off in the League Cup first round with a 9-2 aggregate win over East Fife, followed by an 8-1 margin over Cowdenbeath. Aberdeen were also scoring goals for fun, defeating Berwick 12-1 over two legs in round two. Celtic were shocked to leave Annfield 1-0 down to Stirling Albion thanks to a Lloyd Irvine goal but made light work of the return match when winning 6-1. The third round saw Aberdeen knock out Rangers and Dundee come through on penalties after 210 minutes without a goal against Kilmarnock. Dundee then defeated Aberdeen 1-0 over the two legs of the quarter-finals. Ayr United had come through the early stages with victories over the more fancied Morton, Hearts and Hibs to meet Dundee in the now two-legged semi-finals. Dundee United were to meet Celtic.

Both first legs ended in 1-1 draws. At Dens, Dundee and Ayr played out an exciting second leg with Ayr losing 3-2 after Erich Schaedler hit the winner late on. At Celtic Park, United raced into the lead after four minutes through Willie Pettigrew. Paul Sturrock and Davie Dodds added goals to give the Terrors a 3-0 win.

The all-Dundee final took place at Dens Park in front of 24,466 on a wintry December day. United proved too good for their neighbours and 'hosts' with Davie Dodds putting them ahead just before half-time. Paul Sturrock struck twice in the second half to complete the scoring and give United the trophy.

Buckie Thistle took the scalps of Meadowbank and Stranraer in the first two rounds of the Scottish Cup. The first matches in both ended in 2-2 draws and the replays in 3-2 wins for Buckie, but the Highland club exited to Stirling Albion in the third round. The biggest surprise in that round was St Mirren's 2-0 defeat to Dumbarton at home (Dumbarton had apparently made an approach to Johan Cruyff earlier in the season but sadly the Dutchman's silky skills never graced the bumpy Boghead pitch). St Johnstone had gone 2-0 down to Rangers in Perth after 36 minutes but with nine minutes remaining found themselves 3-2 ahead only for Ian Redford to equalise right at the death. Rangers won the replay 3-1 with a young Alistair McCoist scoring for the Saints. In the quarter-finals, Dundee United routed Motherwell 6-1 while Morton won 6-0 against Clydebank in a replay after a goalless first match.

The semis saw Morton play Rangers at Celtic Park in front of 27,050 spectators. It was reportedly a bit of an ugly match with numerous fouls and bookings and a sending-off. In between that, goals from Colin Jackson and Bobby Russell put Rangers 2-0 up with Andy Ritchie netting for Morton towards the end.

The 40,337 fans at Hampden saw United and Celtic play out a better match but with no goals.

The 32,328 replay crowd saw Celtic lead after five minutes through a Nicholas penalty but by the ninth minute United were in front following goals from Bannon and Hegarty. A spectacular Provan volley restored parity just before half-time. The winner came in the 76th minute through an own goal from Celtic's Mike Conroy to send United into the final.

A crowd of 53,000 saw a dramatic ending to the final, which had seen Dundee United control much of the match but fail to score. In the final 20 minutes Rangers had come into it more and in the dying seconds they were awarded a penalty. Ian Redford's poorly hit strike was saved by the legs of Hamish McAlpine and the match ended all square. The replay was all about Davie Cooper who opened the scoring with the deftest of lobs over the advancing McAlpine with ten minutes gone. His flighted cross in the 21st minute saw Russell at the back post thump in the second goal. United got back into it a few minutes later through Dodds but were 3-1 down by the half-hour mark when Cooper threaded a pass to John MacDonald to score. MacDonald would hit the only other goal in the 77th minute to take the acclaim from the Rangers fans in the crowd of 43,099.

1981/82

Celtic had started the league season with seven straight wins and following their first defeat, to Hibernian in October, they stood two points clear of the pack. By early January, a loss to Rangers still saw them five points clear. There would be three more defeats and although Aberdeen finished strongly it was not enough to catch Celtic, who won it at home on the final day after keeping the champagne on ice following a draw with St Mirren and a defeat to Dundee United. The top scorer was George McCluskey with 21 goals. George had begun to oust the talented Charlie Nicholas from the side with more consistent displays. Nicholas broke his leg against Morton in January and did not finish the season. Celtic ended on 55 points with Aberdeen on 53.

Airdrie finished bottom on 18 points with Partick Thistle also dropping down. Both sides had been

DUMBARTON

Chairman: R A Robertson   Captain: Donald McNeil
Secretary: Manager: William Lamont
Coach: William Lamont   Year formed: 1872
Colours: White shirts with black and gold trim, white shorts and stockings.
Change colours: All gold.

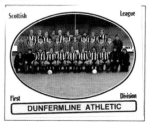

DUNFERMLINE ATHLETIC

Chairman: J C Yellowley   Captain: John Salton
Secretary: Jim McColville   Manager: Harry Melrose
Coach: W Borghwick   Year formed: 1885
Colours: White and black striped shirts, black shorts.
Change colours: Red shirts and stockings, white shorts.

EAST STIRLING

Chairman: Ian Crawford   Captain: Donald Watt
Secretary: P I McKay   Manager: Martin Ferguson
Coach: Andy McCall   Year formed: 1881
Colours: Black and white hooped shirts, black shorts, red stockings.
Change colours: Tangerine shirts, black shorts, tangerine stockings.

FALKIRK

Chairman: A Hardie   Captain: Brian Brown
Secretary: R Shaw   Manager: John Hagart
Coach: John Binnie   Year formed: 1876
Colours: Navy blue shirts with white trim, white shorts, navy blue stockings.
Change colours: White shirts, navy blue shorts, red stockings.

HAMILTON ACADEMICAL

Chairman: M Stepek   Captain: Bobby Graham
Secretary: Joseph Friel   Manager: D McParland
Coach: Pat Barkey   Year formed: 1875
Colours: Red and white hooped shirts, white shorts and stockings.
Change colours: All sky blue.

HEART OF MIDLOTHIAN

Chairman: A Naylor   Captain: Alex MacDonald
Secretary: L W Porteous   Manager: Tony Ford
Coach: W Borthwick   Year formed: 1874
Colours: Maroon shirts with white trim, white shorts, maroon stockings, with white turnovers.
Change colours: White shirts with maroon shorts and stockings.

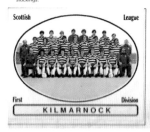

KILMARNOCK

MOTHERWELL

QUEEN OF THE SOUTH

circling the drain as such since the season's start with Dundee escaping on the last day.

In the second tier, David Hay's Motherwell started the season with a defeat to Kilmarnock. They then went on a run of 21 games without defeat and eventually won the league on 61 points, ten clear of Kilmarnock. A poor finish of two defeats and a draw saw Hearts pipped by Killie by one point for second place. Queen of the South finished bottom with 18 points with East Stirling also dropping down.

In the Second Division, Clyde started off with an 11-game unbeaten run before crashing to two losses, but only two more defeats lay ahead of them and they ended on 59 points, nine ahead of Alloa. A last-day win saw Alloa gain promotion on goal difference over Arbroath. Stranraer retained their place at the bottom with 20 points.

The League Cup reverted to sections with the top sides facing each other once more. Celtic lost their first two group games to St Mirren and St Johnstone and failed to qualify, with the Paisley side going through. Rangers topped their group as did Aberdeen and holders Dundee United. The quarter-finals were a whitewash for the Premier Division sides over the two legs with Aberdeen beating

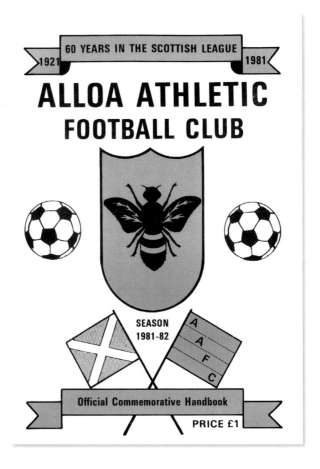

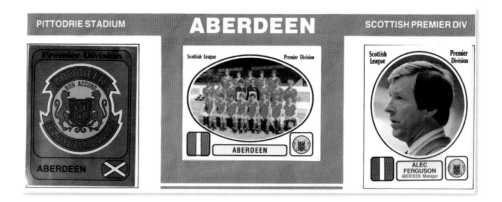

PITTODRIE STADIUM ABERDEEN SCOTTISH PREMIER DIV

Berwick 9-0, Rangers winning 5-0 against Brechin, St Mirren triumphing 7-1 over Forfar and United going through 9-0 against Hamilton.

The semi-finals were once again over two legs. United lost to Aberdeen at Tannadice to a Peter Weir goal but the second leg was a different affair with Paul Sturrock scoring on seven minutes to even the tie, Ralph Milne adding a second in 38 minutes and Sturrock netting a third in the second half to put United into the final.

St Mirren and Rangers drew 2-2 at Love Street in the first leg. Twice Rangers went ahead through Colin McAdam and then an own goal from Jackie Copland. The first equaliser came from a fine solo effort by a young Frank McAvennie, and an Ian Scanlon penalty finished the scoring. The second leg saw Saints go in ahead at half-time through another Scanlon penalty. Jim Bett equalised from the spot in the 69th minute and with two minutes remaining John MacDonald hit the winner to send Rangers into the final.

In the final, 53,777 fans saw United take the lead with a superb goal from Milne in the 48th minute. Sturrock shortly after had the ball in the net but John Holt was flagged as offside. In the 74th minute, Rangers equalised through a wonderful Davie Cooper free kick from the edge of the box and with two minutes remaining a chipped lob from Redford produced the winning goal for the Ibrox club.

1980/81 ▸ 1985/86

Civil Service Strollers drew 3-3 with Cowdenbeath in the first round of the Scottish Cup but lost 6-1 at Central Park. Cowden then drew Gala Fairydean in the next round and lost 3-2 after an initial 1-1 draw. Gala then lost out 2-1 to St Johnstone in the third round. Generally, the third round went to form with no notable surprises although Forfar of the third tier knocked out Hamilton of the second after a replay. Their next scalp was to be Hearts at Tynecastle. Aberdeen eliminated Celtic at Pittodrie with John Hewitt netting the only goal. Forfar were drawn against Queen's Park, who were at the time a division above them. They weren't put off by that and won 2-1 at Hampden to seal a return to the

● *The Forfar team who are searching for Scottish Cup glory. They are:*
BACK ROW (L to R): Billy Gallacher, Ian McPhee, Raymond Farningham, Tom Boardley, Mark Alexander, Colin Craig, John Mitchell. MIDDLE ROW: Ken Brown, James Allan, John Clark, Stewart Kennedy, Alan Brash, Neil Watt, Tom Downie. FRONT ROW: Tom O'Rourke, Alex Carswell (Coach), Steve Hancock, Billy Bennett, Gordon Leitch, Alex Rae (Manager), Robert Morris.

stadium for a dream semi-final against Rangers, who knocked out Dundee.

A small crowd of 15,878 saw Rangers play what was described in the *Glasgow Herald* as 'tip tap' football (way ahead of their time) and not being direct enough. Forfar did create a few chances too but neither side were able to score, and the replay saw only 11,864 turn up – as well as some of the Rangers players. Goals from Derek Johnstone and Jim Bett put their team ahead, but a penalty scored by Alex Brash just before the interval gave the Angus club some hope. However, Davie Cooper made it 3-1 early in the second half and the cup final dream for Forfar was over.

Aberdeen took care of Killie to face St Mirren, who narrowly defeated Dundee United. They served up a nervy affair in the other semi, played at Celtic Park in front of a crowd of 16,782. Keeper Billy Thomson produced some great saves to deny Aberdeen before the Saints went ahead through Frank McDougall in the 61st minute. A penalty converted by Gordon Strachan was the end of the scoring. The replay was more thrilling with both keepers, Thomson and Jim Leighton, at fault for the loss of goals. A crowd of 15,633 saw Aberdeen win 3-2 with St Mirren pegging them back twice. The Dons' scorers were McGhee, Simpson and Weir, with McAvennie and Somner netting for the Saints.

The turnout for the final was a more substantial 53,788. Although Aberdeen on current form were the favourites, it was Rangers who took the lead on 15 minutes through a John MacDonald flying header. Alex McLeish, with a finesse he never really showed again in his career, hit a wonderful lofted ball into the top corner of the net from outside the penalty area to equalise 17 minutes later. That was it for the 90 minutes but Aberdeen swamped Rangers in extra time and goals followed from McGhee, Strachan and Neale Cooper to give the Dons the cup.

1980/81 ▸ 1985/86

1982/83

The title was won on the final day with not two but three teams in contention. It is ironic that Dundee United clinched their third major trophy in the same stadium they had won their first two: Dens Park, the home of their city rivals Dundee. United had started well against Dundee, scoring two goals in the first ten minutes, but a goal from the hosts midway through the first half made for a tense and nervy remainder for their fans. In the end the title was theirs thanks to their 56 points, with Celtic and Aberdeen both behind them on 55.

Despite a defeat to Aberdeen in early October, Celtic were top and then went on to win 11 games in a row before a draw with Dundee left them three points ahead of Aberdeen and four ahead of United. The Tangerine Terrors had lost to Aberdeen that day and were beaten by Rangers the following week. However, they suffered one more defeat that season – to Celtic, whom they beat a fortnight later. This, coupled with a loss to Aberdeen the following week, would really be where Celtic lost the title. As for Aberdeen, a draw to Hibernian in the final weeks may have done it for them. Charlie Nicholas was the top scorer with 29 goals. Kilmarnock finished bottom with a tally of 17 points, with Morton on 20 also dropping down.

Similarly, in the First Division it all came down to the final day. From early on Hearts and St Johnstone were front-runners for the title. With six games remaining Hearts were two points clear but in the proverbial four-pointer St Johnstone beat their rivals 2-1 at Muirton Park to take the initiative. Hearts followed this with three draws and two wins while the Saints recorded three wins and two draws. A Saints victory on the last day against Dunfermline assured them of the title with 55 points as Hearts finished on 54. That result was also the nail in the coffin for Dunfermline's hopes of staying up as the Pars ended up on 31 points, one behind Ayr, to be relegated. Queen's Park finished bottom with 23 points.

In a reversal of fortunes, the Second Division was contested right down to the wire between Brechin City and Terry Christie's Meadowbank Thistle, who fought neck and neck all season. A better run-in by Brechin meant a draw on the final day against Stenhousemuir was enough to give them the championship on 55 points with Meadowbank a point behind. Montrose sat bottom that year on 22 points.

In the League Cup, Celtic topped their group with maximum points with Arbroath, Alloa and Dunfermline making up the section. Dundee United also took full points in a similar grouping. Kilmarnock came through the supplementary round on penalties against Cowdenbeath. Their reward (or rather punishment) was 6-1 and 6-0 defeats to Rangers. Davie Cooper scored four in the first match, all from open play. Dundee United, hoping for a fourth final in a row, beat Aberdeen 4-1 over two legs. Celtic readily took care of Partick Thistle and Hearts overcame St Mirren with the odd goal in five.

Davie Cooper scored in the 84th minute to put Rangers one ahead against Hearts at Ibrox in the first semi. Rangers had found it hard to get past their former player Sandy Jardine marshalling the Hearts defence and goalkeeper Henry Smith. However, they added a second two minutes later through Jim Bett to give them a clear advantage. At Tynecastle, an early penalty saw Bett put Rangers further ahead. Derek O'Connor grabbed one back before half-time but a Derek Johnstone goal eight minutes from the end finished off the contest.

The other semi went down to the final minutes. Celtic had taken command in the first leg with a 2-0 victory over United through a Nicholas penalty and a goal from McGarvey. The second game saw United come back into it, first through an Aitken own goal just after half-time and then in the 64th minute Sturrock scored to restore parity. But United's John Holt was sent off with 12 minutes remaining and Nicholas scored in the last minute to send Celtic through to the final.

A crowd of 55,732 fans witnessed Celtic deservedly win their first League Cup Final in five years. They were slicker than their opponents but Rangers pushed them all the way. Man of the match Davie Provan sent a pass inside to Charlie Nicholas who struck a sweet shot past Jim Stewart without breaking his stride to give Celtic the lead in the 23rd minute. The second goal came in the 31st minute from Murdo MacLeod's thunderbolt. Bett gave Rangers a fighting chance a couple of minutes into the second half with a direct free kick, but they were unable to breach the Celtic goal again.

The Scottish Cup saw Partick Thistle play eight matches and only get as far as the quarter-finals, but first Elgin City knocked out Meadowbank in Edinburgh in the first round. However, City were then unceremoniously dumped out 5-0 by Dunfermline in the third round. Brora Rangers thumped Montrose 5-2 after a replay before being beaten 2-1 by Dundee. Partick Thistle drew 1-1 with Kilmarnock, then 0-0, followed with 2-2 and finally a 1-0 victory thanks to an 86th-minute winner from Mo Johnston. Next up was a 2-2 draw with Clyde, then an abandoned game at Shawfield due to floodlight failure as it stood at 1-1. The rematch saw the Jags win 6-0 with Johnston hitting a hat-trick.

Thistle then faced Aberdeen in the quarter-finals. Aberdeen quickly raced into the lead through a Neale Cooper goal, but the First Division side did not buckle and in the 64th minute equalised with an Ian MacDonald goal. Peter Weir supplied the winner for Aberdeen scoring from a direct free kick. Hearts were one down to Celtic when Willie Johnston was sent off for headbutting Davie Provan in first-half injury time. After that there was no way back and the Edinburgh side lost 4-1. Rangers made hard work of overcoming Queen's Park at Hampden, scraping by 2-1 in the end. St Mirren made lighter work of Airdrie, winning 5-0 at Broomfield.

A crowd of 51,152 attended the semi-final at Hampden as Celtic faced Aberdeen. Nicholas failed a late fitness test and it seemed to knock the stuffing out of Celtic who never really played their normal fluent game. Aberdeen never really showed their flair either and a headed goal by Weir in the 65th minute settled the encounter.

St Mirren and Rangers also played out a nervy match over at Celtic Park with a crowd of 31,102 watching. Sandy Clark scored in the 73rd minute, which seemed to wake the Saints from their stupor, and a Craig Paterson own goal meant a replay. St Mirren were said to have played better in the second match with 25,125 fans watching on but only just, as both sides played out a dull affair that was to end in extra time and controversy. In the 118th minute, Sandy Clark headed a Robert Prytz cross which Billy Thomson got a touch on before Lex Richardson cleared it off the line. Rangers claimed a goal but St Mirren said it never went over the line. Referee Brian McGinlay of Balfron gave the goal.

Some 62,970 watched the final at Hampden which is perhaps remembered most for Alex Ferguson's post-match rant where he claimed that Willie Miller and Alex McLeish won the cup for Aberdeen and that overall, his team's performance was a 'disgrace'. In truth, Rangers had been the better side for much of the match but didn't carve out many clear-cut chances. A misplaced pass by Bobby Russell late in extra time allowed Aberdeen to move upfield and Eric Black was on hand to header in a deflected cross to take the cup north to Aberdeen once more.

1983/84

Aberdeen lost to Hibernian in mid-October to sit fourth and one point behind leaders Dundee United. This was their second defeat of the season, but by the time of their third – to Celtic at the end of March – they were four points clear with two games in hand over the Hoops in second place. The title was won at Tynecastle with a 1-0 victory over Hearts with four games left to play. The Dons drew three of these and lost the other but still sat on 57 points, seven clear of Celtic, who, with Davie Hay in charge, had replaced the departed Charlie Nicholas with Motherwell's Brian McClair. McClair netted 23 goals to be the season's top scorer. Motherwell finished rock bottom on 15 points and were relegated along with St Johnstone on 23 points.

On 12 November Partick Thistle beat Alloa 5-0 to head the First Division table by four points. Mo Johnston left for Watford a few days later and although the Jags maintained their place at the top for several months, the cutting edge had gone from their play. Morton beat them 4-2 on 25 February to top the table for the first time. The Greenock side finished with a flurry, winning seven games out of eight to take the title on 54 points with Dumbarton in second place, three behind. Thistle ended third on 46 points while Alloa finished bottom on 26. Raith were relegated alongside them on 31 points, one away from safety.

Forfar Athletic, managed by Doug Houston, topped the Second Division, clinching a championship for the first time with six games to spare. The Loons won with 63 points, 16 clear of East Fife who were also promoted. Albion Rovers finished bottom on 27 points.

It was all change in the League Cup again. Twelve teams from the Second Division met in the first round and after that it went to the last 32 with each tie over two legs. Celtic made hard work of it against a gallant Brechin City side – a Jim Melrose goal at Glebe Park in the last five minutes was all they had to show from the first leg. It's one more than they got at Celtic Park, however, slinking through with that slim advantage. Aberdeen put Raith Rovers to the sword with a 9-0 thrashing in the first leg with Billy Stark hitting three and Eric Black scoring four. It was only 3-0 in the return match.

At this point, instead of a straightforward last 16, the cup went into four sections. Rangers emerged from their group with a 100 per cent record after new signing Ally McCoist bagged five to add to his one in the previous round. Celtic, Aberdeen and Dundee United all topped their groups to make up the semi-final foursome.

The semis were played in February and March. Rangers were to have a hoodoo over United that

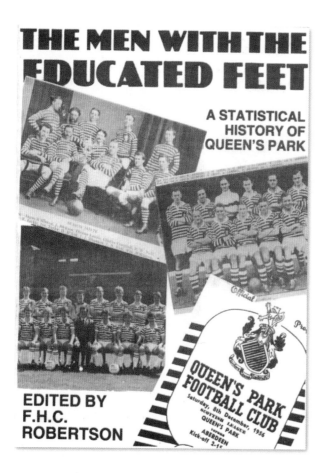

THE MEN WITH THE EDUCATED FEET

A STATISTICAL HISTORY OF QUEEN'S PARK

EDITED BY
F.H.C.
ROBERTSON

season as they didn't lose any of their six matches against them. In the first leg at Tannadice, in front of 14,569 spectators, Davie Dodds put the United side in front in the 68th minute but Rangers, managed once again by Jock Wallace, equalised through Australian Davie Mitchell with five minutes remaining. In the return match, a goal either side of the interval from Clark and Redford saw Rangers through to the final in front of an Ibrox crowd of 35,950.

The other tie was much closer. The first leg at Pittodrie had 23,000 turn up to watch Celtic have the better of the game, particularly in midfield, but they failed to take their chances and left with neither side having an advantage. Some 41,169 attended the second leg, which was a rather tasty encounter, well marshalled by referee Bob Valentine. The decisive moment came in the 54th minute when Tommy Burns was pulled down by Dougie Bell and up stepped young Mark Reid to score the penalty and put Celtic into the final.

The Skol Cup Final, as it was then named, was played at a frenetic pace and would have eight bookings, three penalties and a hat-trick for McCoist. Rangers took the lead a minute before half-time when Macleod was adjudged to have fouled Bobby Russell in the penalty box. McCoist, taking a long run from outside the D, shot cleanly past Bonner in the Celtic goal to give Rangers the lead. When he added a second from a loose ball after Roy Aitken and Clark bustled for a long kick from McCloy in the 61st minute, Celtic looked dead and buried.

A terrific midfield run by Tommy Burns was cut short by Rangers captain John McClelland just outside the area and from the resultant free kick Burns adroitly lofted the dead ball over the Rangers wall for the waiting McClair to volley into the net. In the dying minutes McCoist, uncharacteristically in his own box, felled MacLeod to give Celtic a penalty. Reid stepped up once more to complete the comeback and send the game into extra time.

In the 104th minute Aitken barged into McCoist and Valentine awarded the match's third penalty. McCoist once again took that long run but his shot was poorer and Bonner was able to save it, though the striker managed to smash in the rebound and give Rangers the cup.

Inverness Caley took the scalp of Albion Rovers in the first round of the Scottish Cup, winning 2-1 at home. They followed this with a victory over Gala Fairydean and then beat Stirling Albion 2-1 at Annfield in a replay. However, they crashed 6-0 to Rangers in Inverness in the fourth round. Celtic were also on the goal trail, beating Berwick 4-0, East Fife 6-0 and then Motherwell in the quarter-finals by the same. Also, in the last eight St Mirren beat Renfrewshire rivals Morton 4-3 in a hotly contested match.

In the quarters, Aberdeen and Dundee United's first match ended 0-0. The replay was again a tight affair with McGhee scoring the only goal of the game in the second minute.

Dundee came away from their last-eight match against Rangers at Dens Park frustrated. They felt they had scored a perfectly good goal only for it to be disallowed. The match ended 2-2 but Dundee manager Archie Knox was quite tight-lipped afterwards. Dundee took the game to Rangers at Ibrox and were rewarded by going ahead in the 22nd minute through defender Jim Smith. This was added to just after half-time by Iain Ferguson. However, in a seven-minute period late in the match both John McClelland and Davie McPherson scored for Rangers. Ferguson, though, was to grab a winner with minutes remaining for a well-earned Dundee victory.

The Aberdeen against Dundee semi-final at Tynecastle in front of 17,645 fans was not a classic by any means, hampered by a ferocious wind and a bumpy pitch. Ian Porteous netted for Aberdeen in the 28th minute and with a few minutes remaining Gordon Strachan added a second to send the Dons into their third successive final.

A crowd of 24,690 saw Celtic take the lead in the 30th minute against St Mirren when McClair latched on to a Willie McStay through ball to score. It was against the run of play when Frank McAvennie nodded down for Frank McDougall to level the score eight minutes later, and it took until the 81st minute for Celtic to net the winner through the more famous McStay: Paul.

Celtic fans in the 58,990 crowd would have been disgruntled over some of the decisions made in the final by referee Valentine. Aberdeen's opening goal by Eric Black looked offside but with no flag from the linesmen it stood. Aitken was then sent off for a crunching tackle on Mark McGhee, thus becoming the first player sent off in a cup final since 1929. Celtic had perhaps been the better side up to that point and indeed they were in control for most of the second half too. Their never-say-die attitude eventually rewarded them with a deserved equaliser from Paul McStay in the final minutes.

Extra time was too much for the ten men, however, and in the 98th minute Dougie Bell cracked a shot off the post which fell to Strachan, who flighted it over an all-at-sea Bonner for the onrushing McGhee to win the cup for the Dons.

1984/85

Celtic started the season on an unbeaten run of 11 games including a victory over Aberdeen, but it was not enough for them to top the league. Defeat in their 12th match by Morton meant by the end of that week they were three points behind the Dons. Aberdeen hit a dip at the turn of the year when losing twice to Dundee United, but Celtic were unable to take advantage of it – they inflicted Aberdeen's last defeat of the season in February and still found themselves trailing Fergie's Furies. The Dons won the championship with 59 points with Celtic on 52. The top scorer was Frank McDougall, now of Aberdeen, with 22 goals – a £100,000 buy from St Mirren but within a couple of seasons due to injury his career was over. In 54 league matches he notched up 36 goals for Aberdeen.

Rock bottom were Morton with only 12 points and they were the first club to concede 100 goals in a season since Forfar in 1974/75. Dumbarton also dropped down with 19 points and have as yet still to return to the top flight.

Motherwell won the second tier but looking back it seems as though the title was lost by other sides rather than it being claimed decisively by Well. In early December, Airdrie sat top with a meagre total of 24 points from 17 games, and only 12 points separated them from bottom sides Kilmarnock and Meadowbank. Motherwell had just lost three on the trot and were fifth with 17 points. The Steelmen were only to lose three more games all season. Clydebank ambled their way to the top but too much inconsistency along the way saw their title hopes falter. A final run-in of two draws and a loss saw the Bankies finish on 48 points, two behind Tommy McLean's Motherwell.

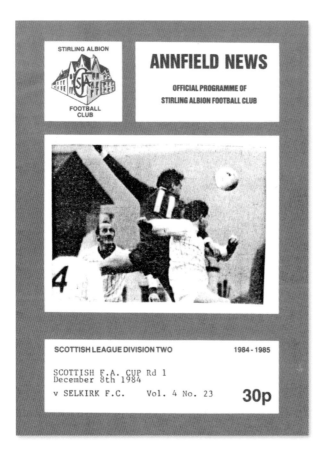

St Johnstone finished bottom on 25 points to be the first club since reconstruction to suffer successive relegations. Meadowbank's run-in of six wins and three defeats was not enough to save them from relegation with 32 points.

In March, Montrose beat Alloa 2-0 to sit on equal points with the Wasps but in second place in the Second Division on goal difference. It was to be the first of four successive defeats for Alloa which allowed Montrose to leapfrog them and win the title with 53 points. Alloa finished three points behind. Arbroath ended bottom on 25 points.

The League Cup changed once again, starting with 12 sides from the Second Division meeting. Then it was on to a 32-team seeded knock-out competition but only over one leg, except for the semi-finals which were over two. The second round saw Airdrie shock Aberdeen 3-1 at Broomfield.

Ally MacLeod was in charge at Broomfield but his side were humbled 4-0 by Celtic in the next round. Cowdenbeath knocked out St Mirren 2-0 at home while Meadowbank travelled five minutes down the road to beat Hibernian at Easter Road 2-1 in extra time. Cowdenbeath would have been happy with the bumper crowd of 9,925 at Central Park in the next round but not so much with the 3-1 defeat to Rangers. Meadowbank's dream, however, lived on as they beat St Johnstone 2-1 at home.

Alan McInally hit an equaliser for Celtic with only seven minutes left at Tannadice. However, Dundee United, who had gone ahead through Sturrock, would win the tie. Youngster John Clark netted the winner two minutes into extra time. At Dens Park, Dundee hit the woodwork but Roddy MacDonald scored the game's only goal to give Hearts the tie in the 41st minute.

The Rangers against Meadowbank semi-final was over by the second half of the first leg as Rangers raced into a 4-0 lead with McCoist netting two of them. The second leg at Tynecastle was not as straightforward as Rangers had Ally Dawson sent off in the first half for retaliation against the home side's Gordon Smith. Meadowbank went ahead in the 76th minute through Smith but McCoist scored in the dying minutes to put a better slant on things for his side.

At Tynecastle, a John Robertson free kick 68 seconds into the game gave Hearts the lead against Dundee United, but two John Clark headers would give United the advantage going into the second leg. Eamonn Bannon increased the Terrors' aggregate lead at Tannadice in the 30th minute from a free kick. Davie Dodds and Billy Kirkwood added to this in the second half before Donald Park grabbed a consolation goal for Hearts.

The final, in front of a crowd of 44,698, was by no means a classic and once again United failed to live up to their high standards at a final in Glasgow. An intricate passing move set up Iain Ferguson to score what proved to be the winner in the 44th minute. United came out and were an improved side in the second half but failed to create any clear-cut chances, so Rangers won the League Cup for the 13th time.

In the Scottish Cup and in front of 250 fans at home, Stirling Albion beating Selkirk was not much of a shock; the fact they won 20-0 was, however. It is the record victory for a senior match in British football in the 20th century. Davie Thomson hit seven with Willie Irvine netting a mere four. Stirling then lost 2-1 to Cowdenbeath in the next round. Inverness Caledonian and Berwick had a seesaw tie which saw the English club travel north twice and finally be beaten 3-0 in the second replay. However, Caley were then dumped out in a 6-0 rout by Hearts in the third round. Meanwhile, city rivals Inverness Thistle beat Kilmarnock 3-0 at home. Celtic took six off Thistle without reply in the next round.

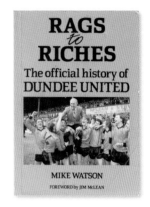

Rangers needed a replay to get past Morton, only to lose out once more at home to Dundee. John Brown, the scorer of the only goal, would go on to play for the Ibrox side. Dundee's 'reward' was a tie against Celtic. Mo Johnston gave the Hoops the lead at Dens Park but Brown equalised to take the match to a replay. Celtic led 1-0 in the second match but within 90 seconds of the restart Dundee had Bobby Glennie sent off and had equalised through Ray Stephen. However, Celtic won the tie with a Johnston goal in the 68th minute. Aberdeen took two goes to get past Hearts but Motherwell and Dundee United both won 4-1 against Forfar and St Mirren respectively.

Both semi-finals went to replays. Aberdeen and Dundee United played out a 'mediocre' goalless match on a boggy Tynecastle pitch in front of

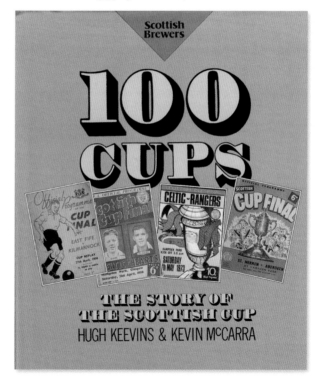

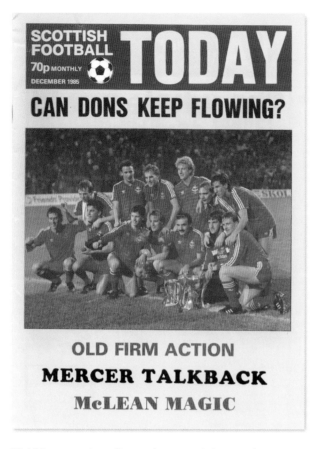

18,485 supporters. Sturrock opened the scoring
five minutes into the rematch at the same venue.
Neale Cooper was sent off for a double booking
on the hour and within three minutes United surged
further ahead with a goal from Stuart Beedie. Ian
Angus scored in the 86th minute to give the Dons
supporters in the 10,771 crowd hope but time was
against them and Aberdeen's grip on the Scottish
Cup was gone.

Motherwell and Celtic played out a 1-1 draw at
Hampden in front of a crowd of 30,536, in which
the second-tier team took the lead early through
Gary McAllister. Tommy Burns drew Celtic level nine
minutes later, but Motherwell held firm and the tie
went to a replay. Celtic played much better in the
rematch but still found it hard to break down the
Motherwell defence. Aitken opened the scoring with
a well-taken goal in the 72nd minute then Johnston

added two more in quick succession to the joy of the Celtic fans in the 25,667 crowd.

The first half of the final, in front of 60,346 spectators, was full of endeavour but not much football. Dundee United made the breakthrough in the 55th minute as Davie Dodds controlled a ball from Maurice Malpas and slipped a pass to Beedie who shot past Bonner in goal. A tactical change for Celtic saw Aitken sent forward into midfield with Burns and McStay being taken off. Almost immediately, Celtic won a free kick and Davie Provan hit an unstoppable shot past Hamish McAlpine to bring his team back into it with 13 minutes remaining.

With six minutes left Aitken latched on to a loose ball and his cross was perfectly met by McGarvey to head into the back of the net. The cup was Celtic's once more.

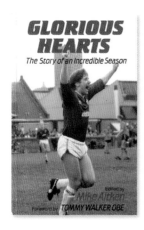

1985/86

On 28 September, Hearts lost 1-0 to Clydebank. After eight games they had lost five, drawn one and won two and were lying third from bottom, seven points behind Celtic at the top. They had also lost to Aberdeen in a League Cup quarter-final, but they would not be beaten again until the last two games of the season and in doing so they lost both the championship and Scottish Cup in the space of a week.

Hearts topped the table in late December after taking over from Aberdeen. A 4-2 defeat to United at Tannadice at the turn of the year saw Celtic sit six points behind the Jambos with three games in hand, although this was to be their final defeat in the league. A run of seven straight wins had them two points and four goals behind Hearts on the final day. Hearts faced Dundee at Dens Park and although players were suffering from a stomach bug on the day, the enormity of the occasion seemed to overcome them. Their play was nervy and disjointed but still with seven minutes remaining all they needed was the draw. Meanwhile, Celtic were running riot at Love Street and beating St Mirren 5-0.

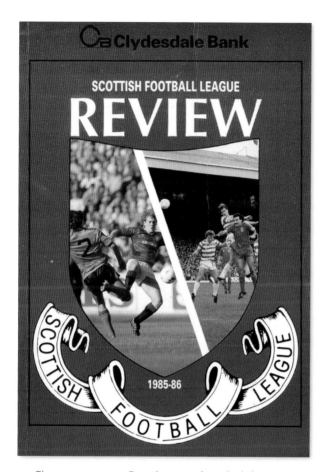

SCOTTISH FOOTBALL LEAGUE

REVIEW

1985-86

SCOTTISH FOOTBALL LEAGUE

Clydesdale Bank

Then a corner to Dundee was headed down by John Brown and substitute Albert Kidd hit the ball into the net. The cheers went up in Paisley and at Easter Road, the home of Edinburgh rivals Hibernian. Kidd rubbed salt into the wounds by adding a second shortly after and the title was Celtic's. In the end Celtic finished on 50 points and a goal difference of plus 29 with Hearts level on 50 points but worse off by three on goal difference. Ally McCoist ended the season as the top scorer with 24 goals. Motherwell and Clydebank made up the bottom two with 20 points each but reconstruction and a move to 12 teams saw them remain in the top flight.

Hamilton, under John Lambie, were front-runners in the First Division and with seven games to go they confirmed promotion before finishing top with 56

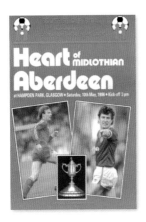

points, 11 clear of Falkirk. Alloa finished bottom on 26 points while Ayr United were also relegated on 31.

Queen of the South and Dunfermline had been at the top of the third tier for the majority of the season and with four games left Queens were a point ahead of the Pars. However, two defeats and two draws saw Dunfermline win the title with 57 points, two clear of the Doonhamers. Meadowbank were way behind in third on 49 points. Stranraer finished bottom with 23.

The first two rounds of the League Cup pretty much ran to form. In round three Rangers travelled to Dens Park and were lucky to get through on penalties. Not such a shock perhaps except their opponents were Forfar and not Dundee. With 21 minutes remaining Forfar were leading 2-0 but Rangers hauled them back to 2-2 and after extra time it went to penalties. Forfar skipper Ian McPhee had a kick to win the tie but shot weakly, allowing Nicky Walker to save, and ultimately the underdogs lost out.

Hibernian hit the goal trail with a 6-0 win over Cowdenbeath, followed with a 6-1 rout of Motherwell. In the quarter-finals they faced Celtic at Easter Road and hit four goals, as did Celtic. The match went to penalties with both Alan Rough and Paddy Bonner saving two each. Pierce O'Leary blasted his over the bar so Hibs headed into the semi-finals. Aberdeen, Dundee United and Rangers also reached the last four.

Rough was once again the hero in the first leg at home to Rangers. Just after half-time he saved a penalty from Ally McCoist, and then Gordon Chisholm on his Hibs debut put his side ahead. Gordon Durie then scored to allow Hibs to head to Ibrox with a 2-0 lead. A Davie Cooper free kick brought Rangers back into the tie but Hibernian held out to reach the final.

At Tannadice, Aberdeen and Dundee United played out a bad-tempered match with eight players booked and Richard Gough sent off. By that time, an Eric Black header had given the Dons the advantage in the tie. Frank McDougall gave Aberdeen a two-goal cushion in the 62nd minute of the second leg. Hamish McAlpine had been carrying an injury since the first half and was immediately substituted, so Paul Hegarty took over in goal, but there would be no further scoring.

A crowd of 40,061 turned up at Hampden for the final and after 12 minutes they all knew Aberdeen had their name on the cup as goals by Black and Billy Stark had given the Dons a commanding lead. There was no way back for Hibs and Black added a third in the 63rd minute. This would be Alex Ferguson's only Scottish League Cup win and the trophy had been claimed without Aberdeen conceding a goal in the entire tournament.

Rather uncharacteristically, Albion Rovers put eight past Gala Fairydean in the first round of the Scottish Cup but went out to Queen's Park in the next round. Nairn put out Meadowbank after a replay but then took a 7-0 hammering by Dundee. Hearts put Rangers out in the third round too. In the quarter-finals, Hibernian once more put four past Celtic at Easter Road but this time with only three in reply, and headed to the semi-finals. Aberdeen took two turns to overcome Dundee. Hearts crushed St Mirren 4-1 at Tynecastle, while Dundee United – thanks to a Gough goal – overcame Motherwell at Fir Park.

In the semis, Aberdeen faced Hibernian at Dens Park with 19,165 fans in the stadium. Once again they proved too good for Hibs with Stark and Black scoring in the first half. Joe Miller added a late third as Aberdeen ran out 3-0 winners. Elsewhere, Hearts' remarkable season continued with a victory at Hampden over Dundee United in front of 30,872. John Colquhoun scored the all-important goal in the 14th minute.

The final itself saw more despair for the Hearts fans in the 62,841 crowd. John Hewitt scored from the edge of the area to put Aberdeen in front after only five minutes, and the second half had barely begun when Hewitt put them further in front. Stark then scored a third in the 75th minute. To rub salt into Hearts' wounds, skipper Walter Kidd was sent off in the dying minutes. Aberdeen thus became the first club outside Celtic and Rangers to collect both cups in the same season. The Dons would repeat the feat in 1989/90 while St Johnstone would become the second non-Old Firm club to do the cup double in 2020/21 when, sadly, due to the coronavirus restrictions there were no spectators in the national stadium to witness this achievement.

Part
two
European Representation

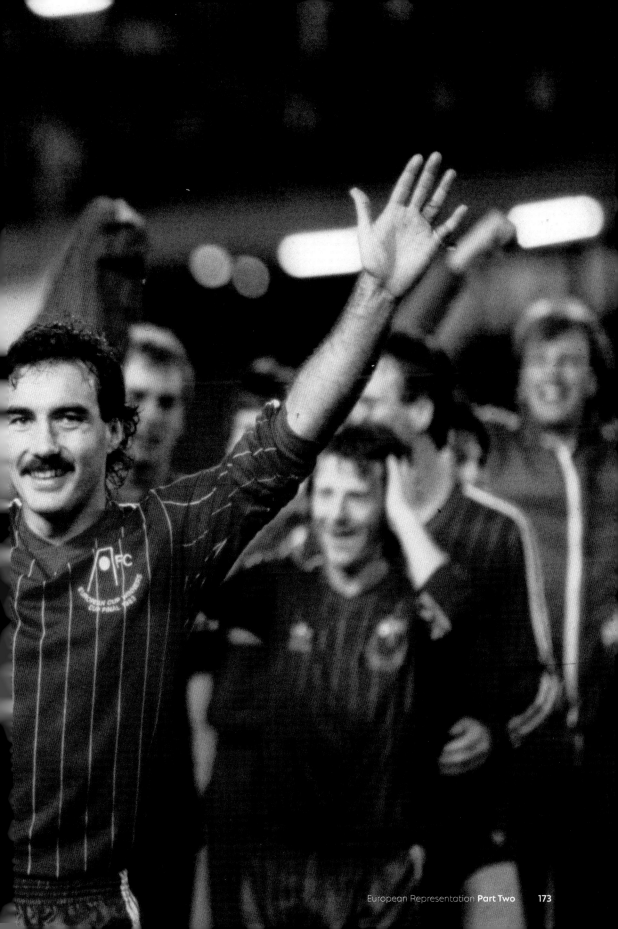

Summary

Season	European Cup	Cup Winners' Cup	Fairs Cup/UEFA Cup
1955/56	Hibernian (SF)	-	-
1956/57	Rangers (1)	-	-
1957/58	Rangers (1)	-	No Representation
1958/59	Hearts (P)	-	-
1959/60	Rangers (SF)	-	No Representation
1960/61	Hearts (P)	Rangers (RU)	Hibernian (SF)
1961/62	Rangers (2)	Dunfermline (QF)	Hearts (2); Hibernian (2)
1962/63	Dundee (SF)	Rangers (2)	Celtic (1); Dunfermline (2); Hibernian (QF)
1963/64	Rangers (P)	Celtic (SF)	Hearts (1); Partick Thistle (2)
1964/65	Rangers (QF)	Dundee (2)	Celtic (2); Dunfermline (3); Kilmarnock (2)
1965/66	Kilmarnock (1)	Celtic (SF)	Dunfermline (QF); Hearts (3); Hibernian (1)
1966/67	Celtic (W)	Rangers (RU)	Dunfermline (2); Dundee Utd (3); Kilmarnock (SF)
1967/68	Celtic (1)	Aberdeen (2)	Dundee (SF); Hibernian (3); Rangers (QF)
1968/69	Celtic (QF)	Dunfermline (SF)	Aberdeen (2); Hibernian (3); Morton (1); Rangers (SF)
1969/70	Celtic (RU)	Rangers (2)	Dunfermline (3); Dundee Utd (1); Kilmarnock (3)
1970/71	Celtic (QF)	Aberdeen (1)	Dundee Utd (2); Hibernian (3); Kilmarnock (1); Rangers (1)
1971/72	Celtic (SF)	Rangers (W)	Aberdeen (2); Dundee (3); St. Johnstone (3)

Notes in brackets reflect stage of competition reached

Season	European Cup	Cup Winners' Cup	Fairs Cup/UEFA Cup
1972/73	Celtic (2)	Hibernian (QF)	Aberdeen (1); Partick Thistle (1)
1973/74	Celtic (SF)	Rangers (2)	Aberdeen (2); Dundee (1); Hibernian (2)
1974/75	Celtic (1)	Dundee Utd (2)	Dundee (1); Hibernian (2)
1975/76	Rangers (2)	Celtic (QF)	Dundee Utd (2); Hibernian (1)
1976/77	Rangers (1)	Hearts (2)	Celtic (1); Hibernian (2)
1977/78	Celtic (2)	Rangers (1)	Aberdeen (1); Dundee Utd (1)
1978/79	Rangers (QF)	Aberdeen (2)	Hibernian (2); Dundee Utd (1)
1979/80	Celtic (QF)	Rangers (2)	Aberdeen (1); Dundee Utd (2)
1980/81	Aberdeen (2)	Celtic (1)	St. Mirren (2); Dundee Utd (2)
1981/82	Celtic (1)	Rangers (1)	Aberdeen (3); Dundee Utd (QF)
1982/83	Celtic (2)	Aberdeen (W)	Dundee Utd (QF); Rangers (2)
1983/84	Dundee Utd (SF)	Aberdeen (SF)	Celtic (3); St. Mirren (1); Rangers (2)
1984/85	Aberdeen (1)	Celtic (2)	Hearts (1); Dundee Utd (3); Rangers(2)
1985/86	Aberdeen (QF)	Celtic (1)	Dundee Utd (3); Rangers (1); St. Mirren (2)

Seasons in European Competitions

Club	European Cup	European Cup Winners' Cup	Fairs/ UEFA Cup	Total	Best Performance
Rangers	9	10	6	25	1971/72 ECWC winners
Celtic	13	6	4	23	1966/67 EC winners
Aberdeen	3	5	7	15	1982/83 ECWC winners
Dundee Utd	1	1	12	14	1983/84 EC semi-finals
Hibernian	1	1	12	14	1955/56 EC semi-finals
Hearts	2	1	4	7	1965/66 FC third round
Dundee	1	1	4	6	1962/63 EC semi-finals
Dunfermline	0	2	5	7	1968/69 ECWC semi-finals
Kilmarnock	1	0	4	5	1966/67 FC semi-finals
St Mirren	0	0	3	3	1980/81 UC second round
Partick Thistle	0	0	2	2	1963/64 FC second round
St Johnstone	0	0	1	1	1971/72 UC third round
Greenock Morton	0	0	1	1	1968/69 FC first round
Totals	**31**	**27**	**65**	**123**	

Factoids

Three European trophies were won by Scottish sides during the Golden Years – Celtic, Rangers and Aberdeen have all triumphed on the continent. In addition, Rangers have twice been runners-up and Celtic have been beaten in another final.

Scotland also supplied 14 beaten semi-finalists over those four decades – Celtic four times; Dundee, Hibernian and Rangers twice each; Aberdeen, Dundee United, Dunfermline Athletic and Kilmarnock once. The split by competition was six in the European Cup, four in the European Cup Winners' Cup, and four in the Inter-Cities Fairs Cup/UEFA Cup.

On two occasions (1968/69, 1970/71), **Scotland had as many as four representatives in the Fairs Cup**, meaning that no fewer than six Scottish clubs were involved in European competitions those seasons. Who needs coefficients?

In terms of **chronological order** of appearance in Europe it reads as Hibernian, Rangers, Hearts, Dunfermline Athletic, Dundee, Celtic, Partick Thistle, Kilmarnock, Dundee United, Aberdeen, Morton, St Johnstone and St Mirren.

The eight post-Golden Years debutants – in alphabetical order – are Airdrie, Falkirk, Gretna, Inverness Caledonian Thistle, Livingston, Motherwell, Queen of the South and Raith Rovers.

Notable scalps have included European trophy winners such as Anderlecht, Ajax, Barcelona (several times), Bayern Munich, Benfica, Borussia Mönchengladbach, Fiorentina, Hamburg SV, Inter Milan, Juventus, Real Madrid and Sporting Lisbon. Closer to home and those noisy neighbours sent packing were Everton, Ipswich Town, Leeds United, West Bromwich Albion and Wolverhampton Wanderers.

Over the period of the Golden Years the **cover price of the home-produced European match programmes** would increase from the equivalent of one penny to 50 pence during which time small, grainy, black and white images of the likes of Hearts skipper Dave Mackay in long, baggy shorts and ankle-high leather boots would give way to full-colour pages of Rangers defender/striker Colin McAdam complete with curly-perm hairstyle, and Aberdeen assistant manager Willie Garner looking like John Motson in a brown sheepskin jacket.

Furthermore, in November 1984 **a ticket for the enclosure at Ibrox Stadium to see Rangers against Inter Milan in the UEFA Cup cost £3**. By comparison, it cost £3.50 to suffer Bow Wow Wow at Tiffany's Discotheque in Glasgow in November 1982 and £4.50 to go mental with The Stranglers at the Glasgow Apollo Theatre in February 1983. Annabella Lwin, Karl-Heinz Rummenigge and Hugh Cornwell. You pays your money.

The Union of European Football Associations
(UEFA) was founded on 15 June 1954 in Basel,
Switzerland, with the Scottish Football Association
a founder member. However, against a backdrop
of a war-ravaged Cold War Europe it was Jacques
Ferran and Gabriel Hanot, two journalists for the
French sports newspaper *L'Equipe*, who were the
driving force behind the creation of the European
Champion Clubs' Cup, which UEFA approved in
April 1955. *L'Equipe* were the initial organisers
of the competition and participating clubs
were selected on the basis that they were both
representative and prestigious.

The inaugural competition comprised 16 clubs, but
with no English representation due to a Europhobe
attitude by the country's football authorities, and
culminated with Real Madrid defeating Reims 4-3
in the final in the Parc des Princes, Paris, on 13 June
1956. As a ridiculous aside, the first Eurovision Song
contest took place in Lugano, Switzerland, on 24
May 1956 – and was won by the host nation. The UK
joined the 'musical fun' in 1957.

Eight different clubs have represented Scotland
in the European Cup and our sides have been
winners once (Celtic in 1966/67), runners-up once
(Celtic in 1969/70) and beaten semi-finalists on six
occasions – Hibernian (1955/56), Rangers (1959/60),
Dundee (1962/63), Celtic (1971/72 and 1973/74) and
Dundee United (1983/84).

———————

Presented by SCOTTISH DAILY EXPRESS

No. 7. L. REILLY, Hibernians F.C.

HIBERNIAN took part in the inaugural Champion
Clubs' Cup in 1955/56 and they weren't even
Scotland's champions – Aberdeen were, but *L'Equipe*
deemed that while the Dons might well be 'Dandy'
they were not 'prestigious' enough. Sore one!

So on 14 September 1955 Hugh Shaw's Hibs flew
the flag, travelled to West Germany and defeated
Rot-Weiss Essen 4-0 in the first leg of their first-
round tie. Eddie Turnbull got the first and third goals
while Lawrie Reilly netted the second and Willie

Ormond the fourth – so that was four goals by three of the 'Famous Five'. Back at Easter Road on 12 October, a crowd of 30,000 witnessed a 1-1 draw – Hibs centre-forward John Buchanan becoming the first player to score a goal on British soil in European competition. The man in the middle was the renowned, English World Cup referee Arthur Ellis, who would achieve even greater stardom in the BBC TV gameshow *It's a Knockout!* in which his dipstick featured regularly.

In the quarter-finals, Hibs defeated the Swedish champions Djurgården 3-1 on 23 November in the first leg, which due to severe weather conditions was not played in Sweden but at Firhill Stadium, Glasgow – so the home of Partick Thistle (aka the 'Maryhill Magyars') saw European action before the likes of Rangers, Celtic, Liverpool, Manchester United, Ajax or Bayern Munich. Once again, Arthur Ellis strutted his stuff. In the second leg at Easter Road just five days later a Turnbull goal separated the sides while Mr Ellis got his Hibs hat-trick so to speak.

About ten weeks after Elvis Presley released 'Heartbreak Hotel', Hibs played their semi-final first leg against Reims on 4 April 1956 at the Parc des Princes and lost by two second-half goals to nil. In the second leg on 18 April not even the fourth appearance by Ellis and a crowd of 44,941 could prevent the Edinburgh side from losing 1-0 and exiting 3-0 on aggregate.

Nevertheless, here's to the trailblazing Hibees and the nearby (and appropriately named) Arthur's Seat!

––––––––––

RANGERS' first two attempts at becoming Europe's best, in 1956/57 and 1957/58, were both ended at the first-round stage. In their first campaign Rangers avoided the preliminary round by way of a bye before defeating the French outfit Nice 2-1 at Ibrox with Max Murray having the honour of netting the Gers' first European goal before Northern Ireland international Billy Simpson hit the winner. A 2-1 reverse in France, with South African Johnny

European Champion
Clubs' Cup

Hubbard netting a penalty, meant a play-off on
neutral ground but at the Parc des Princes, Paris, and
in front of only 11,908 Rangers lost 3-1.

In 1957/58 Rangers overcame French side Saint-
Étienne 4-3 on aggregate in the preliminary round
(Don Kitchenbrand, Alex Scott, Billy Simpson and
Davie Wilson the scorers) but were comprehensively
beaten 6-1 on aggregate by AC Milan in the first
round proper (Max Murray got the consolation goal).
The Italian side went on to reach the final in Brussels
where they lost out to Real Madrid, who lifted the
trophy for the third successive season. Incidentally, the
Scotland 1958 World Cup finals squad would include
four Rangers players with the aforementioned Alex
Scott the youngest member at 21.

In 1959/60 Rangers made it to the semi-finals,
overcoming Anderlecht (7-2 with Andy Matthew
and Sammy Baird contributing two apiece), Red Star
Bratislava (5-4 with Alex Scott netting in each leg)

and Sparta Rotterdam (3-2 in a play-off at Highbury, London, after the aggregate score was tied at 3-3. Two from Sammy Baird plus an own goal got them through). And then it all went horribly wrong. In the semi-final first leg at the Waldstadion, 72,000 saw Eintracht Frankfurt demolish Rangers 6-1, the Gers' goal coming from an Eric Caldow penalty. In the return leg, Rangers collapsed 6-3 (Ian McMillan got a double) to lose 12-4 on aggregate. The Berlin Wall would go up in August 1961 but Rangers' famed 'Iron Curtain' defensive line of the late 1940s and early 1950s was now a fast-fading memory.

Eintracht were in turn demolished 7-3 by Real Madrid in the final at Hampden Park in front of a crowd of around 128,000. Legend has it that the football played by the Spanish side that evening was as good as the first-half display by Partick Thistle at the 1971 Scottish League Cup Final. It was certainly good enough to give Real their fifth successive European Cup.

In 1961/62 the French and East German champions were sent packing before the Belgians spoiled things. Monaco were beaten 3-2 twice. In the principality, Jim Baxter opened the scoring and Scott added a double while back in Glasgow James Christie got a double with Scott netting the winner. The Berlin Wall had only been in place for about three months when Rangers crossed into the 'Russian sector' – to the Friedrich-Ludwig-Jahn Sportpark – and defeated Vorwarts Berlin 2-1 with an Eric Caldow penalty and a goal from Ralph Brand. Rangers' home tie was then played in Malmö, Sweden, as a result of Cold War politics and the East Germans being refused entry visas to Britain. It then took two attempts to complete the tie. Fog caused the abandonment of the first attempt on the evening of 22 November with Rangers leading 1-0 thanks to a goal from 17-year-old apprentice Willie Henderson. The rescheduled match kicked off the following day – at 10am – but not before two of the Vorwarts party had defected to the West. Henderson scored again on his second European debut as Rangers won 4-1 with McMillan

European Champion Clubs' Cup

netting a double and both sides exchanging one own goal.

In the February quarter-finals, Rangers travelled to the Stade de Sclessin in the shadow of steel works and slag heaps and lost 4-1 to Standard Liege with Davie Wilson scoring. A crowd of around 77,000 were at Ibrox hoping for a classic comeback but Rangers could only manage a 2-0 victory through Brand and Caldow and were eliminated 4-3 on aggregate. Liege would lose in the semi-finals to Real Madrid, who in turn were beaten 5-3 by Benfica in the final with a losing hat-trick for Ferenc Puskás.

Less than two months after the infamous Great Train Robbery, the 1963/64 campaign proved to

be short and painful as Rangers were beaten 7-0 on aggregate by Real Madrid in the preliminary round. In the first leg at Ibrox, 81,000 saw the legendary Puskás snatch the only goal of the game four minutes from time. At the Santiago Bernabéu Stadium 90,000 cheered a hat-trick by Puskás as the Spanish champions won 6-0. According to Rangers skipper John Greig, 'Puskás and company had been fortunate to come out on top in the first leg ... but luck had nothing to do with it in the return when the "Galloping Major" mowed us down with ruthless efficiency.' Real Madrid would come up short in the final, however, when they lost 3-1 to Inter Milan.

Rangers' sixth European Cup campaign came in 1964/65, with Scott Symon as manager and in the absence of the away goals rule it took three games to separate them from Red Star Belgrade in the preliminary round. Rangers won the first leg 3-1 at Ibrox with two for Ralph Brand and one for Jim Forrest, but then lost the return match 4-2 in Yugoslavia – goals from John Greig and Ronnie McKinnon keeping the Scottish champions in the tie. A play-off at Arsenal's Highbury would settle matters and Rangers triumphed 3-1, this time with two for Forrest and one for Brand.

A Davie Wilson goal in Glasgow was all that separated Rangers and Rapid Vienna after the first round first leg. In the Prater Stadium, however, Rangers won 2-0 in a match chiefly remembered for Jim Baxter suffering a broken leg in the dying seconds – excessive 'mickey-taking' of an opponent being cited as a contributory factor in the career-changing challenge. In the last eight, Rangers visited the San Siro in Milan to face Inter, the European Cup and Intercontinental Cup holders, and lost 3-1 although the goal from Forrest offered hope. Another massive Ibrox crowd of nearly 80,000 must have thought the dream was on when Forrest put Rangers ahead after only seven minutes but they were unable to further breach Helenio Herrera's 'catenaccio' defensive system and the Italians progressed 3-2 on aggregate. Inter would go on to retain the European Cup, defeating Liverpool in the

European Champion Clubs' Cup

semis before overcoming Benfica 1-0 in the final in their own San Siro home.

Kilmarnock's league success of 1964/65 followed by Celtic's nine in a row meant it was 1975/76 before Rangers, with Jock Wallace as manager, were back in Europe's top competition. In the first round the visitors to Ibrox were Bohemians of Dublin who were eventually overcome 4-1 thanks to goals from Graham Fyfe, an own goal from Irish Olympian Joe Burke, Alex O'Hara and Derek Johnstone. In Dublin, Rangers had to be content with a 1-1 draw as Johnstone scored again but it was enough to see them through to a second-round meeting with Saint-Étienne.

In the first leg in France, Rangers went down 2-0 and then surprisingly lost 2-1 at home with Alex MacDonald's consolation goal coming two minutes from time.

Saint-Étienne went all the way to the final at Hampden where they were arguably the better side but lost out to a second-half Franz Roth rocket and Bayern Munich then held out to lift the trophy for the third successive year. In the first half, however, a shot from Dominique Bathenay hit the crossbar with Bayern's keeper Sepp Maier beaten. A header from team-mate Jacques Santini was also denied by the woodwork. To this day, Saint-Étienne supporters blame/curse 'tes poteaux carres' ('the square posts') which, ironically, were later acquired by the French club and housed in their museum. How's that for masochistic memorabilia?

In 1976/77 Rangers were in the European Cup as Scottish champions and indeed domestic Treble winners but unfortunately that achievement didn't impress FC Zürich who, in the first leg of the first round, visited Ibrox and carved out a valuable 1-1 draw for themselves – the visitors taking the lead in the first minute before Derek Parlane equalised about half an hour later. Over in Switzerland, Zürich again scored early with a goal in the eighth minute, and then held on to their lead to go through 2-1 on aggregate. Zürich would be eliminated at the semi-final stage by Liverpool who went on to lift the trophy for the first time.

Rangers went into the 1978/79 European Cup once again as Treble winners, with former playing legend John Greig experiencing his first season as manager of the Ibrox club. In the opening round the Gers were drawn against the much-fancied Italian aces Juventus, UEFA Cup winners in 1977, but over in Turin the deficit was kept to just 1-0 despite the goal being conceded after just nine minutes. A superb performance at Ibrox saw the Scottish champions progress 2-1 on aggregate – the goals coming from Alex MacDonald and Gordon Smith. In the second round Rangers looked to have slipped up when they drew 0-0 at home to PSV Eindhoven, the current

European Champion Clubs' Cup

holders of the UEFA Cup, but in the second leg in the Netherlands another excellent display resulted in a 3-2 away win. Rangers conceded in the first minute, MacDonald equalised, PSV went 2-1 in front, Johnstone levelled again and then three minutes from time exquisite counter-attacking play ended with Bobby Russell grabbing the winner.

Was Rangers' name on the cup? Alas, no, although confidence and hopes were high when Greig's team returned from Cologne only trailing 1-0. At Ibrox, however, Rangers failed to hit their previous heights and Dieter Müller, the scorer from the first leg, repeated the trick early in the second half before Tommy McLean equalised four minutes from the end. In the semi-finals Cologne were edged out by Brian Clough's Nottingham Forest, who would then win the final with their Scottish skipper John McGovern lifting the trophy and with fellow Scots Kenny Burns (ex-Rangers youth) and John Robertson (ex-Drumchapel Amateurs) in close attendance.

As far as Rangers playing again in the European Cup was concerned, they would have to await the arrival of Graeme Souness in 1986 and the commencement of a championship-winning duopoly with Celtic.

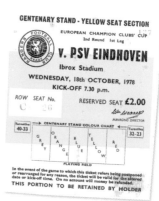

HEARTS had two forays into the European Champion Clubs' Cup but unfortunately both of them ended at the preliminary round stage. In 1958/59 they travelled to Belgium and were mauled 5-1 by Standard Liege but not before Ian Crawford had given the Jambos the lead in the 14th minute. Back in Edinburgh, a modicum of respectability was achieved with a 2-1 victory in front of an impressive crowd of 37,500 – Willie

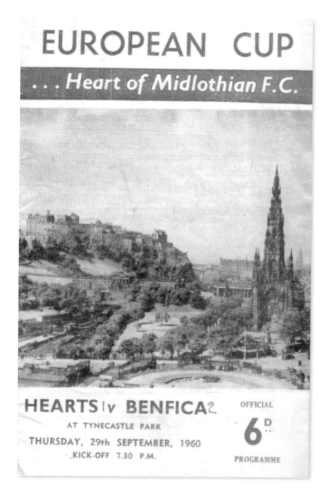

EUROPEAN CUP
... Heart of Midlothian F.C.

HEARTS | v BENFICA 2   OFFICIAL
AT TYNECASTLE PARK
THURSDAY, 29th SEPTEMBER, 1960
KICK-OFF 7.30 P.M.
6 D
PROGRAMME

Bauld scoring both the goals. On the bright side, September 1958 also saw the general release of the very first *Carry On* movie, *Carry On Sergeant*, starring future Dr Who actor William Hartnell. The European Cup space/time continuum would continue with Real Madrid winning the competition for the fourth successive season.

For 1960/61 the great Benfica side were the opposition and they duly won 2-1 at Tynecastle with Alex Young getting Hearts' goal, and then 3-0 at the Stadium of Light. Benfica would go on to win the European Cup that season to become only the second club to get their name on the trophy.

Hearts are arguably Scotland's greatest underachievers in Europe, and the Tynecastle club's

alex young

HEARTS
& SCOTLAND
inside-right

European Champion Clubs' Cup

only appearance at the quarter-final stage would not arrive until the 1988/89 UEFA Cup. Furthermore, they have never managed to qualify for Europe in three successive seasons. In some ways the Jambos are reminiscent of that excellent Edinburgh-born thespian Alastair Sim – not an international star but a class act whose genius was at its peak between 1946 and 1960.

———————

DUNDEE appeared in the 1962/63 European Cup and went all the way to the semi-finals. In the preliminary round they absolutely destroyed Cologne 8-1 at Dens Park – Alan Gilzean got a hat-trick while Bobby Wishart (although some say it was Bobby Seith), ex-Hibee Gordon Smith, Hugh Robertson and Andy Penman also got on the scoresheet with the West German outfit contributing an own goal just for good measure. Over in Cologne, Dundee crashed 4-0 but went through 8-5 on aggregate.

Against a backdrop of the first James Bond movie, *Dr. No*, hitting our cinema screens in October 1962, the Dark Blues then journeyed to Portugal where they narrowly lost 1-0 to Sporting Lisbon. Back at Dens Park, however, another hat-trick from Alan Gilzean plus a goal from Alan Cousin

helped Dundee to a 4-1 win and a 4-2 aggregate triumph. A trip to Brussels in the quarter-finals resulted in a magnificent 4-1 away win against Anderlecht, who had eliminated Real Madrid in the preliminary round, with two goals from Gilzean plus one apiece from Cousin and Smith although some sources credit Andy Penman. Dundee also won the second leg, 2-1, with Cousin and Smith the marksmen.

In the semi-final first leg, AC Milan, roared on by almost 74,000 in the San Siro, took the lead after only three minutes but Dundee hit back through Cousin and the teams went in level at the break. The second half was a different story and four goals for the home side gave them a 5-1 victory. Just over 35,000 packed into Dens Park for the return game and while a miracle comeback was never on, a goal from Gilzean in the 81st minute, his ninth of the competition, gave Dundee a victory nonetheless.

AC Milan, who had eliminated Ipswich Town in the first round, returned to England to defeat Benfica in the final at Wembley and win the European Cup for the first time. On the plus side, by the time of the 1963 final, The Beatles had well and truly arrived.

KILMARNOCK represented Scotland in the 1965/66 competition and in the preliminary round they narrowly defeated Nëntori Tirana. In Communist Albania, which at the time was aligned with China as opposed to the USSR, a 0-0 draw was achieved and then back at Rugby Park a solitary goal from Bertie Black was enough to see Killie through. The following day, *Thunderbirds* appeared on our TV screens for the first time but there would be no International Rescue in the first round proper when the Scottish champions faced Real Madrid and the likes of Francisco Gento and Ferenc Puskás. In the 22nd minute of the first leg Tommy McLean put the home side in front from the penalty spot, but Real hit back to lead 2-1 before a goal from Jackie McInally meant the game finished 2-2. At the Bernabéu a goal from Brian McIlroy midway through the first half gave Kilmarnock the lead, but then the Spanish giants proceeded to turn it on and race to a 5-1 victory. Real Madrid would continue to turn it on to the extent that they won the European Cup for the sixth time that season.

European Champion Clubs' Cup

CELTIC were the sixth different club to represent Scotland in the European Cup, in 1966/67, and they won it at their first attempt – a feat also achieved by Real Madrid in 1955/56, Nottingham Forest in 1978/79 and Aston Villa in 1981/82. Celtic were also the first British/north European side to lift the trophy and did so with 11 Scottish players; indeed all but one of the squad of 15 were born within ten miles of Celtic Park – Bobby Lennox was the 'far-travelled' man from Saltcoats in Ayrshire. Also, by competing in the European Cup, Celtic became the first Scottish club to have participated in all three European competitions.

That great run started with a 5-0 aggregate win over FC Zürich (2-0 at Celtic Park and 3-0 in Switzerland). Tommy Gemmell got three of the goals while the other two were by striker Joe McBride. In the second round, away and home victories were again achieved, 3-1 in both Nantes and Glasgow, with the goals being shared between Lennox and Steve Chalmers (two apiece – one away, one home) plus McBride in France and Jimmy Johnstone at Celtic Park.

By the time of the quarter-finals, Celtic had lost McBride through injury, and away to Vojvodina of Yugoslavia the Bhoys went down 1-0, their only reverse of the campaign. In Glasgow, however, it was business as usual with a 2-0 win – although they did have to wait until the 90th minute for Billy McNeill's clincher after Chalmers had levelled the tie in the 58th minute. Almost 75,000 were in Celtic Park to see their favourites defeat Dukla Prague 3-1 in the semi-final first leg with a goal from Jimmy Johnstone and a brace from Willie Wallace – McBride's replacement. A goalless draw was achieved in Czechoslovakia as Jock Stein's side moved closer to immortality.

In the final at the Estádio Nacional in Lisbon on Thursday, 25 May the good guys (Celtic, playing attacking football) overcame the bad guys (the defensive-minded Inter Milan) 2-1, and by 42 goal attempts to five! The Italian champions, who had eliminated the holders Real Madrid in the quarter-finals and whose line-up included five players who

would help Italy lift the European Championship the following year, took the lead after only seven minutes due to the award of a dubious penalty which was converted by Sandro Mazzola. Celtic had to wait until the 63rd minute for their deserved equaliser – a powerful 25-yard shot from Tommy Gemmell. With six minutes remaining history was made when Chalmers scored the winner by diverting a low drive from Bobby Murdoch into the back of the net. At full time a friendly pitch invasion ensued which forced veteran keeper Ronnie Simpson to step lively and retrieve his false teeth from his bunnet in the back of the goal! 'Celtic V-E Night '67!' shouted the *Daily Record* headlines and looking back, all you need is love, the Lisbon Lions, Jock Stein and fast, beautiful football.

European Champion Clubs' Cup

The 1967 Summer of Love came and went, however, and in defending their title in 1967/68 Celtic's celebratory champagne went somewhat flat when the European champions lost 3-2 on aggregate to Dynamo Kiev in the first round. In the first leg at Parkhead the Soviet champions were 2-0 ahead after half an hour before Lennox pulled one back in the second half. In Kiev, Lennox gave Celtic the lead after 67 minutes but the home side made sure of progression with an equaliser one minute from time.

Dynamo were eliminated by Górnik Zabrze in the second round, and the Poles in turn lost in the quarter-finals to the eventual winners Manchester United, managed by Bellshill's Matt Busby. Scotland striker supreme Denis Law missed the final due to injury, although his fellow Scot and former Celt Pat Crerand collected a winners' medal that evening at Wembley.

Going back to late 1967, and while the existence of a European Super Cup would have pitted Celtic against Bayern Munich (it could so easily have been Rangers) there was instead a 'confrontation' with Racing Club of Argentina in the Intercontinental Cup, with the South American side resorting to incessant cynical fouling and spitting over the course of three games. On 18 October almost 84,000 were inside Hampden Park to see Celtic win 1-0, Billy McNeill the scorer. On 1 November Racing won the return match in Buenos Aires 2-1 (as an aside, a copy of the match programme went for £261 in an eBay auction in January 2021). A Tommy Gemmell penalty had given the Bhoys an early lead and in my book Celtic became world champions on away goals but as I was not in charge of things, a third game in 'neutral' Uruguay was required which took place on 4 November and is often referred to as the 'Battle of Montevideo'. Celtic players retaliated against the assaults and abuse and had four men sent off while Racing, who scored the only goal of the farce/game, were reduced to nine men. Apparently, Jock Stein commented after the match that he would not take a team to South America again for all the money in the world. I sometimes wish Ally MacLeod had said something similar a decade or so later.

Celtic's third venture into the European Cup in 1968/69 saw the Parkhead men reach the quarter-finals although they should arguably have gone further. Following the invasion of Czechoslovakia in August 1968 by Warsaw Pact troops, protests led to the withdrawal of Eastern Bloc teams. A re-draw was required and Celtic's campaign started with a 2-0 away defeat to Saint-Étienne. In Glasgow, though, goals from Gemmell (a penalty), Jim Craig, Chalmers and McBride put Celtic through to the second round 4-2 on aggregate. Red Star Belgrade then visited Celtic Park and although Bobby Murdoch put the home side in front after only three minutes, by half-time it was 1-1. The second half was a different story as Celtic turned it on to romp to a 5-1 victory with two-goal Jinky Johnstone 'inspired' by the promise of not having to fly to Belgrade for the second leg if the Bhoys could achieve a four-goal lead. Lennox and Willie Wallace scored the other goals. In Belgrade, Celtic drew 1-1 with Wallace again on the scoresheet.

In the quarter-finals, Celtic did the hard bit first via a goalless draw with AC Milan in a San Siro snowstorm but at Parkhead, an uncharacteristic error by skipper Billy McNeill allowed Pierino Prati to score after 12 minutes and 1-0 it finished.

Milan then eliminated the holders Manchester United in the semis before going on to lift the cup for the second time by defeating Ajax 4-1 in the final with Prati nabbing a hat-trick.

In July 1969, America put the first men on the moon but more importantly, two months later the Scottish champions got off to a winning start in the 1969/70 European Cup with a 2-0 aggregate win over FC Basel. In the St. Jakob Stadium, Celtic earned a goalless draw and then won 2-0 at Parkhead thanks to Gemmell and Harry Hood. They then had to rely on the toss of a coin to get past Benfica in the second round after they had defeated the Portuguese side 3-0 at Celtic Park with Gemmell,

European Champion Clubs' Cup

Wallace and Hood scoring, only to lose by the same score in Lisbon. Penalties weren't used back then so a silver two-guilder piece belonging to the Dutch referee was used to settle things when Billy McNeill twice called 'Heads' correctly – firstly to win the right to spin the coin and secondly to take Celtic through to the quarter-finals. Incidentally, in the same round Galatasaray eliminated Spartak Trnava by the same monetary method.

In the last eight, Celtic powered to another 3-0 victory, at home to Fiorentina, thanks to Bertie Auld, Willie Wallace and an own goal. In Florence,

Fiorentina were the better side but the deficit was kept to 1-0 and Celtic became the first British team to defeat an Italian club in the European Cup over two legs. The semis produced a 'Battle of Britain' tie against Don Revie's Leeds United with the English media all but writing off Celtic's chances. In the first leg at Elland Road, George Connelly scored for the visitors in the very first minute and 1-0 to the Glasgow club was how it ended. Celtic switched their home tie to the larger Hampden Park to try to accommodate demand and the crowd of 136,505 is a European record which may never be broken. On the pitch it was Leeds' turn to take an early lead – Billy Bremner scoring in the 14th minute to give the Yorkshire club a half-time advantage. Six minutes into the second half, Celtic were 2-1 in front with John Hughes and Bobby Murdoch doing the honours and they duly became the first British club to appear in two European Cup finals.

Being Scottish, I am totally biased of course when I say that Celtic deserved a happy, nay ecstatic, ending to the campaign, but it wasn't to be. In Milan's San Siro Celtic lost 2-1 to a Feyenoord side which included future Parkhead manager Wim Jansen. The Hoops took the lead in the 30th minute through Tommy Gemmell but Rinus Israel equalised just two minutes later and with no more goals in the 90 minutes the final went into extra time. In the 117th minute came a 'dagger to the heart' from Swedish striker Ove Kindvall who took the European Cup to the Netherlands for the first time. As an aside, the 12 Celtic players involved in the match were all Scottish.

In 1970/71 the Dutch did Celtic in again but this time at the last-eight stage. In the first two rounds it was goals galore starting with a 14-0 aggregate win over Finland's KPV Kokkola – 9-0 at Celtic Park including a first-half hat-trick for Hood and a double for Paul Wilson, followed by a 5-0 away win which featured a Wallace brace. In round two Waterford were overwhelmed 10-2 on aggregate – 7-0 in the Republic of Ireland with a Wallace hat-trick plus doubles for Bobby Murdoch and Lou Macari, then a surprisingly narrow 3-2 victory in Glasgow thanks to John Hughes and Jimmy Johnstone's pair.

In Amsterdam, however, three second-half goals gave Ajax a 3-0 win – Johan Cruyff, Barry Hulshoff and Piet Keizer scoring. At Hampden Park (Celtic Park was undergoing reconstruction works), Johnstone scored after 27 minutes but Celtic couldn't add to their lead and went out 3-1 on aggregate. Ajax went on to win their first European Cup that season by defeating Panathinaikos, managed by Ferenc Puskás, 2-0 in the final at Wembley. Earlier, the defending champions Feyenoord had been eliminated in the first round by UTA Arad of Romania.

Celtic's tenth European campaign, 1971/72, would see much drama at the semi-final stage but it all started with a surprising 2-1 defeat away to 1903 Copenhagen – Lou Macari on target – but this was

followed up with a 3-0 victory at home with a double for Wallace plus one for Tommy Callaghan. In the second round, Maltese champions Sliema Wanderers visited the East End of Glasgow and were thumped 5-0; Macari got a double with one each for Hood, Jim Brogan and Gemmell – the latter transferring to Nottingham Forest in December 1971. Over on the sunshine island, the home side went ahead in the first minute thanks to a goal from Ronnie Cocks before Celtic hit back through Hood and Lennox on the notorious, sun-baked, sandy playing surface of the Empire Stadium, Gzira, which was replaced by the modern Ta' Qali stadium in 1981.

The quarter-finals provided opposition in the shape of Újpesti Dózsa, and over in Budapest Celtic carved out a 2-1 victory – Macari in addition to an own goal. In the return leg, the visitors took the lead after only five minutes and held it until that man Macari equalised in the 62nd minute and 1-1 it finished. Another semi-final beckoned and this time old friends Inter Milan stood in the way of a third final for the Celts. A goalless draw in the San Siro elicited cries of 'Ya beauty!' and 'Who do you think we'll play in the final?' Cue that old, well-worn phrase, 'Alas, it was not to be.' After 120 goalless minutes at Celtic Park, to the dreaded penalties it went. Inter scored five out of five but Celtic netted four with Dixie Deans skying the first one. Where was that lucky silver two-guilders coin when you needed it?

That very same evening, 19 April, across the city at Ibrox Park, Rangers overcame Bayern Munich to reach the final of the Cup Winners' Cup. Policing issues aside (the aggregate attendances totalled around 155,000), Glasgow – and Scotland – came agonisingly close to having representatives in the finals of the two major European competitions in the same season for the second time in five years. As it transpired, Inter had used up all their luck in the semis, and in the final they lost 2-0 to Ajax Amsterdam in Rotterdam. The Feyenoord supporters must have loved that one.

The 1972/73 season saw another Scandinavian start for Celtic at Hampden, with works ongoing at the Parkhead stand, against the Norwegian part-timers of Rosenborg and a narrow 2-1 victory thanks to Macari and Deans. In Trondheim, Rosenborg held a 1-0 lead on the night and away goals advantage for about 50 minutes before goals from Macari, Hood and Dalglish's first in Europe saw the Hoops go through. In the second round, at Celtic Park, Újpesti Dózsa were back in town and were a goal to the good at half-time before two strikes from Dalglish gave the home side victory. In Budapest, three first-half goals would give Újpesti a place in the last eight as well as revenge for the previous season's elimination.

In the quarter-finals, Újpesti would lose to Juventus on the away goals rule and the Turin club ultimately lost in the final to Ajax who lifted the trophy for the third successive season.

There was more Scottish semi-finals heartbreak in 1973/74. A flying start to the campaign was achieved

European Champion Clubs' Cup

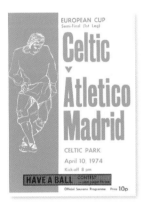

with a 6-1 win in Finland against TPS Turku as Tommy Callaghan grabbed a double, followed by a 3-0 win in Glasgow with Jimmy Johnstone netting twice. Sandwiched in between those matches, the Scotland national team, with five Celtic players in the starting line-up, defeated Czechoslovakia at Hampden to qualify for their first World Cup finals since 1958. Back to the European Cup and Vejle of Denmark then paid a visit to Parkhead and surprised everyone by going home with a 0-0 draw, but across the North Sea a Bobby Lennox goal was enough to ensure Celtic progressed.

While waiting for the quarter-finals Slade released the perennial hit single 'Merry Xmas Everybody' but spring eventually arrived and Celtic then travelled to Switzerland where two goals from Otto Hitzfeld helped FC Basel to a 3-2 win. After 90 minutes at Celtic Park it was 3-2 to Celtic and 5-5 on aggregate, but a goal from Steve Murray in the 114th minute put the Bhoys through to the last four.

And so to the drama, the mayhem, the injustice of Celtic against Atlético Madrid. The basic statistics show that the first leg at Parkhead finished goalless, and that Atlético had three players sent off and seven booked with three yellow cards for Celtic. The 'Shame-Game' was quite possibly the dirtiest match Celtic have ever been involved in as the home side were subjected to 90 minutes of assaults. UEFA should have expelled Atlético from the competition but hit them with a fine instead.

As a lighter aside, the back cover of the match programme featured an advert for 'Easy! Easy!' – the official single by the Scotland World Cup squad as well as for the album *Scotland Scotland*. Only fair, I suppose, seeing as the squad included those four well-known Celtic tenors, Danny McGrain, Davie Hay, Jimmy Johnstone and Kenny Dalglish.

Back to the pantomime villains from Madrid and Atlético won the return match 2-0 to prove that sometimes cheats *do* win unfortunately. Thankfully, Atlético did not win the cup itself – but it was a close thing as they led Bayern Munich 1-0 in extra time before Schwarzenbeck equalised in the 120th minute. There was no penalty shoot-out lottery back then but in a Brussels replay two days later the West German side triumphed 4-0. Danke-schoen!

Celtic's ninth consecutive European Cup campaign in 1974/75 proved to be a Greek tragedy, ended at the first-round stage by Olympiakos. At Celtic Park the first leg finished 1-1 with Celtic having to rely on a Paul Wilson equaliser ten minutes from time. In the return leg on the outskirts of Athens, Celtic were 2-0 down within 25 minutes and that's the way it finished, with Lennox getting his marching orders four minutes from time as a result of two bookable offences. No European odyssey this time, the referee wasn't a 'Homer', and Celtic went out 3-1 on aggregate.

In the final in Paris, a Leeds United side including Scottish internationals David Stewart, Frank Gray, Billy Bremner, Peter Lorimer, Joe Jordan and late substitute Eddie Gray were mugged 2-0 by Bayern Munich. No danke-schoen this time.

Preceded by the death of Elvis Presley four weeks earlier, Jock Stein's last European campaign was the 1977/78 European Cup, which was also Celtic's 16th successive on the continent before they took a one-year sabbatical in the Anglo-Scottish Cup, but his side only got as far as the second round. It was, indeed, the end of several eras. Against Jeunesse d'Esch of Luxembourg, Celtic won 11-1 on aggregate (5-0 at home, including a double from Joe Craig, and 6-1 away with braces from veteran Lennox and Icelandic international Jóhannes Eðvaldsson). Wacker Innsbruck, winners of five Austrian championships in the 1970s, then visited Celtic Park to be narrowly beaten 2-1, Craig netting the opener and Tommy Burns hitting the winner. The return leg was played in Salzburg but we'll avoid any *Sound of Music* allegories and just say that Celtic, 3-0 down at half-time, had a proverbial mountain to climb (sorry). There were no goals in the second half thanks in the main to goalkeeper Peter Latchford, Andy Lynch was dismissed late on and Celtic said, 'So long, farewell, auf wiedersehen, good night.' I just couldn't help myself.

European Champion Clubs' Cup

In the final at Wembley, Liverpool retained the trophy by defeating FC Brugge 1-0 – the scorer being Kenny Dalglish who had signed from Celtic the previous summer. Alan Hansen (ex-Partick Thistle) and Graeme Souness (ex-Tynecastle Boys Club) also collected winners' medals.

The 1979/80 season saw Celtic reach the quarter-finals with Billy McNeill as manager. The campaign got off to a poor start, however, when Celtic lost 1-0 away to Partizan Tirana and then at Celtic Park; just to make things interesting, an own goal from Alan 'Snoopy' Sneddon after 15 minutes put the Albanians 2-0 ahead on aggregate. The Bhoys hit back with four goals before half-time thanks to a double from Roy Aitken, plus one apiece from Roddie MacDonald and Vic Davidson, and 4-1 it finished to send the Hoops through 4-2 on aggregate. In the second round Celtic just shaded it against Dundalk, 3-2 at Parkhead and 0-0 in the Irish Republic. The scorers for the Hoops were MacDonald, George McCluskey and Burns.

In the last eight, the giants of Real Madrid visited Glasgow and were beaten 2-0 by goals from McCluskey and Johnny Doyle. Hopes were high in front of 110,000 at the Bernabéu but Celtic were overpowered 3-0 after McCluskey missed a glorious chance to open the scoring in the fifth minute and out they went. Real would be eliminated in the semis by Hamburg SV, who in turn lost to Brian Clough's Nottingham Forest in the final in the Bernabéu with Scotland's John Robertson netting the winner, Scotland's John McGovern, as skipper, collecting the trophy for the second time, while Scotland's Frank Gray (ex-Parkhead ball boy), Kenny Burns and John O'Hare (ex-Drumchapel Amateurs) also took winners' medals home with them.

In 1981/82 it was a quick in-and-out affair after being drawn against Juventus. At Parkhead a second-half goal by Murdo MacLeod gave Celtic a 1-0 victory in the first leg. In the Stadio Communale, however, two first-half goals from the hosts were enough to see Juventus through to the second round – where they were eliminated by Anderlecht.

Aston Villa gave England its sixth consecutive success by defeating Bayern Munich in the final. Scots Ken McNaught, Allan Evans (ex-Dunfermline Athletic) and Des Bremner (ex-Hibernian) collected winners' medals while Scotland under-21 international Andy Blair was an unused substitute.

After an impressive start in 1982/83, Celtic's 20th European campaign was all over by Christmas. Ajax were overcome in the first round despite the first leg ending 2-2 at Celtic Park. The home side's first-half equalisers were scored by Charlie Nicholas and Frank McGarvey respectively. In Amsterdam's Olympic Stadium, Nicholas beat two defenders then gloriously chipped the keeper to give the Celts the lead after 33 minutes, but Ajax equalised midway through the second half. An excellent display by goalkeeper Pat Bonner helped keep the visitors in the tie and two minutes from time a beautiful left-footed shot from McCluskey gave Celtic victory. After the game, glorious, gorgeous George swapped shirts with Johan Cruyff.

Away to Real Sociedad in the second round first leg, Celtic played well but conceded two late deflected goals to lose 2-0. In Glasgow they conceded an early goal but battled on and two powerful shots from Murdo MacLeod beat Spain's international keeper Luis Arconada to give Celtic a 2-1 victory on the night but out they went 3-2 on aggregate. Sociedad would lose out in the semi-finals to the eventual tournament winners Hamburg SV.

In the summer of 1983 Celtic sold Charlie Nicholas to Arsenal, apparently against the wishes of manager Billy McNeill, who shortly thereafter left Parkhead to take up the managerial reins at Manchester City. Both Nicholas and McNeill would later return to Celtic Park – and to differing degrees of success.

European Champion Clubs' Cup

ABERDEEN have had three entries into the European Cup – it should have been four – but instead they had a wait of 25 years, until 1980/81, to take their rightful place in Europe's top club competition. Belated 'justice' also meant that the Dons had now competed in all three European competitions, and 1980/81 was their tenth season in Europe.

In the first round first leg, a narrow 1-0 victory over Austria Vienna at Pittodrie was achieved thanks to a goal from Mark McGhee. The second leg was goalless, so mission accomplished. In the second round, however, the mighty Liverpool came a calling and the visitors returned to Merseyside with a 1-0 lead. At Anfield, Alex Ferguson's Aberdeen were given a 4-0 footballing lesson with ironically three of the four goals coming from Scots – a Willie Miller own goal plus strikes from Kenny Dalglish and Alan Hansen. It's unusual for a Scottish international goalkeeper, especially one as talented as Jim Leighton, to concede four goals at Anfield. Usually they keep clean sheets in Liverpool, like Alan Rough against Wales in 1977. Just sayin'.

Anyway, some consolation would come in seeing Liverpool go on to lift the European Cup for the third time – with three Scots featuring: the aforementioned Dalglish and Hansen plus Graeme Souness.

In 1984/85 much was expected of a stylish Aberdeen side who in the two previous seasons had won the European Cup Winners' Cup then reached the semis in defence of their crown. It all went wrong, however, in the very first round. At Pittodrie, two goals from Eric Black had the Dons in control until Dynamo (East) Berlin narrowed the gap with a late strike. On the wrong side of 'Checkpoint Charlie',

East German striker Andreas Thom gave the home side the lead after 50 minutes but 18 minutes later Ian Angus grabbed an equaliser and the Dons' noses were in front until a goal for Dynamo six minutes from the end took the tie into extra time. There were no more goals in the half hour added so to the dreaded penalties it went, and Aberdeen lost 5-4. Black was the unfortunate player who missed the decisive penalty after earlier misses from Bernd Schulz and Willie Miller.

Dynamo would lose to Austria Vienna in the second round while Juventus would defeat Liverpool in the ill-fated final of 1985. Dynamo Berlin (who were the secret police outfit) would, however eventually go on to win ten consecutive East German championships. On the world stage, the Live Aid concert at Wembley Stadium in July 1985 would offer hope (as well as practical help) to millions while in the world of sport, Scots golfer Sandy Lyle won the 1985 Open Championship.

Aberdeen reached the quarter-finals in 1985/86 but like Rangers' campaign in 1978/79 there was a feeling they could, and should, have made it to the semis at least. In the first round ÍA Akraness were beaten comfortably enough, 3-1 in Iceland and then 4-1 at Pittodrie with striker John Hewitt netting in both legs. The second round was much tighter – goalless against Servette in Geneva followed by a 1-0 victory in Aberdeen, Frank McDougall scoring, with a League Cup Final victory against Hibernian in between. In the last eight, IFK Gothenburg took a 2-2 draw back to Sweden. Twice Aberdeen took the lead, through Joe Miller and John Hewitt, but twice they were pegged back with the second equaliser coming in the 89th minute. Over in the same Ullevi stadium where Aberdeen worked their magic in the 1983 Cup Winners' Cup Final, a goalless draw meant they were eliminated from the European Cup on the away goals rule. They would, however, have the consolation of lifting the Scottish Cup in May 1986 while the following month, Alex Ferguson, in a caretaker capacity, led his country (with four Aberdeen players in his squad) at the Mexico World Cup finals.

European Champion Clubs' Cup

In the first season of the ban on English clubs competing in Europe, Steaua Bucharest won the European Cup by defeating Barcelona – managed by Terry Venables and including former Aberdeen striker Steve Archibald – on penalties in the final after 120 goalless minutes. Ironically, Barça had eliminated Gothenburg in the semis – on penalties.

———

DUNDEE UNITED, like Hibs, Dundee and Kilmarnock, have had one shot at the European Cup and like Hibs and Dundee they came unstuck at the semi-final stage but Jim McLean's side came so damn close to getting to that 1983/84 final in Rome against Liverpool that their near miss *still* irks me (some consolation can be found in the chapter 'The Battle of Britain' in Simon Turner's excellent book *If Only – An Alternative History of the Beautiful Game*).

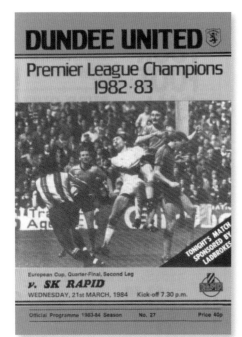

Back to the real story and in the first round United swept past the Maltese champions Hamrun Spartans 3-0 in the Ta' Qali stadium with John Reilly, Eamonn Bannon and Derek Stark scoring, and then 3-0 at home thanks to Ralph Milne plus two from Billy Kirkwood. Just prior to the commencement of the second-round tie against Standard Liege, Neil Kinnock was elected leader of the Labour Party – and another 'hard luck story' beckoned. United's number one, Hamish McAlpine, was the less busy of the two keepers in the goalless first leg in Belgium, and at Tannadice the Terrors did their stuff with a 4-0 win through a Milne brace plus one each from Paul Hegarty and Davie Dodds.

In the last eight, another European goal from defender Stark gave United a half-time lead over Rapid Vienna in the Gerhard Hanappi Stadion before the home side fought back to win 2-1. Back in Dundee, Davie Dodds scored the only goal of the game to put United through on the away goals rule.

On 11 April the Romans ventured north of the Antonine Wall to Tannadice Park and were repelled, skilfully but peaceably, 2-0 with second-half goals from Stark and Dodds. Two weeks later, however, the Stadio Olimpico became a modern-day Colosseum with 70,000 fans baying for blood, and United players being pelted with fruit and other objects in the pre-match warm-up. Milne missed a good early chance to score a crucial away goal and Roma then proceeded to level the tie by half-time. After the break the home side went 3-0 in front thanks to a dodgy penalty award and when the full-time whistle sounded United management and players were subjected to physical and verbal abuse from gloating Roma players.

In the European Cup Final itself, in the very same Stadio Olimpico, justice was eventually done when Liverpool claimed the trophy for the fourth time by winning 4-2 on penalties after the teams were tied at 1-1. The Scots who collected winners' medals were Alan Hansen, Graeme Souness, Kenny Dalglish and Steve Nicol. Gary Gillespie was also a non-playing substitute.

As an aside, United had become the seventh Scottish club to have participated in all three European competitions. Kilmarnock and Motherwell would also achieve the treble, albeit post-1986.

––––––––––

Nowadays, the bloated, misnamed Champions League competition means that a club (usually a very rich one) can be crowned champions of Europe when they weren't even the champions of their own country in the first place – although I daresay that if fifth-in-the-table Hibs had done the business back in 1955/56 there would have been no complaints from me. Relatively few countries, however, have produced European champions – Scotland is the smallest but arguably the greatest. There, I said it!

European Cup Winners' Cup

In light of the success of the European Champion Clubs' Cup there was a desire to create an additional competition (the Inter-Cities Fairs Cup was also up and running but was not under the auspices of UEFA), which led to a tournament for national cup winners to run in tandem with the tournament for national league champions. All that was required was for some countries to initiate their own cup competitions!

Eight clubs represented Scotland in the Cup Winners' Cup during the Golden Years (St Mirren, Motherwell, Airdrie and Kilmarnock would join that list before the competition ceased in 1999). Scotland has produced two winners, Rangers in 1971/72 and Aberdeen in 1982/83, and two runners-up – Rangers in 1960/61 and again in 1966/67. Our beaten semi-finalists are Celtic (1963/64 and 1965/66), Dunfermline Athletic (1968/69) and Aberdeen (1983/84).

———————

RANGERS competed in the semi-official pilot tournament of 1960/61 which comprised just ten teams. Nevertheless, they reached the final and in so doing helped promote and increase the popularity of the competition. In the preliminary round Ferencváros of Hungary were overcome 5-4 on aggregate and in the quarter-finals, Borussia Mönchengladbach were thumped 3-0 in West Germany and 8-0 at Ibrox – with Ralph Brand grabbing a hat-trick and Jimmy Millar a double. That must have felt good, coming as it did a mere six months after Rangers were on the receiving end of a thumping from Eintracht Frankfurt in the European Cup semi-final.

At the semi-final stage of the Cup Winners' Cup, Rangers got it right, overpowering English FA Cup winners Wolverhampton Wanderers 2-0 in Glasgow with Alex Scott and Ralph Brand netting. On 19 April, seven days after the Soviets put the first man into outer space, Rangers travelled to Molineux and Scott scored again in a 1-1 draw to go through 3-1 on aggregate.

Hintere Reihe v. l.: Greig, D. Smith, McKinnon, Provan, Ritchie, Watson, Johansen, Wood, Millar.
Vordere Reihe v. l.: Manager S. Symon, Henderson, Willoughly, A. Smith, Forrest, McLean, Johnston, Wilson, Kinnaer.

The inaugural final was the only one to be played over two legs but in the first game, at Ibrox on 17 May, a crowd of around 80,000 saw Rangers go down 2-0 to Fiorentina, the beaten European Cup finalists in 1957. Over in Florence ten days later, the Italian side triumphed 2-1 with Alex Scott on the scoresheet for the Light Blues in a 4-1 aggregate defeat. Jim Baxter played in both legs, as did other Rangers greats such as Bobby Shearer, Eric Caldow, Ian McMillan, Ralph Brand and Davie Wilson, and 60 years on, the souvenir programme from the first leg was going for £150 on eBay.

Rangers' second adventure in the Cup Winners' Cup came in 1962/63 when they defeated Seville 4-2 on aggregate in the preliminary round – 4-0 at Ibrox with a hat-trick from Jimmy Millar plus a goal from Brand. In the Ramón Sánchez Pizjuán Stadium, Rangers conceded two first-half goals

European Cup Winners' Cup

but held out despite several of their players being kicked, punched, bitten and spat at. In the first round proper, however, Rangers travelled down to White Hart Lane and lost 5-2 to Bill Nicholson's great Tottenham Hotspur side. Two of Spurs' goals came from John White (ex-Falkirk) while fellow Scottish internationals Bill Brown (ex-Dundee) and Dave Mackay (ex-Hearts) also starred. Brand and Millar got Rangers' goals. In the return leg at Ibrox, which had been postponed the week previous due to fog, Spurs won 3-2 with Jimmy Greaves netting the opening goal. Brand then Wilson had twice drawn Rangers level before a last-minute sickener compounded matters further.

Tottenham went on to lift the Cup Winners' Cup that season, skelping the holders Atlético Madrid 5-1 in the final and in so doing becoming the first British club to win a major European trophy.

In 1966/67 Scot Symon's Rangers would, once again, reach the final with the journey beginning with a 1-1 draw against Glentoran in Belfast – a George McLean goal being cancelled out by an equaliser for the home side in the final minute. Rangers got their act together in the second leg and won 4-0 with Willie Johnston, Dave Smith, Dennis Setterington and George McLean on target. In the second round, Rangers eliminated the holders Borussia Dortmund, winning 2-1 at Ibrox through Kai Johansen and Alex Smith before drawing 0-0 in West Germany.

Real Zaragoza, conquerors of Everton, were next and a 2-0 for the Gers at Ibrox with Dave Smith and Alex Willoughby scoring was followed by a 2-0 reverse in Spain, which included Dave Smith missing a penalty in extra time. Skipper John Greig correctly called 'Tails' on the coin-toss decider. Big, Bad John was given the French two-franc piece as a souvenir. Rangers faced Slavia Sofia in the semi-finals. A narrow 1-0 win in Glasgow with Davie Wilson's goal was followed by another one in a grassless Levski National Stadium with Willie Henderson on target and Rangers were through to their second Cup Winners' Cup Final in six years.

K ♣ 1972 Barcelona Team K ♣

Willie Waddell
Manager 1972 Barcelona Team

On 31 May, six days after Celtic won the European Cup, Rangers had the chance to play their part in creating a unique piece of footballing history – but those jammy Germans ruined everything (okay, so I'm no big loss to diplomacy efforts). In the final in Nuremberg, Rangers generally outplayed Bayern Munich, squandered several good goalscoring opportunities, had a Roger Hynd goal disallowed and lost 1-0 in extra time to a lob from Franz 'The Bull' Roth.

As an aside, watching the two European finals of 1967 on black and white television as an awestruck eight-year-old schoolboy are my earliest footballing memories. For some unknown reason, however, I recall absolutely nothing about the 1966 World Cup finals. Thankfully, the English media are kind enough to show highlights every now and again to help fill in the gaps in my memory bank.

The 1969/70 campaign would end with manager Davie White losing his job although it began well enough with a first-round victory over Steaua Bucharest – 2-0 at Ibrox with both goals courtesy of Willie Johnston, followed by a goalless draw in Romania. It all went wrong, however, in another Warsaw Pact nation when the Gers went down 3-1 at Górnik Zabrze – the great Włodzimierz Lubanski scored twice while a goal from Swedish international Örjan Persson gave Rangers hope. At Ibrox things looked promising when Jim Baxter gave Rangers the lead after 18 minutes, and then the roof fell in as the visitors scored three times to win 6-2 on aggregate.

Out of Europe early on, indifferent league form and failure to land a domestic trophy throughout his tenure all combined to seal White's fate and he was gone just 24 hours later. Górnik would go on to reach the Cup Winners' Cup Final where they lost to Manchester City.

But there was glory in 1971/72 for Willie Waddell's Rangers, who eliminated four western Europe sides before defeating a club from the epicentre of the Soviet Communist Empire. No official match programme was produced for the

European Cup Winners' Cup

final itself although there is other associated memorabilia to be had.

First up were the French club Rennes and although Rangers took the lead in Brittany through Willie Johnston, they had to settle for a 1-1 draw before an Alex MacDonald goal at Ibrox put them through. The second-round opponents were the better-known Sporting Lisbon who had won the competition in 1964. In the first leg in Glasgow, Rangers were cruising after only 30 minutes at 3-0 to the good with two goals from Colin Stein and another from Willie Henderson, but two second-half goals for the visitors laid the foundations for a night of high drama in the return match.

In Lisbon the 90 minutes went like this: 1-0 to Sporting; 1-1 (Colin Stein); 2-1 to Sporting; half-time; 2-2 (Stein); 3-2 to Sporting; extra time; 3-3 (Willie Henderson); 4-3 to Sporting, full time. The referee then got confused and failed to appreciate that away goals in extra time also counted as double so instructed a penalty shoot-out to decide the tie. Sporting won it, Rangers trooped off dejectedly, the Sporting fans headed home happy, and eventually the referee was alerted to the error of his ways and the Gers were, correctly, awarded the win. A farce worthy of London's West End – but with a happy ending for the visitors.

Once upon a time Torino, Rangers' quarter-final opponents, and not their city neighbours Juventus, were top dogs in Italian football – indeed in 1961 they paid £100,000 for Denis Law, the first time that a British club had been involved in a six-figure transfer. In the shared Stadio Communale a goal from Willie Johnston gave Rangers a half-time lead before Torino equalised in the 61st minute but Rangers held firm to earn a draw. In the return at Ibrox, Alex MacDonald scored the only goal one minute after the restart and Rangers were through to the semis, where they were greeted by old foes Bayern Munich whose squad included future World Cup winners Sepp Maier, Franz Beckenbauer, Paul Breitner, Uli Hoeneß, Gerd Müller and Hans-Georg Schwarzenbeck.

At the end of the first leg when we took a look at the old Bavarian scoreboard it read 'Bayern Munich 1 Rangers 1'. In front of 80,000 at Ibrox, Rangers finished the job with first-half goals from Sandy Jardine and Derek Parlane – a third Cup Winners' Cup Final, in Barcelona, awaited.

In the five weeks preceding the final the UK singles chart was topped by 'Amazing Grace' as performed by The Pipes and Drums and Military Band of the Royal Scots Dragoon Guards. I like to think that piece of music was more inspirational to Greig, McCloy, Jardine and co than the subsequent number one – 'Metal Guru' by T. Rex.

On 24 May, a bearded (and semi-fit) John Greig skippered Rangers to a 3-2 victory at the Camp Nou. Rangers were 3-0 up after 49 minutes with Colin Stein opening the scoring and Willie Johnston adding a double. It wasn't all over, however, as Dynamo Moscow fought back to score in the 60th and 87th minutes but Rangers hung on to collect their holy grail. Sadly, the achievement was detracted from by the subsequent pitch invasion by jubilant Rangers supporters which was 'mishandled' by 'over-zealous' Spanish police. Things turned ugly and ultimately Rangers copped a fine and a one-year ban from European competition. While the aftermath may be subject to debate, the history books show that a Scottish club, comprising an all-Scottish XI, had brought a second European trophy back to Scotland. Slainte!

Due to the one-year ban we can but speculate as to whether or not Rangers would have been good enough to become the only club to successfully defend their Cup Winners' Cup title. By the time of the 1973/74 competition key players such as Colin Stein and Willie Johnston had left; indeed, they were gone even before the first (unofficial) European Super Cup matches against Ajax Amsterdam took place in January 1973 with the Dutch masters winning 6-3 on aggregate. Jock Wallace was also now the manager.

In the first round of the 1973/74 Cup Winners' Cup, Rangers recorded a 2-0 victory in Turkey

against Ankaragücü, Alfie Conn and Tommy McLean the scorers. At Ibrox it was 4-0 with two from skipper John Greig plus one apiece from Alex O'Hara and Derek Johnstone. In the second round, however, the opposition were the excellent Borussia Mönchengladbach side who would twice win the UEFA Cup in the 1970s and boasted players such as Berti Vogts, Rainer Bonhof, Jupp Heynckes and Allan Simonsen. In the first leg at the Bökelbergstadion, Heynckes scored twice as the West German club ran out 3-0 winners. The match programme for the return game recalled the Cup Winners' Cup tie of 1960 when Rangers triumphed 8-0, but on this occasion the Ibrox club had to settle for a 3-2 victory on the night with Alfie Conn, Colin Jackson and Alex MacDonald doing the honours.

Mönchengladbach would reach the semi-finals before being eliminated by the holders AC Milan, who in turn were defeated by the East German outfit FC Magdeburg in the final in Rotterdam.

The 1977/78 campaign would begin with a preliminary round tie against Young Boys of Bern, and a goal from Greig gave Rangers a narrow 1-0 win at Ibrox. In Switzerland, Johnstone and Gordon Smith earned Rangers a 2-2 draw and a place in the first round proper. FC Twente, UEFA Cup finalists in 1975, then visited Ibrox and earned a 0-0 draw before winning 3-0 in the Netherlands. Twente would reach the semi-finals before losing to Anderlecht who would in turn win the competition for the second time in three years.

In 1979/80, with Greig now at the managerial helm, Rangers performed well before letting slip a glorious chance of reaching the last eight. Lillestrøm were beaten home and away in the preliminary round, 1-0 at Ibrox through Smith's goal and 2-0 in Norway thanks to MacDonald and Johnstone. Next up were Fortuna Düsseldorf, beaten finalists in the previous season's competition. Rangers managed a narrow 2-1 win at home with MacDonald and Tommy McLean on target, followed by a hard-earned 0-0 draw in West Germany.

Then along came Valencia, although in the first leg in Spain Rangers managed a 1-1 draw when McLean cancelled out the opener by Mario Kempes, an Argentine hero of the 1978 World Cup finals. In Glasgow, Rainer Bonhof gave the visitors the lead before the Gers equalised through Johnstone – who could have been a Scottish hero of the 1978 World Cup if only Ally MacLeod had played him and not Joe Harper against Iran (let it go, Robert)! Anyway, Kempes then scored twice to give Valencia a 3-1 win on the night and a 4-2 aggregate scoreline.

Valencia would go on to win the Cup Winners' Cup by defeating Arsenal in the final on penalties,

European Cup Winners' Cup

EUROPEAN CUP WINNERS' CUP
FIRST ROUND — SECOND LEG

RANGERS v. DUKLA PRAGUE

IBROX STADIUM, WEDNESDAY 30th SEPTEMBER, 1981
KICK-OFF 7.30 p.m. **£2·50**

R. C. OGILVIE, *Secretary*

BROOMLOAN ROAD STAND — ORANGE SECTION

FRONT

ENTER BY TURNSTILES 61–70

Row	Seat No.
T	3

THIS PORTION TO BE RETAINED BY THE HOLDER

despite Kempes missing his spot-kick. Willie Young (ex-Aberdeen) would collect a runners-up medal.

The 1981/82 campaign was over by 30 September when Rangers crashed out 4-2 on aggregate to Dukla Prague in the first round. The damage was done in the first leg in Czechoslovakia courtesy of a 3-0 defeat. In Glasgow, Dukla took the lead after 24 minutes to effectively kill the tie, although goals from Jim Bett and John MacDonald gave Rangers a 2-1 victory on the night. Dukla would lose in the second round to Barcelona, the eventual winners of the competition.

In 1983/84 Rangers compete in what would be their final Cup Winners' Cup campaign and John Greig's managerial career would also come to an end. It all started so promisingly with a first-round 18-0 aggregate win over the part-timers of Valletta. It finished 8-0 in Malta with defender Dave McPherson netting four of them and Swedish international Robert Prytz hitting a double. I was at Ibrox for the return when Rangers hit ten (the most goals I've seen in a game of professional football) and which included a John MacDonald hat-trick as well as braces for Australian international Davie Mitchell and Ian Redford.

The second round provided much tougher opposition in the shape of FC Porto but at Ibrox,

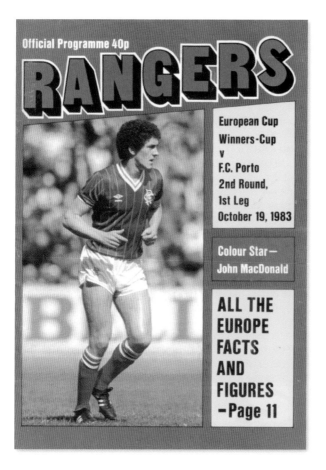

Official Programme 40p

RANGERS

European Cup
Winners-Cup
v
F.C. Porto
2nd Round,
1st Leg
October 19, 1983

Colour Star—
John MacDonald

ALL THE
EUROPE
FACTS
AND
FIGURES
–Page 11

Rangers lead 2-0 through Sandy Clark and Davie Mitchell with four minutes remaining when a glitch from the Girvan Lighthouse (aka goalkeeper Peter McCloy) gifted the visitors a valuable away goal. Under intense pressure from all and sundry, failure to win or look likely to win a league title being the main cause, Greig resigned prior to the second leg in Portugal for which assistant manager Tommy McLean was put in charge. Porto scored a second-half goal though to win 1-0 and progress on the away goals rule, thus ending another era.

Porto eliminated the holders Aberdeen in the semi-finals but would fail to lift the trophy. A European Cup, however, would come their way in 1987.

European Cup Winners' Cup

DUNFERMLINE ATHLETIC enjoyed two Cup Winners' Cup campaigns in the 1960s. Their first started in September 1961 when John Leyton topped the UK singles charts with 'Johnny Remember Me' and their second ended in April 1969 with The Beatles and 'Get Back' at number one.

In 1961/62 the Pars, with Jock Stein as manager, made their European debut at home to St Patrick's Athletic and a 4-1 victory was achieved with Harry Melrose, George Peebles, Charlie Dickson and Tommy McDonald on target. In the return at Tolka Park, Dublin it was 4-0 to the Fifers – doubles from Peebles and Dickson. Vardar Skopje were then overcome with a resounding 5-0 win at East End Park thanks to Alex Smith, Melrose, Peebles and another brace from Dickson. Dunfermline could then afford the 2-0 reverse in Yugoslavia.

In the quarter-finals first leg in February 1962 Dunfermline travelled to a wet and windy Budapest where they lost 4-3 to Újpesti Dózsa. By all accounts the match was a cracker with Smith putting the visitors in front after just 40 seconds. McDonald then made it 2-0 with just eight minutes gone and then a third goal was ruled out for offside. Újpesti woke up, however, and at the break it was 2-2. In the second half the home side then surged to a 4-2 lead before McDonald made it 4-3 with five minutes remaining to set things up nicely for the return leg. Seven days later 24,000 piled into East End Park but alas (a word synonymous with Scottish football) Dunfermline couldn't work their early magic and in the 51st minute Bene beat goalkeeper Eddie Connachan to win the match and the tie.

Újpesti would lose to the holders Fiorentina in the semi-finals and after a replayed final, Florence's finest lost to Atlético Madrid. In the Hampden final, Glasgow's Tom 'Tiny' Wharton reffed a 1-1 draw in front of 27,000. A second game was required, played four months later, on 5 September, curiously in the Neckarstadion, Stuttgart. The Madrid side triumphed 3-0 in front of 38,000.

For the 1968/69 competition George Farm was in charge and he oversaw Dunfermline's run to

the semi-finals. It began with a trip to Cyprus and some fun in the sun as Apoel Nicosia were thrashed 10-1 with doubles for Hugh Robertson, Willie Renton and Willie Callaghan, whose brother Tommy also got on the scoresheet. It was a much closer game in the return with Dunfermline winning 2-0 – Pat Gardner and Willie Callaghan the scorers.

It was a sunny start though an ultimately tight result in the second round when, after Olympiakos were beaten 4-0 in Fife thanks to two goals from Alex Edwards and one apiece from Jim Fraser and Barrie Mitchell, on the outskirts of Athens a Greek tragedy loomed into view in the return as Dunfermline trailed 3-0 after 32 minutes. However, they held on to progress 4-3 on aggregate.

In the quarter-finals it was Scotland against England and after the first leg in Fife, West Bromwich Albion and their Scots duo Bobby Hope and Asa Hartford were delighted to go back down the road with a 0-0 draw. A crowd of 25,000 visited East End Park for the first leg and another 7,000 returned to that venue to view the second leg on two specially erected giant screens. In the return at The Hawthorns, Gardner's second-minute goal was enough to see the Pars through to the last four.

But Slovan Bratislava spoiled everything by drawing 1-1 in Scotland then winning 1-0 in what is now the capital of Slovakia. In the first leg Jim Fraser gave Dunfermline the lead seconds before half-time and with eight minutes remaining the Fifers missed a glorious chance to go 2-0 in front. From that let-off the visitors duly equalised. Apparently it was somewhat bruising in the return in Bratislava – five players were booked and Gardner was sent off with half an hour remaining, and just to rub salt in the wounds the goal came from a defensive error.

In the final, Slovan defeated Barcelona 3-2 in Basel to become the first Eastern Bloc side to win the Cup Winners' Cup.

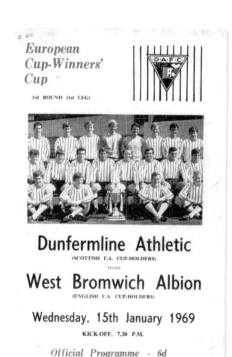

European Cup-Winners' Cup

3rd ROUND (1st LEG)

Dunfermline Athletic
(SCOTTISH F.A. CUP-HOLDERS)

versus

West Bromwich Albion
(ENGLISH F.A. CUP-HOLDERS)

Wednesday, 15th January 1969

KICK-OFF, 7.30 P.M.

Official Programme - 6d

DUNFERMLINE

WILLIE CALLAGHAN
RIGHT BACK

European Cup Winners' Cup

CELTIC's first appearance in the Cup Winners' Cup was in 1963/64 as beaten Scottish Cup finalists. This was Celtic's second European campaign overall and under Jimmy McGrory they reached the semi-finals; indeed they should have made it to the final itself.

In the first round FC Basel were given a damn good thrashing – 5-1 in Switzerland with John Hughes grabbing a hat-trick and 5-0 at Celtic Park with under 10,000 seeing a Johnny Divers double. Dynamo Zagreb were then beaten 3-0 at Parkhead thanks to two from Stevie Chalmers and one from Hughes, while in Yugoslavia Bobby Murdoch gave Celtic the lead before the home side came back to win 2-1, although the Hoops went through 4-2 on aggregate. In the quarter-finals Celtic defeated Slovan Bratislava 1-0 at home with Murdoch on target, and again away when Hughes scored.

In the last four, two goals from Stevie Chalmers and one from Jimmy Johnstone gave the Bhoys a 3-0 lead against MTK Budapest after the first leg in Glasgow and a trip to Brussels for the final would probably have been do-able for thousands of Celtic supporters. An advert in the match programme for Cotter Coach Tours offered an eight-day trip to the Belgian coast for 27 guineas (£28.35). However, in the return leg in the Nep Stadium, the general consensus was that Celtic were tactically naïve, played too open a game and paid the penalty by losing 4-0.

It would take Sporting Lisbon, conquerors of Manchester United, a replay to overcome MTK – Magyar Testgyakorlok Kore just in case you were wondering – and lift the trophy.

Stein was in charge for the 1965/66 campaign, which again ended in semi-final heartbreak. It began with another convincing first-

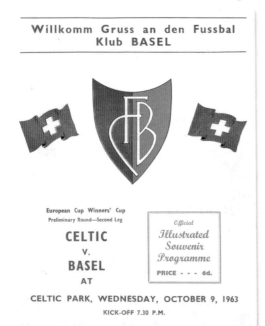

Willkomm Gruss an den Fussbal Klub BASEL

European Cup Winners' Cup
Preliminary Round—Second Leg

CELTIC
V.
BASEL
AT
CELTIC PARK, WEDNESDAY, OCTOBER 9, 1963
KICK-OFF 7.30 P.M.

Official
Illustrated
Souvenir
Programme
PRICE - - - 6d.

round performance against Go Ahead Deventer, winning 6-0 in the Netherlands with Charlie Gallagher and Johnstone both netting a brace and an associated match programme fetching £352 on eBay in 2020, and 1-0 at home through Joe McBride. The second round also brought away and home victories against Aarhus – 1-0 in Denmark with McBride scoring and 2-0 at Celtic Park through Billy McNeill and Johnstone.

The quarter-final opponents were from further afield – Dynamo Kiev, who travelled to Glasgow for the first leg and were defeated 3-0 with Tommy Gemmell netting and Murdoch adding two. Thanks to another goal from Gemmell, Celtic got a 1-1 draw in the away leg, which was moved from Kiev to Tbilisi due to the poor weather conditions in the Ukraine. It was January after all.

There were three British teams in the last four but none of them would win the competition – I find that somewhat annoying. Anyway, as holders West Ham United were coming unstuck against the eventual winners Borussia Dortmund, Celtic and Liverpool were also facing off for the right to play in the final at Hampden Park. The first leg went in Celtic's favour with a goal from Bobby Lennox although several other good chances were spurned. However, in the return game at Anfield just five days later, two second-half goals saw Bill Shankly's Liverpool through. A last-minute goal by Lennox was controversially disallowed for offside – when it clearly wasn't. Another one for the 'Robbed' file.

Torrential rain kept the Hampden attendance down to around 42,000 – they saw Dortmund triumph 2-1 after extra time against a Liverpool side containing four Scots – Ayrshire goalkeeper Tommy Lawrence, skipper Ron Yeats (ex-Dundee United), Willie Stevenson (ex-Rangers) and Ian St John (ex-Motherwell).

The 1975/76 campaign was another where you felt Celtic should have done better – especially as nine successive European Cup seasons had seen them really hit the heights. The first round was straightforward enough with a 9-0 aggregate win

over Valur (2-0 in Iceland and 7-0 at Celtic Park with Jóhannes Eðvaldsson scoring against his former club and Harry Hood nabbing a brace). In the second round Celtic travelled to Portugal and drew 0-0 with Boavista, goalkeeper Peter Latchford saving a penalty, and then completed the job in Glasgow, 3-1 through Kenny Dalglish, Eðvaldsson and Dixie Deans.

In the quarter-finals the Hoops were drawn against Sachsenring Zwickau and probably most people this side of the Iron Curtain thought 'semi-finals for Celtic' – quietly ignoring the fact that the East German side had eliminated Panathinaikos and Fiorentina thus far. For the first leg at Parkhead, Celtic had three players sidelined with a flu bug while apparently Paul Wilson played with a temperature of 102 degrees – I think that must be

Fahrenheit. Lennox missed a penalty before Dalglish gave the home side a 1-0 lead at half-time. The Celtic pressure was relentless, forcing 21 corners to Zwickau's one but they couldn't add to their lead and the sucker-punch equaliser duly arrived two minutes from time. Over in the Russian Sector, Celtic – with several regulars missing as the flu bug persisted – lost 1-0 and I expect a recuperating Jock Stein was raging. Sachsenring then lost to the eventual tournament winners Anderlecht in the semi-finals.

On the plus side, Brotherhood of Man won the Eurovision Song Contest with 'Save Your Kisses for Me'. Superb.

The 1980/81 season saw Billy McNeill in charge for a surprisingly short campaign. It started comfortably enough with a 6-0 preliminary round win over Diósgyőri at Celtic Park with a hat-trick for Frank McGarvey, a double from George McCluskey plus one from Dom Sullivan – all the goals coming in the second half. In the return leg in Hungary, Charlie Nicholas opened the scoring before the home side fought back to win 2-1.

In the first round proper it was a sterner, eastern European test in the shape of Romania's Politehnica Timişoara although Celtic appeared to be in command when leading 2-0 at half-time thanks to a brace from Nicholas. Second-half chances were squandered, however, and ten minutes from time the visitors grabbed a vital away goal. Celtic then lost 1-0 in Romania with the Greek referee reportedly being a contributory factor.

PT lost in the very next round to West Ham United but the competition was won by Dinamo Tbilsi who defeated their East German comrades Carl Zeiss Jena in the final in Düsseldorf in front of a crowd of under 5,000. Again, salvation was to be found in Eurovision with Bucks Fizz and 'Making Your Mind Up' winning the competition for the UK.

The 1984/85 adventure ended in controversy. In the first round David Hay's side lost 1-0 away to Ghent but at Celtic Park two goals from Frank McGarvey and another from Paul McStay saw the

European Cup Winners' Cup

Hoops triumph 3-1 on aggregate. In the second round Celtic lost 3-1 in Austria to Rapid Vienna but the away goal from Brian McClair gave the visitors hope and in the return leg Celtic were inspired and won 3-0 on the night through McClair, Murdo MacLeod and Tommy Burns, progressing 4-3 on aggregate. Or so we all thought. The match was subsequently voided by UEFA following appeals by Rapid Vienna over a bottle-throwing incident which they claimed had felled and injured one of their players. Everyone knows it did nothing of the kind! UEFA bungled it completely and ordered the match to be replayed at a neutral venue at least 300km from Glasgow.

Celtic chose Old Trafford and in a victory for the dark side, Rapid Vienna won 1-0 in Manchester. The Austrian side would go all the way to the final where eventually justice was delivered by Everton who won 3-1. Andy Gray (ex-Dundee United) scored the opener and he had fellow Scot Graeme Sharp (ex-Dumbarton) for company.

Following on from the misbehaviour of some Hoops fans at Old Trafford, UEFA ordered that Celtic play the home leg of their 1985/86 first-round tie behind closed doors. Just to add insult to injury, they were then drawn against Atlético Madrid – the club who 12 years previous had kicked them out of the European Cup at the semi-final stage. In the first leg in Spain, Celtic earned a creditable 1-1 draw with Mo Johnston grabbing the equaliser, but in the surreal surroundings of an empty Celtic Park the hosts did not play well – Murdo MacLeod missing from six yards early on – and eventually trailed 2-0 before Roy Aitken pulled one back. Incidentally, the fact that there was no crowd didn't deter Celtic from producing a match programme. Back then, behind-closed-doors matches were something of a rarity, a novelty even.

English clubs were also banned from European competitions at that time and Atlético Madrid would go on to reach the Cup Winners' Cup Final by eliminating Bangor City of Wales in the second round. The trophy would be won by Dynamo Kiev, who eliminated Rapid Vienna at the quarter-finals stage, 9-2 on aggregate. It's funny how things sometimes work out isn't it?

———————

DUNDEE qualified for the 1964/65 Cup Winners' Cup by virtue of reaching the final of the 1964 Scottish Cup, where they lost 3-1 to treble-winning Rangers. Bob Shankly's Dens Parkers' only appearance in this competition began with them receiving a bye to the second round. So far so good, but at that stage they drew Real Zaragoza of Spain who were holders of the Inter-Cities Fairs Cup.

In the first leg at home on 18 November, Dundee got off to the perfect start when Stephen Murray put them in front after only two minutes. According to the *Glasgow Evening Times*, however, the injured Scotland international Alan Gilzean (who would move to Spurs the following month) was sorely missed as the Dark Blues squandered several chances and the visitors hit back – twice – to go 2-1 ahead. Doug Houston netted the equaliser with three minutes remaining, however, and '21,000 sent their bunnets flying in glee'.

In Spain, Dundee and Real were level pegging 1-1 at half-time, Hugh Robertson having netted for the visitors but again it wasn't to be and in the second half Los Magníficos edged 2-1 ahead to clinch the tie 4-3 on aggregate. Zaragoza would eliminate Cardiff City in the quarter-finals before being knocked out in the semis by West Ham United who, skippered by Bobby Moore, went on to lift the trophy at Wembley.

European Cup Winners' Cup

ABERDEEN's first foray into Europe came via the 1967/68 Cup Winners' Cup following on from being beaten Scottish Cup finalists to the all-conquering Celtic team of 1966/67. A dramatic debut saw Eddie Turnbull's Dons defeat KR Reykjavík, Iceland's oldest club, 10-0. Central defender Frank Munro got the first goal and went on to net a hat-trick with Jim Storrie and Jimmy Smith both hitting a double. Aberdeen won the return leg 4-1 with two for Storrie and one apiece for Munro and Martin Buchan, and to be fair to Reykjavík they were a strictly amateur club at the time. Their captain was a lawyer by profession although that doesn't necessarily make him a bad person.

In the second round first leg, the Scottish side lost convincingly to Belgian outfit Standard Liege 3-0 in the Wallonia region. In the return leg, in the Grampian region, Aberdeen gave it a right good go but just came up short, beating Liege 2-0 with goals from Frank Munro and Harry Melrose. Liege would reach the quarter-finals before losing in a Milan play-off to AC Milan who went on to defeat Hamburg SV in the final in Rotterdam.

In 1970/71 Aberdeen represented Scotland as Scottish Cup holders but this time suffered a first-round exit – to Honvéd of Budapest. At Pittodrie, after going 1-0 behind, a 3-1 victory was achieved with Arthur Graham, Joe Harper and Stevie Murray scoring. In Hungary it was the same scoreline for the hosts with Murray netting for the visitors late on to keep Aberdeen in the tie. Extra time couldn't resolve matters so to a penalty shoot-out it went, the Dons' first, and they lost 5-4 with Jim Forrest's kick striking the bar.

Honvéd were then eliminated in the second round by holders Manchester City, who in turn lost to Chelsea at the semi-final stage. Chelsea then defeated Real Madrid in a replayed final when utilising the services of Motherwell-born defender

John Boyle and winger Charlie Cooke (ex-Aberdeen and Dundee).

The 1978/79 competition saw Alex Ferguson's Aberdeen fail to get beyond Christmas in the Cup Winners' Cup. The Bulgarian outfit Marek Stanke Dimitrov – now known as FC Marek – were defeated in the first round 5-3 on aggregate. A 3-2 defeat in Dupnitsa was overcome via a 3-0 victory at Pittodrie. Drew Jarvie and Joe Harper got the away goals and both of them also netted on home soil, in addition to Gordon Strachan.

The Dons were, however, undone in the second round by Fortuna Düsseldorf after slumping to a 3-0 defeat in the first leg in West Germany. In the return game Aberdeen scored twice early in the second half through Chic McLelland and Jarvie but alas the third goal would not come, so Fortuna progressed – all the way to the final. Barcelona would lift the cup, however, the first of their four triumphs in this competition.

In the glorious campaign of 1982/83 Aberdeen played 11 European matches, winning eight, drawing two and losing just the once, scoring 25 goals and conceding six. It began with a preliminary round tie in August against Sion, winning 7-0 at Pittodrie with Eric Black grabbing a double and then 4-1 in Switzerland which included two for Mark McGhee. The first round was a lot tighter with a narrow 1-0 win at home to Dinamo Tirana – John Hewitt the scorer – followed by a goalless draw in Albania. Round two brought Lech Poznań to Aberdeen where they were beaten 2-0 by McGhee and Peter Weir, and just for good measure the Dons also won in Poland, 1-0 with Dougie Bell on the scoresheet.

In the last eight they faced the giants of Bayern Munich, who had eliminated Tottenham Hotspur in the second round. No problem – a fifth consecutive Euro clean sheet for goalkeeper Jim Leighton as a 0-0 draw was achieved in the Olympic Stadium followed by an enthralling/nerve-wracking 3-2 win at Pittodrie. Twice the visitors took the lead only to be pulled back via goals from Neil Simpson and then Alex McLeish (a headed goal from a 'deliberate

European Cup Winners' Cup

mix-up' of a free kick from Strachan) before John Hewitt got the winner 11 minutes from time. Waterschei of Belgium, who would subsequently merge with KFC Winterslag to become KRC Genk, were put to the sword 5-1 in the first leg of the semi-final in Aberdeen with McGhee netting a double, although in Belgium, the Dons would suffer their only reverse of the competition, a 1-0 defeat.

The final, on 11 May 1983, pitted Aberdeen against Real Madrid, who at that time had appeared in ten previous European finals, at the Ullevi stadium in Gothenburg – a venue celebrating its 25th anniversary and which witnessed Pelé's first World Cup appearance, for Brazil against the USSR in 1958. This type of book can't do Aberdeen's magnificent performance justice, and nor those of Celtic in 1967 and Rangers five years later, so the basics will have to do. Eric Black opened the scoring after only seven minutes but eight minutes later Real were level, Juanito having equalised from the penalty spot. There was more scoring in regulation time so an extra 30 minutes was required, and John Hewitt got the winner in the 112th minute. Fergie's Red Furies had overcome 'Football Royalty' to give Scotland its third European trophy. Incidentally, Real Madrid – and likewise Liverpool and Inter Milan – never did add the Cup Winners' Cup to their collection of European Cups and UEFA Cups.

Even Margaret Thatcher winning her second successive UK General Election, on 9 June 1983, couldn't take the sheen off Aberdeen's achievement. Aberdeen then 'trumped' Maggie later in the year by defeating Hamburg SV to lift the European Super Cup. A 0-0 draw at the Volksparkstadion in November was followed up with a 2-0 win at Pittodrie just five days before Christmas with two second-half goals from Neil Simpson and Mark McGhee. Thank you, Santa.

In 1983/84 Aberdeen gave a robust defence of their title before being stopped at the last-four stage. It began with a narrow 3-2 aggregate win over Akraness – commonly known as ÍA – which demonstrated that Icelandic football had come a

EUROPEAN
CUP WINNERS' CUP
ABERDEEN FC
REAL MADRID CF
FINAL TIE OF MAY 11th 1983
GOTHENBURG • SWEDEN

ULLEVI

SVENSKA
FOTBOLLFÖRBUNDET
Pris: 5 Sek.

ABERDEEN v FC PORTO (Portugal)
WEDNESDAY 25th APRIL 1984
EUROPEAN CUP-WINNERS' CUP
SEMI-FINAL — SECOND LEG.
32 PAGE OFFICIAL PROGRAMME 50p

WELCOME TO PITTODRIE

long way since Aberdeen made their Euro debut 16 years previous. The Dons trailed in Reykjavík before a double from Mark McGhee gave them a 2-1 victory. But there was no victory at home when a Gordon Strachan penalty was cancelled out in the 89th minute with an Áskelsson spot-kick. In the second round a goalless draw was achieved in Beveren before Aberdeen beat the Belgian side 4-1 at Pittodrie with two from Strachan and one each from Neil Simpson and Peter Weir.

The first leg of the quarter-finals resulted in a 2-0 reverse against Újpesti Dózsa in Budapest which was overturned by an excellent 3-0 win in Aberdeen and a superb Mark McGhee hat-trick. By the time of the semi-finals, 1984 had well and truly arrived and I suspect that most Dons fans would like to have seen

European Cup Winners' Cup

both of the 1-0 defeats by Porto banished to Room 101. George Orwell's basement torture chamber would later be clogged up with the likes of Skonto Riga, Bohemians of Dublin and Sigma Olomouc – but that is another story.

In the Cup Winners' Cup Final of 1984, Porto would lose 2-1 to Juventus.

———

HIBERNIAN had their solitary attempt to win the Cup Winners' Cup in 1972/73, as Scottish Cup runners-up, and in so doing became another of the nation's teams to have competed in all three major European competitions. By rights, Hibs should have had Rangers for company that season but no matter, they flew the flag alone and headed

off to Portugal to face the 1964 Cup Winners' Cup winners, Sporting Lisbon. Arthur Duncan scored Hibs' goal in a narrow 2-1 defeat but back in Edinburgh the Hibees turned it on to crush their illustrious opponents 6-1. Alan Gordon netted a brace while Jimmy O'Rourke went one better. In the second round the Easter Road scoring spree continued with a 7-1 hammering of FC Besa of Albania – another hat-trick for O'Rourke, two for Duncan and one apiece for Alex Cropley and John Brownlie. In the land where King Zog and Norman Wisdom are fondly remembered, Hibs got a 1-1 draw for an 8-2 aggregate win.

By the time the quarter-finals came around, in March 1973, Hibs had the League Cup in their trophy room while the UK (along with Denmark and the Republic of Ireland) had joined the European Economic Community. Hibs headed outside of the community, however, to the Yugoslav seaport of Split following a 4-2 win over Hajduk at Easter Road in the first leg – an Alan Gordon hat-trick bringing the competition tally to six for the striker who earlier in his career had scored more than 50 goals for city rivals Hearts. Hibs were fancied to make it to the semis but in Titoland they crashed 3-0 to go out 5-4 on aggregate.

A Leeds United side containing several Scottish internationals defeated Hajduk in the semis before a highly questionable refereeing performance in the final in Salonika contributed to AC Milan's success.

DUNDEE UNITED had one Cup Winners' Cup campaign during the Golden Years, in 1974/75, after finishing runners-up to Celtic in the previous season's Scottish Cup Final – the Tangerines' first such occasion. Further appearances in the Cup Winners' Cup would come in 1988/89 and 1994/95.

In the first round, Jim McLean's side faced Eastern Bloc opposition in the shape of Jiul Petroşani of Nicolae Ceauşescu's Romania. In the bastion of democracy that is Dundee, the home side comfortably won 3-0, David Narey with Jackie Copland and Pat Gardner the scorers. It was not so comfortable behind the Iron Curtain, however, with United going down 2-0 but hanging on to win 3-2 on aggregate. In the second round, Turkish outfit Bursaspor visited Tannadice and left with a 0-0 draw. In the return leg Bursaspor won 1-0 to reach the last eight in what was their first foray into European competition.

The general consensus was that United should have been good enough to make it to the quarter-finals but underperformed over the two legs, which was a very disappointing outcome. Also disappointing was the fact that no programmes were produced for either of United's two home ties in the competition, which that season was won by Dynamo Kiev, conquerors of Bursaspor, who in the final defeated Ferencváros – surprise conquerors of Liverpool at the second-round stage.

HEARTS too had but one appearance in the Cup Winners' Cup, in 1976/77 – qualifying as Scottish Cup runners-up to Treble winners Rangers the season previous – although two more participations were achieved towards the end of the life of the competition in 1996/97 and 1998/99. Thanks to the 1976/77 campaign, Hearts became the fifth Scottish club to complete the European participation 'treble'.

In the first round first leg, Hearts visited East Germany (aka the German Democratic Republic) to face Lokomotive Leipzig. Hearts lost 2-0 but in the second leg they turned in a fabulous performance to win 5-1 and go through 5-3 on aggregate. Roy

Kay, Willie Gibson with a brace, Jimmy Brown and Drew Busby got Hearts' goals. As an aside, in earlier competitions of the Fairs Cup the German Railwaymen had been stopped in their tracks by both Kilmarnock and Hibs.

In the second round of the Cup Winners' Cup the wheels came off Hearts' bogie in the shape of Hamburg SV of West Germany. A 4-2 defeat in the Volksparkstadion, with goals from Donald Park and Busby, offered hope but back in Edinburgh John Hagart's boys crashed 4-1 and went out 8-3 on aggregate with Gibson netting the consolation goal. Further consolation came via Hamburg, featuring internationals Manfred Kaltz and Felix Magath, going on to win the competition.

———————

There is a school of thought which suggested that if only the champions, plus the current holders, could participate in a Champion Clubs' Cup then only the actual national cup winners could participate in a Cup Winners' Cup and if clubs had won the league and cup double they should have been afforded the opportunity to compete in both of the associated European competitions!

That ruling, if applied, would have had an adverse affect on plenty of Scottish clubs, not least Rangers' successful 1971/72 campaign, but in an alternative universe, perhaps Rangers won the Cup Winners' Cup in 1964/65 (at the expense of Dundee's entry) while Celtic triumphed in 1967/68 (with Aberdeen getting bumped). Okay, so I've taken things too far.

Inter-Cities Fairs Cup /UEFA Cup

The Inter-Cities Fairs Cup was a competition set up in 1955 to promote international trade fairs and as such was initially only open to teams from cities that hosted such events. Eventually competitions featured a 'one city, one team' rule which meant qualification could be determined by geography instead of success on the football field.

As a result, when Clyde finished third in Scotland's top flight in 1966/67 behind fellow Glasgow sides Celtic and Rangers, they were prevented from competing in the 1967/68 Fairs Cup. Clyde argued that they were not a Glasgow club but a Rutherglen club – at the time, the municipal boundary between Glasgow and Lanarkshire dissected Shawfield Stadium – but their regular participation in the Glasgow Cup competition counted against them. As such, Scotland's Fairs Cup representatives that season would be Rangers (second place), Hibernian (fifth) and Dundee (sixth). Fourth-placed Aberdeen went into the 1967/68 Cup Winners' Cup as runners-up to Celtic in the 1967 Scottish Cup Final.

The tournament was organised by a Fairs Cup Committee chaired by future FIFA president Stanley Rous, but in 1971/72 the competition was replaced by UEFA's very own UEFA Cup complete with a new trophy.

During the Golden Years 13 clubs represented Scotland in the Fairs Cup and its successor competition, and on four occasions the semi-finals were reached – Hibernian (1960/61), Kilmarnock (1966/67), Dundee (1967/68) and Rangers (1968/69). Dundee United subsequently reached the final in 1986/87.

———————

There was no Scottish representation in the first two Fairs Cup competitions, but like the European Champion Clubs' Cup the pioneering **HIBERNIAN** were Scotland's first participant, in the 1960/61 tournament having finished seventh in the league the season previous. In the first round, which ran from September to November, Hugh Shaw's Hibs

were awarded a walkover victory against Lausanne Sports of Switzerland which took them through to the last eight.

TV soap *Coronation Street* first appeared on our screens on 9 December 1960 and less than three weeks later Hibs travelled to the Camp Nou and drew 4-4 with Fairs Cup holders Barcelona in the quarter-final first leg. God bless Elsie Tanner! Hibs twice led by two goals – to let that slip once is unfortunate but to do it twice is bordering on careless, surely? Joe Baker grabbed a double while John MacLeod and Tommy Preston got the others.

The return match in Edinburgh took place in February and the Hibees came back from 2-1 down to win 3-2 and go through 7-6 on aggregate. Baker, Preston and former Forres Mechanics forward Bobby Kinloch were the scorers. Incidentally, the match programme cost six old pennies (2.5 pence) and included a photograph of the actual Fairs Cup which to be blunt looked more like a snooker trophy than a piece of soccer silverware.

Against AS Roma in the semi-final first leg at Easter Road, Baker and MacLeod were back on the scoresheet but the game finished 2-2. In Rome, Hibs led 3-1 through Kinloch plus two from Baker with 25 minutes remaining but ultimately it finished 3-3 and 5-5 on aggregate, but with no away goals rule to take Hibernian through a play-off was arranged for 27 May. It took place in Rome and the home team romped to a 6-0 victory. The two-legged final didn't take place until September/October of the following season when the Romans beat the Brummies 4-2 on aggregate. Incidentally, in the first leg at St Andrew's the referee was Scotsman Bobby Davidson while the Birmingham City line-up included future Celtic hero Bertie Auld.

In the 1961/62 competition Hibs, following an eighth-place finish in the league, opened with a 3-3 draw with Belenenses at Easter Road – a double from John Fraser plus a Sammy Baird penalty after the home side trailed 3-0. A much-improved performance in Portugal gave Hibernian a 3-1 win with two goals from John Baxter and one from Eric Stevenson.

In the second round Hibs were blown away 5-0 on aggregate by Red Star Belgrade, losing 4-0 in Yugoslavia and 1-0 in Scotland. On the bright side, Elvis Presley was at number one in the UK singles charts with '(Marie's the Name) His Latest Flame'. Valencia would beat Barcelona in an all-Spanish Fairs Cup Final.

The 1962/63 campaign began with a convincing 4-0 home win against Stævnet with John Byrne netting a double. Hibs, with Walter Galbraith now in charge, also won the away leg in Denmark 3-2 with Stevenson hitting a brace. In the second round against a City of Utrecht XI, Hibs would win 1-0 in the Netherlands through Duncan Falconer and 2-1 at Easter Road thanks to Baker and Stevenson with 16-year-old Jimmy O'Rourke making his debut.

It all went pear-shaped in Spain in the quarter-finals, however, when the Hibees crashed 5-0 to the holders Valencia, who had eliminated Celtic and Dunfermline Athletic in the two previous rounds. Some honour was retrieved though with a 2-1 victory in Edinburgh with Preston and Baker scoring. Valencia would go on to retain the Fairs Cup, defeating Dynamo Zagreb in the final.

In 1965/66 it took three first-round games to separate Bob Shankly's Hibs and old foes Valencia with the Spanish club ultimately triumphing again. In the first leg at Easter Road, Hibernian won 2-0 with goals from Jimmy Scott after five minutes and a headed effort from John McNamee on the stroke of full time. Valencia matched that result in Spain and in the play-off back in the Mestalla Stadium the home side won 3-0 with Hibs hitting both bar and post. In the third

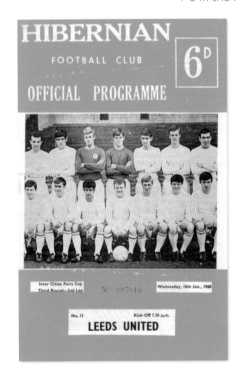

round Valencia would lose to Leeds United 2-1 on aggregate with a teenage Peter Lorimer netting one of the goals.

In 1967/68 Scotland's three Fairs Cup representatives all got beyond the second round before being beaten by the eventual winners Leeds United. Hibs were the first to go, in the third round, losing 1-0 at Elland Road with Glaswegian Eddie Gray scoring in the 4th minute, then drawing 1-1 at Easter Road. Colin Stein scored in the fourth minute and Jack Charlton equalised for the visitors in the 87th.

Earlier, Hibs had pulled off a couple of remarkable victories starting with a 3-0 success against Porto in Edinburgh, with two goals for Peter Cormack and one for Stevenson. It was just enough as the away leg was lost 3-1, a Pat Stanton penalty registering their goal. In the second round Hibs then crashed 4-1 away to Napoli with Stein scoring, but in an amazing game at Easter Road they won 5-0. Bobby Duncan, Pat Quinn, Cormack, Stanton and Stein were the 'Neapolitan Famous Five'.

In 1968/69 Hibs again made it to the third round with a string of impressive results, beginning with a 3-0 victory against Olimpija Ljubljana in Yugoslavia with Stevenson, Stein and Peter 'the next George Best' Marinello scoring, which was followed up with a 2-1 win at home thanks to Joe Davis's brace. In the second round Lokomotive Leipzig were beaten 3-1 in Edinburgh by a Joe McBride hat-trick and 1-0 in East Germany by Colin Grant. The winning run came to an end though in West Germany, losing 1-0 to Hamburg SV. At Easter Road, Hibs won 2-1 with a McBride double but went out on the away goals rule. In the quarter-finals Hamburg were due to play Göztepe of Turkey but they chose to withdraw from the competition, apparently fearing potential repercussions should they not return from Izmir in time to fulfil a Bundesliga fixture against Bayern Munich. So much for Teutonic efficiency.

In 1970/71 Hibs, managed by Willie MacFarlane, contested the Fairs Cup for the seventh time – a Scottish record. Just two months after some Scottish heroics in the Commonwealth Games at nearby

PETER CORMACK
HIBERNIAN
INSIDE RIGHT

Inter-Cities Fairs Cup /UEFA Cup

Meadowbank Stadium (think Lachie Stewart, Ian Stewart, Ian McCafferty, Rosemary Stirling and Rosemary Payne), Hibs kept the flag flying with a resounding 6-0 victory over Malmö at Easter Road. McBride got a hat-trick, Arthur Duncan a double and Jim Blair one. In Sweden, a 3-2 victory was achieved to give a 9-2 aggregate win.

In the second round Hibs squeezed past Vitória de Guimarães 3-2 on aggregate, winning 2-0 in Edinburgh through Duncan and Stanton but losing 2-1 in Portugal with Johnny Graham scoring. In the third round, however, Bill Shankly's Liverpool did the double over Hibs – winning 1-0 at Easter Road and 2-0 at Anfield. Liverpool would be eliminated by Leeds United at the semi-final stage and the Elland Road side went on to lift the Fairs Cup for the second time with Billy Bremner and Peter Lorimer adding to their medals collection.

The 1973/74 season was Hibs' tenth in Europe – the third Scottish club to achieve this milestone – and although the Edinburgh club were beaten at the second-round stage, technically Eddie Turnbull's side were 'undefeated' and were only eliminated via a penalty shoot-out. In the first round, Keflavík were bested 2-0 at Easter Road by Jim Black and Tony Higgins followed by a 1-1 draw in Iceland with skipper Pat Stanton netting. Against old adversaries Leeds in the second round, two goalless draws were played out, before Stanton, who had netted a hat-trick the previous weekend, saw his spot-kick hit an Easter Road post. Bremner converted the winning penalty for the Yorkshire outfit.

Leeds and their sizeable Scottish contingent would lose out in the third round to Vitória Setubal but by the end of the season they would be crowned English champions.

Scotland, who initially included Hibs central defender John Blackley, were unbeaten in the three matches they played in the 1974 World Cup finals. In the 1974/75 UEFA Cup campaign, however, Hibs could only manage that feat for two games when in the first round they beat Rosenborg of Norway 3-2 away followed by a 9-1 rout at Easter Road – with

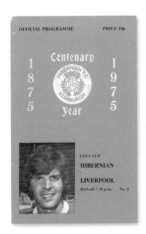

doubles for Joe Harper, Iain Munro, Pat Stanton and Alex Cropley plus one from Alan Gordon. In the second round, Juventus – with the likes of Pietro Anastasi and Jose Altafini in their ranks – were way too slick, winning 4-2 in Edinburgh (although Hibs led 2-1 via goals from Stanton and Cropley) and 4-0 in Turin. Juventus would reach the semi-finals before losing to FC Twente who in turn lost to Borussia Mönchengladbach in the final.

A second successive runners-up spot in the League got Hibs into the 1975/76 UEFA Cup where in the first round they met Liverpool, who had finished as runners-up in England. An excellent 1-0 victory was achieved in Edinburgh thanks to a Joe Harper goal but at Anfield, Hibs lost 3-1 as an Alex Edwards equaliser was swamped by a John Toshack hat-trick. Bob Paisley's Liverpool went on to win the UEFA Cup (the only match they lost en-route was at Easter Road) as well as the English League title.

In 1976/77, Sochaux of France were overcome in the first round. Jim Brownlie secured a 1-0 win at Easter Road while a 0-0 away draw was accomplished in Hibs' 60th European match overall. The Hibees slipped up, however, in the next round when, after defeating Östers IF 2-0 in Edinburgh through Blackley and Brownlie, they slumped to a 4-1 defeat in Sweden – Bobby Smith grabbing the visitors' goal nine minutes from time. Östers would take an 8-1 aggregate pummelling from Barcelona in the third round and Juventus would win the tournament – their first European success.

The 1978/79 UEFA Cup was Hibs' 14th European campaign – the next one wouldn't come along until 11 seasons later. In round one IFK Norrköping were beaten 3-2 at Easter Road by two goals for Tony Higgins and one for Willie Temperley, while it was goalless in Sweden. In the second round Hibs lost 2-0 to Strasbourg in France but couldn't quite manage to pull it back at Easter Road, only winning 1-0 with a goal from Ally MacLeod. Strasbourg lost to MSV Duisburg in the third round while Borussia Mönchengladbach won the competition for the second time and Berti Vogts was still their skipper.

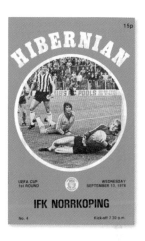

Inter-Cities Fairs Cup /UEFA Cup

HEARTS, managed by Tommy Walker, made it a first and second for Edinburgh when they competed in the 1961/62 Fairs Cup – after having finished seventh in the League the season previous. Both capital clubs participated that same season and like their Easter Road rivals, Hearts were eliminated at the second-round stage. In the first round, Hearts delivered that rare treat – a Scottish win in Belgium – beating Royale Union Saint-Gilloise 3-1 after trailing 1-0. Bobby Blackwood got the equaliser followed by two from Norrie Davidson. The Jambos won 2-0 at Tynecastle, Willie Wallace and Robin Stenhouse the scorers.

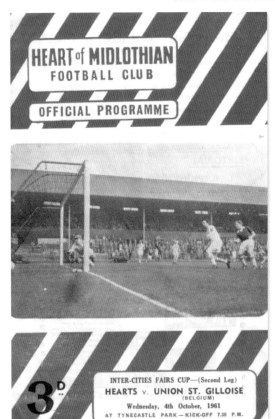

Inter Milan then visited Tynecastle and won 1-0 before thumping Hearts 4-0 in the San Siro with two goals coming from Englishman Gerry Hitchens. As a nostalgic memorabilia aside, the programme for the Tynecastle game features an advert for an old favourite of mine – McEwan's Export – alongside a pen pic of Hitchens, while next to Luis Suárez is a wonderful British Railways advert featuring services to Callander, Melrose and St Andrews, pre-Beeching axing.

Inter would lose in the quarter-finals to the eventual winners Valencia.

The 1963/64 campaign consisted of three matches against Lausanne-Sport which swung one way then the other. In the away leg Hearts were 2-0 up after 49 minutes through Tommy Traynor and Danny Ferguson but ended the game 2-2. In Edinburgh, a goal from John Cumming in the 19th minute gave the Jambos a 1-0 lead at half-time but their Swiss visitors fought back to equalise then take the lead in the 88th minute before Johnny Hamilton levelled things in the dying seconds. A play-off took place back in Lausanne where Hearts found themselves 2-0 behind after 20 minutes before coming storming back to level it in the second half through Willie Wallace and Danny Ferguson. A third goal for Lausanne, in extra time, proved to be the winner. Lausanne then crashed out in the next round to Real Zaragoza, the eventual tournament winners.

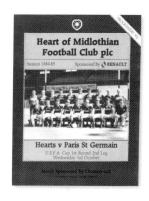

In 1965/66 Hearts once again joined Hibs in the Fairs Cup – the 'one city, one club' rule coming into play the following season. Dunfermline Athletic were Scotland's third representative in that campaign. While Hibs went out at the first round, Hearts made it to round three albeit with the help of a bye initially. In the second round Vålerengens IF were beaten 1-0 at Tynecastle by Willie Wallace and 3-1 in Norway by two from Don Kerrigan and another from Tommy Traynor.

In the third round in January, Real Zaragoza, the tournament winners from 1964, lay in wait but it would take three games to bring the tie to a conclusion. A 3-3 draw in the first leg at Tynecastle – Alan Anderson, Wallace and Kerrigan the Hearts scorers – was followed by a 2-2 draw in Spain with Anderson and Wallace on target. The play-off in March was back at La Romareda and Zaragoza scraped home 1-0. They would eliminate Dunfermline in the quarter-finals before going on to reach the final.

Nineteen years and a competition name change later saw Hearts, now managed by Alex MacDonald, appear in the 1984/85 UEFA Cup – but sadly not for long. They lost it in France, going down 4-0 to Paris Saint-Germain in the first round first leg, followed by a 2-2 draw at Tynecastle – John Robertson with two equalisers on the night. PSG lost to Hungary's Videoton in the next round.

Inter-Cities Fairs Cup /UEFA Cup

Jimmy McGrory's **CELTIC** made their European debut in the 1962/63 Fairs Cup competition thanks to a third-place finish and off they went to visit the holders Valencia in the first round first leg. In Spain the Celts went down 4-2 with both goals coming from Bobby Carroll – in his last season at the club. Back at Celtic Park, a 2-2 draw ensued with Pat Crerand plus an own goal putting Celtic on the scoresheet, so the holders progressed 6-4. They would go on to retain the trophy that season.

Celtic's second and final attempt at winning the Fairs Cup came in 1964/65. It was not a competition that held fond memories as the Hoops went out at the second-round stage to Barcelona – losing 3-1 in the Camp Nou, with goalkeeper Ronnie Simpson making his debut and John Hughes getting the goal. A 0-0 draw at Celtic Park confirmed their exit. Barcelona were eliminated by Strasbourg in the next round, on the toss of a coin. In the first round Celtic had ousted Leixões of Portugal, drawing 1-1 away with Bobby Murdoch scoring before winning a bad-tempered match at Parkhead 3-0, Murdoch and two for Stevie Chalmers doing the damage. Celtic played the entire second half with ten men following a bad tackle on Charlie Gallacher.

It was 1976/77 before Celtic again appeared in Europe's number three competition (now named the UEFA Cup) and Jock Stein's side would surprisingly fall at the first hurdle to Wisla Kraków. In the first leg at Parkhead, Celtic led 1-0 at half-time through Roddy MacDonald then trailed 2-1 before an equaliser from Kenny Dalglish in the final minute saved their blushes. In the return game in Poland, Celtic were sunk by two second-half goals to lose 4-2 on aggregate. Wisla would lose in the next round to RWD Molenbeek on penalties.

In 1983/84, Celtic's journey to the third round with Davie Hay in charge began with a 1-0 home win over Aarhus through Roy Aitken, followed by a much more convincing 4-1 victory in Denmark with Murdo MacLeod, Frank McGarvey, Aitken and Davie Provan scoring. In the second round, however, Celtic lost 2-0 away to Sporting Lisbon before an exhilarating

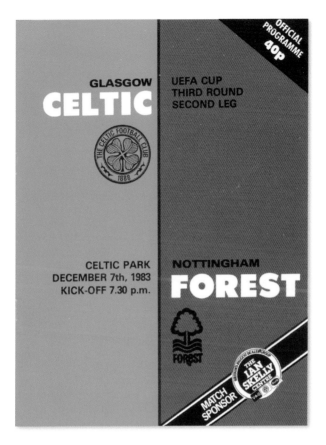

GLASGOW **CELTIC**

UEFA CUP
THIRD ROUND
SECOND LEG

OFFICIAL PROGRAMME 40p

CELTIC PARK
DECEMBER 7th, 1983
KICK-OFF 7.30 p.m.

NOTTINGHAM **FOREST**

MATCH SPONSOR

performance at Parkhead saw them triumph 5-0 through Tommy Burns, Tom McAdam, Brian McClair, MacLeod and McGarvey.

Brian Clough's Nottingham Forest were next although the hard bit appeared to have been done with a 0-0 draw at the City Ground. At Celtic Park, however, Forest hit Celtic on the counter to lead 2-0 before MacLeod netted what proved to be a consolation goal 11 minutes from time. Nottingham Forest would lose out at the semi-finals stage, in dubious circumstances, to Anderlecht who in turn lost to Tottenham Hotspur in the final. Steve Archibald (ex-Aberdeen) played in both matches for Spurs while Stirling-born Ally Dick made a substitute appearance in the second leg.

A couple of decades later, Martin O'Neill's Celtic reached the 2003 UEFA Cup Final in Seville where they lost 3-2 to a talented but sometimes theatrical Porto side.

Inter-Cities Fairs Cup /UEFA Cup

DUNFERMLINE ATHLETIC appeared in the 1962/63 Fairs Cup following on from finishing fourth in the league and in the first round Jock Stein's boys did Scotland proud by slaying the English giants Everton, who had also finished fourth, 2-1 on aggregate. A narrow 1-0 defeat at Goodison Park was overturned in the second leg through goals from George Miller and Harry Melrose. Everton would go on to be crowned English champions that season.

In the second round first leg, however, the Pars crashed 4-0 away to Valencia who had eliminated Celtic in the previous round. An amazing return game at East End Park six days before Christmas finished 6-2 for Dunfermline to see the tie finish 6-6 with Melrose, Jim MacLean, George Peebles, Alex Smith and two for Jackie Sinclair accounting for their goals, while 16-year-old Alex Edwards gave the holders hell out on the right wing. With no away goals rule, penalties or coinage available to settle things a third match was required. The play-off took place in February 1963 in Lisbon – London or Paris might have been fairer but the big freeze of the winter of 1962 and into '63 probably put paid to that. In the Estádio do Restelo (where Belenenses FC, Metallica, The Police and The Smashing Pumpkins have all starred) the Spanish side triumphed 1-0 and went on to win the competition.

Scotland had three representatives in the 1964/65 tournament and Willie Cunningham's Dunfermline faired the best, reaching the third round. In the first round Örgryte were defeated 4-2 at East End Park, John McLaughlin and Jackie Sinclair both nabbing a brace with the visitors twice having taken the lead, while a 0-0 draw was achieved in Sweden. In the second round VfB Stuttgart were beaten 1-0 in Fife by a Tom Callaghan drive from the edge of the penalty box before another goalless draw away from home. The result in West Germany was particularly sweet as seven minutes from time the West Germans were awarded a dubious penalty which future Scotland goalkeeper Jim Herriot saved, but only after he had recovered from a right hook from one of the Stuttgart players.

But there was Spanish/Basque heartbreak next. A narrow 1-0 away defeat to Athletic Bilbao was followed by a 1-0 victory at home – Dunfermline's fifth game in 11 days. Alex Smith got the winner while Alex Ferguson had a goal disallowed. Bilbao won the coin toss to take the third match back to the San Mamés Stadium where they triumphed 2-1, albeit with the aid of another soft penalty award. Smith again got the Fifers' goal. Athletic lost in the semi-finals to Juventus who in turn lost to Ferencváros in the final.

In 1965/66, Dunfermline, having finished third in the league the season previous, were again the highest achievers of the Scottish Fairs Cup trio and reached the last eight before being stopped by Spanish opposition for the third successive campaign. Following a bye in the first round, Dunfermline demolished KB 5-0 at home with two from Bert Paton plus Jim Fleming, Hugh Robertson and Tommy Callaghan also scoring, then 4-2 in Copenhagen thanks to Alex Edwards, Paton, Fleming and Ferguson. In the third round Spartak Brno were beaten 2-0 at East End Park by Paton and a Ferguson penalty while a 0-0 draw was achieved in Czechoslovakia.

In the quarter-finals, the Pars defeated Real Zaragoza 1-0 in Fife through Paton's goal but lost 4-2 in Spain after extra time with Ferguson scoring both Dunfermline goals. Zaragoza would reach the final before losing out to domestic rivals Barcelona.

In 1966/67 the Pars only got as far as the second round before being frustrated by the eventual tournament winners. In the first round, however, they were off to that famous athletics venue, the Bislett Stadium, to face Frigg Oslo FK. The home side took the lead in the first minute but Dunfermline fought back to win 3-1 through Callaghan plus two from Fleming. At East End Park, Frigg again took the lead in the first minute before Dunfermline again fought back to win 3-1 with Callaghan on target plus two from Pat Delaney.

In the second round Dynamo Zagreb were beaten 4-2 in Fife by Delaney, Edwards and a brace

Inter-Cities Fairs Cup /UEFA Cup

from Ferguson, but the Pars went down 2-0 in Yugoslavia to go out on the away goals rule.

In 1969/70 the Pars competed in the Fairs Cup for the fifth time, having again finished third, but it would be 35 years before they would once again grace a European competition. In 1969 the third round was reached and the run began with an impressive 4-0 win over Bordeaux thanks to a double for Paton plus Barry Mitchell and Pat Gardner scoring at East End Park, which 'cushioned' a 2-0 defeat in the return match. Next up were Gwardia Warsaw who were beaten 2-1 in Dunfermline by McLean and Gardner, and 1-0 in Poland with Willie Renton scoring.

In the third round the Pars narrowly lost 1-0 to Anderlecht in Brussels but in the second leg McLean netted after nine minutes, then six minutes later Edwards's penalty hit the post. Barry Mitchell, however, made it 2-0 30 seconds after the restart. Anderlecht then fought back to draw level before McLean made it 3-2 to Dunfermline, which was not enough and the Fifers went out on the away goals rule. Anderlecht would reach the final before losing to an Arsenal side which featured four Scots – skipper Frank McLintock, goalkeeper Bob Wilson, Eddie Kelly and George Graham.

Looking back, Dunfermline Athletic enjoyed a total of seven European campaigns throughout the 1960s, so for a while anyway, Fife did swing.

––––––––––

PARTICK THISTLE made their European debut in the 1963/64 Fairs Cup by virtue of finishing third in the league – and travelled to Belfast to face Glentoran. A 4-1 away win was achieved with Billy Hainey scoring Thistle's first goal in European competition while Ernie Yard netted a brace, and they followed it up with a 3-0 win in Glasgow including George Smith's double. Against Spartak Brno of Czechoslovakia in the second round, Thistle raced into a 3-0 lead at Firhill in the first leg before being pegged back to 3-2. The return leg didn't go well at all, however, and after a marathon 14-hour journey apparently, Willie Thornton's Thistle were comprehensively beaten 4-0 and went out 6-3 on aggregate.

Thistle's second appearance on the European stage was in the 1972/73 UEFA Cup – achieved as a result of their sensational victory over Celtic in the 1971 League Cup Final. Alas, the Jags' performance in Europe wasn't quite so sensational and

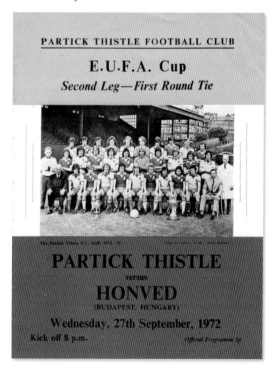

PARTICK THISTLE FOOTBALL CLUB

E.U.F.A. Cup

Second Leg—First Round Tie

PARTICK THISTLE

versus

HONVED

(BUDAPEST, HUNGARY)

Wednesday, 27th September, 1972

Kick off 8 p.m.   *Official Programme 5p*

Inter-Cities Fairs Cup /UEFA Cup

Davie McParland's 'Bright Young Things' (including future internationals Alan Rough, Alex Forsyth and Ronnie Glavin) crashed out in the first round to some real Magyars – Honvéd of Budapest. Behind the Iron Curtain, a narrow 1-0 defeat raised hopes for the second leg but in front of a Maryhill crowd of 17,000, the visitors triumphed 3-0 to win 4-0 on aggregate. As personal disappointments go it is right up there with striking out at the fifth-year school disco and failing my driving test for the fourth time. The Jags would not frighten European opposition again until the 1995/96 Intertoto Cup.

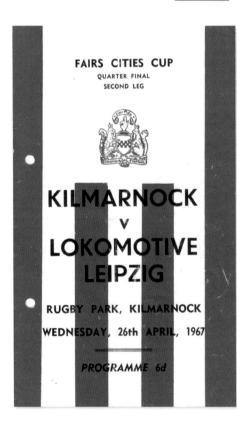

FAIRS CITIES CUP
QUARTER FINAL
SECOND LEG

KILMARNOCK
v
LOKOMOTIVE LEIPZIG

RUGBY PARK, KILMARNOCK
WEDNESDAY, 26th APRIL, 1967

PROGRAMME 6d

KILMARNOCK made their European debut in the 1964/65 Fairs Cup as league runners-up in 1963/64 and it was a case of pain – losing 3-0 away to Eintracht Frankfurt – followed by ecstasy as they thrashed the 1960 European Cup runners-up 5-1 at Rugby Park. Just to make things interesting, Eintracht scored first in the return leg before goals from Ronnie Hamilton, Brian McIlroy, Jim McFadzean, Jackie McInally and Hamilton again seconds from the end clinched a stunning comeback. The newspapers were fulsome in their praise of Willie Waddell's team – 'Hail Killie Tigers' and 'Here was a game that will be remembered as long as football is played in Ayrshire' are just two examples.

In the second round, however, the Ayrshire club came unstuck against the Toffees when Everton won 2-0 at Rugby Park then 4-1 at Goodison with Brian McIlroy grabbing the consolation goal. Everton then lost to Manchester United in the third round with Scotsman David Herd netting the decisive goal. At the end of 1964/65 Manchester United would be crowned champions of their country, as would Kilmarnock.

The 1966/67 season began with Malky McDonald's side receiving a bye to the second round where Royal Antwerp were edged 1-0 in Belgium by Jackie McInally's goal and then thrashed 7-2 in Kilmarnock with doubles for McInally, Gerry Queen and Tommy McLean plus one for Craig Watson. In round three another Belgian side, La Gantoise, were ousted but it was much closer this time. At Rugby Park, Kilmarnock won 1-0 thanks to Eric Murray but lost 1-0 in Gent after 90 minutes before scoring twice in extra time through McInally and McLean to go through. In the quarter-finals, Killie lost 1-0 away to Lokomotive Leipzig but won the return leg 2-0, Jim McFadzean and Brian McIlroy scoring.

By the time the semi-final against Leeds United came along in May, Celtic and Rangers were waiting to take part in the finals of the European Cup and Cup Winners' Cup respectively, so, incredibly, Scottish clubs were still chasing a European triple crown. However, not for the first time, Don Revie's side's spoiling tactics spoiled things by winning 4-2 at Elland Road where McIlroy got the Killie goals, then surviving an onslaught at Rugby Park to draw 0-0. In the final, played over two legs in August and September, Leeds – with Billy Bremner, Peter Lorimer, Eddie Gray and Willie Bell featuring to different degrees – lost out to Dynamo Zagreb.

In 1969/70 Walter McCrae's Kilmarnock made it to the third round, along with Dunfermline Athletic, and began their run with a 5-4 aggregate win over FC Zürich. Killie lost 3-2 in Switzerland with Jim McLean and Ross Mathie scoring before winning the return 3-1 thanks to Jackie McGrory, Eddie Morrison and Tommy McLean. In the second round Slavia Sofia were beaten 4-1 at Rugby Park by two for Mathie plus Jim Cook and John Gilmour both netting, which proved just enough to see Killie through following a 2-0 defeat in Bulgaria.

In the last 16 Kilmarnock could only draw 1-1 at

Inter-Cities Fairs Cup /UEFA Cup

home with Dinamo Bacău – Mathie giving the home side a lead they couldn't hold let alone build upon – and in Romania the Ayrshire side went down 2-0. In the quarter-finals, Bacău lost 9-1 on aggregate to eventual winners Arsenal.

Scotland's Fairs Cup allocation was extended to four clubs for the second time in 1970/71 and it was Kilmarnock who benefited via seventh place in the league with the higher-placed Hearts and Dundee losing out on the one city, one club rule of the time. Unfortunately, Killie bowed out from European competition at the first-round stage and did not reappear until 1997/98, by which time, incidentally, the price of the match programme had increased from a pre-decimal one shilling (five 'new' pence) to £1.50. Killie's surprise conquerors were Coleraine when, after grabbing a 1-1 draw in Northern Ireland, Mathie's goal having given the Ayrshire side a second-half lead they held for all of four minutes, they surrendered a 2-0 half-time lead at Rugby Park earned via Tommy McLean and Eddie Morrison to lose 3-2 and go out 4-3 on aggregate. I really wish our clubs wouldn't do that sort of thing. It's rather annoying as well as upsetting.

———

DUNDEE UNITED, with long-serving manager Jerry Kerr in charge, made their European debut in the 1966/67 Fairs Cup thanks to a fifth-placed league finish. United received a bye in the first round, but thereafter the draw provided tough ties, although a sensational start was achieved in the shape of away and home victories over Barcelona. In the Camp Nou, goals from Billy Hainey and Norwegian striker Finn Seemann had the Black and Whites (the Tangerine colour arrived in 1967) leading 2-0 before Barça pulled one back eight minutes from time. At Tannadice a crowd of 28,000 saw the Fairs Cup holders beaten 2-0, Ian Mitchell and Billy Hainey the scorers.

United's reward was a third-round tie against Juventus. In Turin, the Italian Black and Whites

– I Bianconeri – won 3-0, but in Dundee they were beaten 1-0, the goal coming from Denmark's Finn Døssing. Juventus would lose out in the quarter-finals to the eventual winners, Dinamo Zagreb.

In 1969/70, Dundee United were drawn against the holders Newcastle United, who proved too strong for the Tannadice club – now sporting their Tangerine Terrors look. The Magpies won 2-1 in Dundee, Ian Scott netting for the home side, and 1-0 at St James' Park. Newcastle would lose out to Anderlecht on the away goals rule in the quarter-finals.

As a twee aside, the programme for the game at Tannadice included a 'Meet the Wife!' page which included photographs of the better halves of Donald MacKay, Doug Smith, Alec Stuart and Kenny Cameron plus the wording 'Usually it's goals we like to see but you'll agree these "Mrs" are charming.' All that was missing was a 'Phwoarr!'

Jerry Kerr's final full season in charge was 1970/71 – Jim McLean would take the helm in December 1971 – although it would be the 1980s before United would see appearances in the last eight and beyond. In the first round first leg at Tannadice, the home side, just to be sporting, gave Grasshopper Club Zürich two goals of a start before strikes from Ian Reid, Stuart Markland and Alex Reid in the last 25 minutes made it 3-2 for the Tayside escapologists. A goalless draw in Switzerland followed, thus enabling a trip to Prague in the second round.

In the Letná Stadion a first-half equaliser from Tommy Traynor had United looking good before two second-half goals from Sparta gave the home side a 3-1 victory. Back in Dundee, a goal from Alan

U.E.F.A. CUP 1st ROUND 1st LEG
DUNDEE UNITED v. **R.S.C. ANDERLECHT**
WEDNESDAY, 19th SEPTEMBER, 1979. Kick-off 7.30 p.m.
Official Programme 1979/80 ● No. 4 ● Price 15p

Inter-Cities Fairs Cup /UEFA Cup

Gordon in the 31st minute meant United had almost an hour to grab a second and victory on the away goals rule. But the Sparta keeper performed heroics (as opposed to United squandering chances) and the visitors progressed 3-2 on aggregate. Sparta would be eliminated by the eventual winners, Leeds United, in the third round.

Two months after Tom Watson won his first Open Championship at nearby Carnoustie, Dundee United competed in the 1975/76 UEFA Cup – their first time in the renamed competition, achieved via finishing fourth in the league the previous season. Also worthy of mention was the third UK/Iceland 'Cod War', which ran from November 1975 to June 1976, and as a 'pre-emptive strike' Dundee United defeated Keflavík 2-0 in Iceland with a double for David 'Birdseye' Narey and 4-0 at Tannadice thanks to two for Henry Hall plus Paul Hegarty and Paul scoring.

In the second round we switched fish from cod to robalo and the warmer waters off Portugal but when Porto visited Dundee in the first leg their takeaway was a 2-1 victory – Alex Rennie scoring for United. For their part, United then achieved a 1-1 draw away from home through Paul Hegarty but it was not enough. In the third round, Hamburgers were the order of the day as HSV eliminated United's conquerors.

The 1977/78 campaign ended in disappointment at the first-round stage – just like Aberdeen's did. However, also like Aberdeen, this marked the start of a club record number of successive seasons in European competitions – 14 in total. In 1977, though, a 1-0 home win over Danish side KB with Paul Sturrock scoring was followed by a 3-0 collapse in Denmark. Defeats on the football field as well as in nightclubs have proven that sometimes Copenhagen isn't always wonderful.

But 1978/79 in the UEFA Cup was not a case of third time lucky as United exited in the first round again. This time Standard Liege turfed them out, winning 1-0 in Belgium and collecting a goalless draw at Tannadice. The Belgian club would lose out to Manchester City in the second round.

A second successive league placing of third meant an appearance in the 1979/80 competition but again United found goals hard to come by. A notable scalp, however, in the shape of Anderlecht, was taken in the first round as a result of a goalless draw in Dundee and a 1-1 draw in Brussels with Frank Kopel netting the vital goal. But in the second round United lost twice to Diósgyőri VTK, 1-0 at home and then 3-1 in Hungary with former Manchester United defender Kopel again on the scoresheet. In the third round the Hungarian outfit were slaughtered by Kaiserslautern 8-1 on aggregate.

In 1980/81 United continued to blow hot and cold. Their campaign started with a 0-0 draw against Śląsk Wrocław in Poland followed by a resounding 7-2 victory at Tannadice which featured braces for Davie Dodds and Willie Pettigrew. In the second round United drew 1-1 at home to Lokeren with Willie Pettigrew scoring, then 0-0 in Belgium to exit the competition on the away goals rule, having gone unbeaten in individual matches. Lokeren would be eliminated at the last-eight stage by the eventual beaten finalists, AZ Alkmaar.

Like the season before, United's compensation for a November exit from the UEFA Cup would be a December League Cup Final victory. Ipswich Town would win the 1980/81 UEFA Cup, ably assisted by Glasgow boys Alan Brazil and John Wark, the latter of whom scored a record 14 goals in the course of the campaign.

In 1981/82, Dundee United, in their tenth Euro campaign, reached the quarter-finals, to become the first Scottish club to stay in the UEFA Cup beyond

Inter-Cities Fairs Cup /UEFA Cup

Christmas. United players David Narey and Paul Sturrock were also included in Scotland's 1982 World Cup finals squad.

The rollercoaster of results began with a stunning 5-2 away win against Monaco thanks to doubles for Davie Dodds and Eamonn Bannon plus one from Billy Kirkwood, before losing the home leg 2-1 with Ralph Milne scoring. Another impressive scalp was taken in round two as Borussia Mönchengladbach were hammered 5-0 at Tannadice with Milne, Kirkwood, Hegarty, Sturrock and Bannon on target after the first leg had been lost 2-0. And then the Belgians of Winterslag – now KRC Genk – were bested by another 5-0 drubbing in Dundee thanks to Bannon, Narey, Hegarty and two from Milne, following on from a goalless draw away.

In the quarter-finals Radnički Niš were defeated 2-0 at home by Narey and Dodds. The semi-finals beckoned, but United conceded three second-half goals in Yugoslavia. Radnički would then lose to Hamburg SV in the semis.

The 1982/83 season brought another last-eight appearance and this time the run began with the elimination of PSV Eindhoven, with a 1-1 draw at Tannadice earned by Davie Dodds followed by a 2-0 win in the Netherlands thanks to Billy Kirkwood and Paul Hegarty. Another away win followed, Milne scoring twice and Sturrock adding the other in a 3-1 success against Viking in Stavanger, and then progress was assured with a goalless draw at home. United's solitary home win of the campaign was a 2-1 victory over Werder Bremen through Milne and Narey, with a 1-1 draw – Hegarty scored then Rudi Völler equalised for Werder – being achieved in West Germany.

In the quarters, United came unstuck against Bohemians of Prague by losing 1-0 in Czechoslovakia then drawing a blank at home. It was a tie United should have won but as compensation, they finished the season as Scottish champions for the first (and, to date, only) time in their history. Bohemians lost in the semis to the eventual winners, Anderlecht.

After narrowly failing to reach the European Cup Final the season previous, United went out in the third round of the 1984/85 UEFA Cup. Their campaign began with a 1-0 away defeat to AIK Stockholm but three second-half goals at Tannadice – one from Paul Sturrock and two from Milne – saw United through. In the second round, Linzer ASK were beaten 2-1 in Austria by Kirkwood and Bannon and 5-1 in Dundee by two from Tommy Coyne plus Paul Hegarty, Richard Gough and Dave Beaumont scoring.

In the third round first leg, Dundee United travelled south to Old Trafford to face Ron Atkinson's Manchester United and got themselves an enticing 2-2 draw with equalisers from Hegarty and Sturrock cancelling out leads from Gordon Strachan and Bryan Robson. At Tannadice, however, the home side twice fought back to draw level through goals from Davie Dodds and Hegarty before conceding a third to lose 3-2 on the night and go out 5-4 on aggregate. Manchester United would surprisingly lose on penalties to Videoton in the quarter-finals and the Hungarian side went on to reach the final, where they lost to Real Madrid.

The 1985/86 campaign resulted in another third-round exit when much more was expected. In the first round Bohemians of Dublin were beaten 5-2 at Dalymount Park by a hat-trick for Sturrock and a brace for Bannon, but in the return United had to be content with a 2-2 draw with Milne and Ian Redford having put them 2-0 up. Vardar Skopje then visited Tannadice and United managed to win this one, 2-0 thanks to Redford and Gough. A 1-1 draw after Hegarty had given United the lead was then achieved in Yugoslavia.

Next up was Neuchâtel (which translates as Newcastle) Xamax, a club I had never heard of at the time but who would go on to become Swiss champions in 1987 and 1988. At Tannadice, former Mönchengladbach and Real Madrid hero Uli Stielike gave the visitors a half-time lead before goals from Dodds and Redford made it 2-1 to United. In Switzerland, Redford gave the visitors the lead (and great expectations) after 17 minutes but the home side said, 'What the Dickens?' and fought back to win 2-1 after 90 minutes and then 3-1 after extra time. It was enough to give the Tangerine Terrors the Pip. Anyway, Neuchâtel would lose in the quarter-finals to Real Madrid, who went on to lift the trophy for the second successive season.

The following season, United would go all the way to the final where sadly they were beaten by IFK Gothenburg. In the summer of 1986, however, five of their players would have the honour of being included in Scotland's squad for the World Cup finals in Mexico.

_____

DUNDEE's initial foray into the Fairs Cup in 1967/68, on the back of finishing sixth in the league, also meant that the Dens Parkers completed the set of competing in the three European tournaments. Bobby Ancell's side had a smashing run to the semi-finals which began with a 4-2 aggregate win over AFC DWS of Amsterdam. Although the first leg in the Netherlands was lost 2-1 with George McLean on target, a 3-0 win was achieved at Dens Park thanks to Sammy Wilson and two for McLean. In the second round FC Liege were beaten 3-1 in Dundee by two goals for Alex Stuart and one for Sammy Wilson and then 4-1 in Belgium with McLean netting all four for the visitors.

As the Fairs Cup that season had 48 entrants as opposed to an easier-to-manage 32 or 64, it meant that four clubs (including Dundee and Rangers) received byes into the quarter-finals. In the last eight there were 1-0 home and away victories against FC Zürich – Jim Easton scoring at Dens Park and Wilson netting in Switzerland. In the semi-final first leg in Dundee, Paul Madeley put Leeds United in front after 26 minutes with Bobby Wilson equalising ten minutes later and 1-1 it finished. The second leg was played on 15 May and in the 80th minute Eddie Gray netted the only goal of the game to put the Yorkshire club into their second successive Fairs Cup

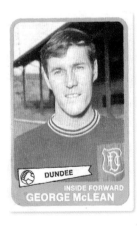

INSIDE FORWARD
GEORGE McLEAN

Final. Leeds, with three Scots in their side, became the first English team to triumph in European football's third competition, overcoming Ferencváros in a two-legged final played in August and September.

If – like UEFA – you choose to determine that the Fairs Cup and UEFA Cup are two distinct and separate tournaments, then Dundee's appearance in the inaugural UEFA Cup of 1971/72 meant that they were the first Scottish club to have competed in all FOUR European competitions. You can only take this anorak thing so far, however, so we'll continue to interpret the Fairs Cup and UEFA Cup as being one and the same – just like Sean Connery and Roger Moore.

Dundee, having finished fifth, made it to the third round after beginning with a 5-2 aggregate win over Akademisk of Denmark with Alex Bryce netting a brace at Dens Park. In the second round Dundee took the notable scalp of West Germany's Cologne – overcoming a 2-1 away defeat with a 4-2 win at Dens with John Duncan grabbing himself a hat-trick and Jimmy Wilson also netting.

Unfortunately, in the third round, old foes AC Milan awaited as did a comprehensive 3-0 defeat at the San Siro. Back in Scotland, however, Dundee ran the Italian aces close with a superb 2-0 victory on the night – Gordon Wallace and Duncan the scorers – but lost 3-2 on aggregate. Milan would be eliminated in the semi-finals by a Tottenham Hotspur side featuring former Dens Park hero Alan Gilzean. Spurs would go on to lift the new trophy, a handle-free, towering octagonal and mottled silver edifice which sits atop a marble base, by defeating a Wolves team, which included Scots Frank Munro (ex-Dundee United and Aberdeen) and Glasgow-born Jim McCalliog, in the final.

Inter-Cities Fairs Cup /UEFA Cup

Another fifth-placed finish put Davie White's Dundee into the 1973/74 UEFA Cup but even the signing of Lisbon Lion Tommy Gemmell couldn't prevent an early exit courtesy of FC Twente. In the first round first leg at Dens Park the visitors won 3-1, with George Stewart netting for Dundee, and over in the Netherlands the Dutch outfit won 4-2 with David Johnston and Jocky Scott replying. Twente would lose out to Ipswich Town in the third round.

Dundee entered the 1974/75 UEFA Cup as Scottish League Cup holders. It was also the first time that they competed in Europe in successive seasons, but unfortunately they departed early as victims of RWD Molenbeek. A narrow 1-0 defeat in the first round first leg in Belgium offered hope, as did Duncan's goal which put Dundee 1-0 ahead after ten minutes at Dens Park. It's the hope that kills you though as the visitors went 2-1 in front, then Jocky Scott equalised in the 51st minute before two more goals for the Belgian outfit gave them a 4-2 victory on the night. RWD would win their only Belgian title come the end of 1974/75 and Dundee's next European adventure would not be until the 2001/02 Intertoto Cup.

————

RANGERS competing in the 1967/68 Fairs Cup was probably considered a bit of a 'comedown' at the time but it also meant that the Ibrox side had competed in all three European competitions. Furthermore, it was Rangers' tenth season in Europe – the first Scottish club to hit double figures – and it would begin with Scott Symon in charge and end with Davie White in the manager's chair.

A year after reaching the Cup Winners' Cup Final, Rangers went out in the quarters to Leeds United – the second of the three Scottish representatives to be eliminated by the Yorkshire club that season. In the first round, Dynamo Dresden had been overcome after a 1-1 draw in East Germany with Alex Ferguson netting which was followed up with a 2-1 win at Ibrox courtesy of Andy Penman and

John Greig. Cologne of West Germany provided the second-round opposition and Rangers squeezed through after winning 3-0 in Glasgow with two for Ferguson and one from Willie Henderson, before losing the away leg 3-1 with Henderson grabbing the vital goal.

Rangers then received a bye to the last eight and in the first leg 80,000 were inside Ibrox to see a goalless draw with Don Revie's Leeds. At Elland Road, however, Rangers lost 2-0 to the eventual tournament winners with Peter Lorimer scoring the second goal.

Alphabetically speaking, Rangers were Scotland's fourth entrant in the 1968/69 competition, and they got the furthest, reaching the semi-finals. Vojvodina were edged out in the first round with Rangers winning 2-0 at Ibrox thanks to John Greig and Sandy Jardine but going down 1-0 in Yugoslavia. In round two, Dundalk were beaten home and away, 6-1 at Ibrox thanks to braces for Willie Henderson and Alex Ferguson plus Greig and an own goal and 3-0 in the Republic of Ireland via Willie Mathieson and two for Colin Stein. The third-round opponents, Dutch side AFC DWS, were also beaten in both legs, 2-0 in the Netherlands via Johnston and Henderson and 2-1 in Glasgow with Dave Smith and Stein scoring.

In the last eight a 4-1 win over Athletic Bilbao at Ibrox was just enough of a cushion to overcome a 2-0 defeat in Spain. Rangers' scorers were Ferguson, Andy Penman, Örjan Persson and Stein. In the home leg of the semi-final against Newcastle United, Penman had his penalty saved, other chances were squandered and the game finished 0-0. In the return at St James' Park, United won 2-0 and crowd trouble added to the pain.

Newcastle United would win the Fairs Cup by defeating Újpesti Dózsa 3-0 at St James' Park and 3-2 in Budapest with Scottish international Bobby Moncur

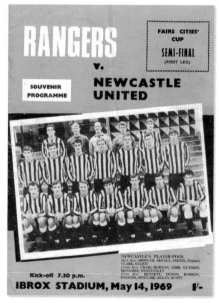

Inter-Cities Fairs Cup /UEFA Cup

getting three goals across the two legs – he only scored three goals in 296 league appearances for the Magpies. Tommy Gibb (ex-Partick Thistle), Jim Scott (ex-Hibernian) and Jackie Sinclair (ex-Dunfermline Athletic) were three other Scots who picked up winners' medals.

In 1970/71 the first round, draw pitted Rangers against Bayern Munich – a reminder that there were seasons when the Bavarian giants did not win their own league or cup competition. In the first leg at the old Grünwalder Stadion a first-half goal from Franz Beckenbauer was all that separated the teams. Back at Ibrox, however, a crowd of almost 83,000 saw Bayern kill the tie ten minutes from time when Gerd Müller scored direct from what Rangers believed was the award of an indirect free kick. Colin Stein got the consolation equaliser not long after. Bayern would lose to Liverpool in the quarter-finals but Rangers' oh so sweet revenge would come the following season in the Cup Winners' Cup. Memorabilia-wise, for the first leg a large single news sheet headed 'Die Neustadion Zeitung' went for £588 on eBay in 2020.

In the early 1980s, Rangers were struggling on all fronts and in their first appearance in the UEFA Cup, in 1982/83, John Greig's team went out in the second round. A West German scalp is always one to be savoured, however, and in round one Rangers eliminated Borussia Dortmund – drawing 0-0 away then winning 2-0 at Ibrox with Davie Cooper and Derek Johnstone scoring. Rangers then defeated another West German outfit in Glasgow – Cologne 2-1, the scorers being Johnstone and John McClelland, who had enjoyed an excellent World Cup finals with Northern Ireland in Spain in 1982. In Cologne, however, it all went horribly wrong as Rangers crashed 5-0. Cologne then lost to Roma in the third round.

Jock Wallace was in charge for the 1984/85 campaign which again ended in the second round. In the first round first leg, Rangers twice took the lead in Dublin against Bohemians through Ally McCoist and Dave McPherson but lost 3-2 on the night. At Ibrox, two goals in the last six minutes saved Rangers' bacon – Craig Paterson and Ian Redford the scorers.

Rangers then lost 3-0 in the San Siro to Inter however; an excellent game of football at Ibrox had seen them win 3-1 via David Mitchell plus two from Iain Ferguson. The home side had 35 minutes to improve on that scoreline but couldn't quite manage it so out they went. Inter went on to reach the semi-finals before losing to eventual winners Real Madrid.

In 1985/86 Rangers, like Marty McFly, were in real need of a Flux Capacitor which would take them back (or forward) in time to when they were able to give a better account of themselves. In September and October Rangers struggled against the little-known CA Osasuna, winning 1-0 at Ibrox through Craig Paterson before losing 2-0 in Spain. Osasuna would lose in the second round to Waregem of Belgium.

In April 1986, Graeme Souness arrived at Ibrox and proceeded to turn things around. 'Great Scot!' as Marty's friend Doc Brown was to say.

Walter Smith's Rangers later reached the 2008 UEFA Cup Final in Manchester where they would lose 2-0 to Zenit Saint Petersburg. Where was Lenin when you needed him?

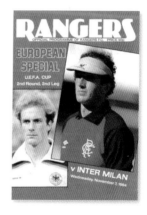

ABERDEEN's only sortie into the Inter-Cities Fairs Cup was in 1968/69 having finished fifth in the league the season previous, when Eddie Turnbull's Dons overcame Slavia Sofia before losing out to Real Zaragoza. In the first round first leg a 0-0 draw was achieved in Bulgaria which was then followed up with a 2-0 win at Pittodrie – Davie Robb and Ian Taylor hitting the net. In round two the Dons recorded a 2-1 victory at home through Jim Forrest and Jimmy Smith but then crashed 3-0 in Spain. In the third round, Zaragoza would lose to eventual winners Newcastle United on the away goals rule.

Inter-Cities Fairs Cup /UEFA Cup

In 1971/72 the Fairs Cup had just been replaced by the UEFA Cup and Jimmy Bonthrone's Aberdeen appeared courtesy of finishing second in the league. A fine start was made with a 2-0 win in Spain against Celta Vigo, Joe Harper plus an own goal doing the damage, then a 1-0 home victory with Harper again finding the net. In the second round the Dons travelled to Turin where George Murray contributed an own goal in a 2-0 defeat to Juventus. At Pittodrie, Pietro Anastasi added to the goal he scored in the first leg before Joe Harper hit a late equaliser. It was 3-1 on aggregate to Juventus who were eliminated in the quarter-finals by Wolverhampton Wanderers with Jim McCalliog contributing one of the goals in a 3-2 aggregate win.

A second successive runners-up spot meant UEFA Cup football in 1972/73 – but for one round only.

The Dons lost 3-2 at home to Borussia Mönchengladbach with Joe Harper and Drew Jarvie scoring and then 6-3 in West Germany with two for Harper plus another one for Jarvie, to crash out 9-5 on aggregate.

Borussia, featuring the super-cool Günter Netzer, would reach the UEFA Cup Final where they would lose to Bill Shankly's Liverpool, who included the also-cool Peter Cormack (ex-Hibs) and Glasgow-born Brian Hall who apparently moved to Merseyside to study for his Maths degree because he was 'a Beatles nut'.

Finishing fourth in the league got the Dons into the 1973/74 UEFA Cup (their third successive appearance) and they got as far as the second round. In the first round Finn Harps were overpowered 4-1 at Pittodrie by Bertie Miller, Arthur Graham and two from Jarvie, and 3-1 in Ballybofey with Davie Robb, Graham and Miller scoring.

Then Tottenham Hotspur visited Aberdeen and went home with a 1-1 draw after Jim Hermiston's penalty equalised for the Dons. In north London Spurs ran out 4-1 winners on the night with Jarvie scoring in the second half while in the first, the referee was persuaded to change his mind on an Aberdeen penalty award with the home side leading 1-0 at the time. Tottenham would go on to reach their second UEFA Cup Final in three seasons but would lose out to Feyenoord with future Celtic manager Wim Jansen picking up another European winners' medal.

The 1977/78 campaign ended at the first-round stage courtesy of a narrow and extremely annoying 2-1 aggregate defeat by RWD Molenbeek. In the first leg, Billy McNeill's team did the difficult bit by managing a 0-0 draw in Belgium. At Pittodrie, however, they trailed 1-0 at half-time before eventually losing 2-1, Jarvie netting what proved to be a consolation goal. In the second round RWD lost out on penalties to Carl Zeiss Jena but on a more positive note, this campaign marked the start of 15 successive seasons in European competitions for the Dons – who, incidentally, had three of their players included within Scotland's squad for the 1978 World Cup finals in Argentina.

In 1979/80, with Alex Ferguson in charge, Aberdeen disappointingly came a cropper at the first-round stage yet again, albeit to Eintracht Frankfurt who went on to win the competition – all four semi-finalists that year were West German clubs. In the first leg at Pittodrie, the match was drawn 1-1 with Harper scoring a second-half equaliser, but the away tie was lost 1-0.

In 1981/82 Aberdeen eventually managed to get beyond the second round of a European competition – at the 11th time of asking. An impressive start was made via the elimination of the holders, Ipswich Town, in the first round. The Dons managed a 1-1 draw down at Portman Road via a John Hewitt equaliser then won 3-1 at Pittodrie thanks to a Gordon Strachan penalty, John Wark equalising from the spot, then two goals from Peter Weir. (Scotland's 1982 World Cup finals squad would include four Aberdeen players plus three from Ipswich Town.)

Inter-Cities Fairs Cup /UEFA Cup

In the second round, Argeş Piteşti were beaten 3-0 in Aberdeen with Strachan, Weir and Hewitt scoring, before a 2-2 draw in Romania, another Strachan penalty plus Hewitt completing a comeback from 2-0 down at half-time. Hamburg SV came to Pittodrie for the third round and were beaten 3-2 with Eric Black, Andy Watson and Hewitt grabbing the Dons goals but crucially Horst Hrubesch got a second for the visitors three minutes from time. In West Germany, Aberdeen went down 3-1 with Mark McGhee on target to go out 5-4 on aggregate. Hamburg went on to reach the final where they lost to IFK Gothenburg.

———————

GREENOCK MORTON's only European sortie to date was the 1968/69 Fairs Cup when they got as far as London and a first-round tie with Chelsea. A visit to Chelsea in the swinging 1960s was surely a good trip and on the day of that first round first leg, 18 September, the UK singles charts included acts such as The Beatles with 'Hey Jude', Amen Corner with 'High in the Sky' and Mama Cass with 'Dream a Little Dream of Me'.

Hal Stewart's Morton had finished their 1967/68 league campaign in sixth place, as had Dave Sexton's Chelsea, but Scottish clubs had been afforded four places in the enlarged 1968/69 Fairs Cup and Scottish Cup winners Dunfermline Athletic – who had finished fourth – were in the Cup Winners' Cup. Morton attacked at Stamford Bridge but Chelsea won 5-0 with Scotland international Charlie Cooke grabbing one of the goals.

In the second leg at Cappielow, Morton performed much better but lost 4-3 on the night, to go out 9-3 on aggregate. In front of a crowd of around 8,000, goals from Danish international Børge Thorup, Joe Mason and Tony Taylor put the home side, featuring a young Joe Harper and a tough Stan Rankin, 3-1 in front before the Blues – with the likes of Peter 'The Cat' Bonetti, Ron 'Chopper' Harris and Bobby Tambling – staged a comeback. Chelsea would be eliminated in the second round by AFC DWS of Amsterdam on the toss of a coin.

ST JOHNSTONE became the 12th club to represent Scotland in Europe when Willie Ormond's outfit made their debut in the inaugural 1971/72 UEFA Cup competition – qualification having been achieved via finishing third. In the first round the Saints travelled to West Germany to face Hamburg SV, with seasoned internationals Willi Schulz and Uwe Seeler still in their ranks. The home side managed a narrow 2-1 win with 18-year-old Jim Pearson netting for St Johnstone. In the return leg, at the now much missed Muirton Park, the Perth side did Scotland proud with an emphatic 3-0 victory – Henry Hall, Pearson and Gordon Whitelaw the scorers.

In the second round first leg, Vasas of Budapest visited Muirton and were beaten 2-0 – a John Connolly penalty plus Pearson again. Over in Hungary the Saints went down 1-0 but progressed to the third round 2-1 on aggregate. In late November, Željezničar Sarajevo came a calling and were defeated 1-0 thanks to a John Connolly goal but it would not be enough, for in the return leg the Saints crashed to a 5-1 defeat. The Yugoslav side were 2-0 up after only four minutes before wing-half Benny Rooney netted to make it 2-1 and put the Saints in front on the away goals rule. Sadly it wasn't to be but at the end of this great European adventure, the main thing was that ultimately the Scottish party all got home safely – the wintry conditions had resulted in a hairy return journey with the wings of the aircraft icing up and forcing the pilot to make an emergency landing shortly after take-off. St Johnstone would not return to European competition until 1999/2000 by which time the club had relocated to McDiarmid Park.

For their part, Željezničar went out on penalties to Ferencváros in the quarter-finals.

ST MIRREN made their European debut in the 1980/81 UEFA Cup thanks to finishing third in the Premier Division, so they passed on the opportunity to defend the Anglo-Scottish Cup won in 1979/80 – I don't see why they couldn't have been allowed a go

Inter-Cities Fairs Cup /UEFA Cup

at both competitions. Anyway, an excellent start was made when goals from Doug Somner and Billy Abercromby gave Jim Clunie's Saints a 2-1 win over Elfsborg in Sweden. Back in Scotland the home side failed to find the net but at the other end, Scotland international goalkeeper Billy Thomson kept a clean sheet. At home in the second round first leg against the mighty Saint-Étienne (whose squad included six players who would make the France 1982 World Cup squad), Thomson once again kept the opponents out but unfortunately once again Peter Weir, Frank McDougall and friends couldn't find a way through at the other end. In France, Michel Platini, Johnny Rep and co. won the 'Battle of the Saints' 2-0. Saint-Étienne would lose to eventual winners Ipswich Town in the quarter-finals.

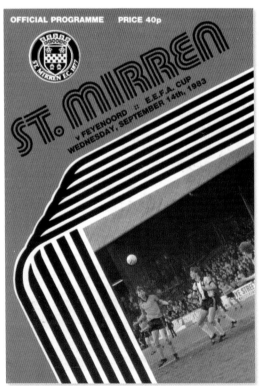

The Paisley club were back in the UEFA Cup in 1983/84 with Ricky McFarlane as manager but came unstuck in the first round against former European Cup and UEFA Cup winners, Feyenoord, who had none other than Johan Cruyff within their ranks. A 1-0 defeat was suffered at Love Street with a young Ruud Gullit finding the net, which was followed by a 2-0 reverse in the Netherlands. Feyenoord would be eliminated in the second round by eventual winners Tottenham Hotspur.

A third UEFA Cup campaign beckoned in 1985/86 for Alex Miller's St Mirren, which included the likes of Campbell Money, Tony Fitzpatrick and Frank McGarvey – the last of the 'New Romantics' if you will. In the first round an away trip to Prague ended in a 1-0 defeat to Slavia – St Mirren's sixth successive European match in which they had failed to score. At Love

Street, however, two goals from McGarvey and another from Brian Gallagher ensured an impressive 3-0 victory and progression to the second round – and a Scotlandesque finale. The first leg, away to Hammarby of Sweden, went well – a 3-3 draw was achieved with Gallagher hitting a hat-trick. In Paisley, things looked good too when McGarvey scored to put the Saints ahead 4-3 on aggregate but the last five minutes were a complete horror show. Hammarby equalised but their increasingly nervous-looking hosts still led on the away goals rule. Hammarby scored again, but the goal was disallowed. Cue the theme tune from *The Great Escape*, but in mid-whistle Hammarby scored once more and this time it counted. Defeat from the jaws of victory, disaster for Scotland; sometimes you just have to laugh. Hammarby stopped laughing in the next round, however, when they lost to Cologne.

————————

In the not too distant future the political map of Europe would be redrawn. Germany would reunify while the Soviet Union, Yugoslavia and Czechoslovakia would all fragment to give us new nations such as Russia, Ukraine, Georgia, Croatia, Serbia and Slovenia. International recognition would also mean new entrants from San Marino, Liechtenstein and Gibraltar to name but a few.

Competition-wise, the UEFA Cup would be rebranded as the Europa League in 2010, following the European Cup becoming the Champions League in 1993, with qualifying matches for both commencing as early as June. As such, for most Scottish clubs nowadays, remaining in European competition beyond Christmas is a significant but all too rare achievement.

Part
three
Other Competition Winners

Coronation Cup

Year	Winners	Runners-up	Score	Attendance
1953	Celtic	Hibernian	2-0	117,000

Other participants: Aberdeen, Rangers, Arsenal, Manchester Utd, Newcastle Utd, Spurs

Texaco Cup

Year	Winners	Runners-up	Score
1970/71	Wolves	Hearts	3-2 (agg)

Other participants: Airdrie, Dundee, Dunfermline, Hearts, Morton, Motherwell

1971/72	Derby County	Airdrie	2-1 (agg)

Other participants: Airdrie, Dundee Utd, Hearts, Falkirk, Morton, Motherwell

1972/73	Ipswich Town	Norwich City	4-2 (agg)

Other participants: Ayr Utd, Dundee, Dundee Utd, Hearts, Kilmarnock, Motherwell, St. Johnstone

1973/74	Newcastle Utd	Burnley	2-1 (agg)

Other participants: Ayr Utd, Dundee Utd, East Fife, Hearts, Morton, Motherwell, St. Johnstone

1974/75	Newcastle Utd	Southampton	3-1 (agg)

Other participants: Aberdeen, Ayr Utd, Hearts, Rangers

Anglo-Scottish Cup

Year	Winners	Runners-up	Score
1975/76	Middlesbrough	Fulham	1-0

Scottish participants: Aberdeen, Ayr Utd, Dundee, Falkirk, Hearts, Motherwell, Queen of the South, St. Johnstone

1976/77	Nottingham Forest	Orient	5-1

Scottish participants: Aberdeen, Ayr Utd, Clydebank, Dundee Utd, Kilmarnock, Motherwell, Partick Thistle, Raith Rovers

1977/78	Bristol City	St. Mirren	3-2

Scottish participants: Alloa Athletic, Ayr Utd, Clydebank, Hibernian, Motherwell, Partick Thistle, Stirling Albion, St. Mirren

1978/79	Burnley	Oldham Athletic	4-2

Scottish participants: Celtic, Clyde, Hearts, Moreton, Motherwell, Partick Thistle, Raith Rovers, St. Mirren

1979/80	St. Mirren	Bristol City	5-1

Scottish participants: Berwick Rangers, Dundee, Dunfermline Athletic, Hibernian, Kilmarnock, Morton, Partick Thistle, St. Mirren

1980/81	Chesterfield	Notts County	2-1

Scottish participants: Airdrie, East Stirling, Falkirk, Hearts, Kilmarnock, Morton, Partick Thistle, Rangers

Summer Cup

Year	Winners	Runners-up	Score
1963/64	Hibernian	Aberdeen	3-1 (replay after 4-4 agg)
1964/65	Motherwell	Dundee Utd	3-2 (agg)

Drybrough Cup

Year	Winners	Runners-up	Score	Attendance
1971/72	Aberdeen	Celtic	2-1	25,000

Other participants: Airdrie, Arbroath, Dumbarton, East Fife,
Partick Thistle, St. Johnstone

1972/73	Hibernian	Celtic	5-3 (aet)	49,462

Other participants: Aberdeen, Dumbarton, Montrose, Rangers,
St. Mirren, Stirling Albion

1973/74	Hibernian	Celtic	1-0 (aet)	49,204

Other participants: Dundee, Dunfermline, Montrose, Raith Rovers,
Rangers, St. Mirren

1974/75	Celtic	Rangers	2-2 (4-2 pens)	57,558

Other participants: Airdrie, Dundee, Hibernian, Kilmarnock,
Queen of the South, Stirling Albion

1979/80	Rangers	Celtic	3-1	40,609

Other participants: Aberdeen, Berwick Rangers, Clydebank,
Dundee Utd, Dunfermline, Kilmarnock

1980/81	Aberdeen	St. Mirren	2-1	6,994

Other participants: Airdrie, Albion Rovers, Ayr Utd, Celtic, Falkirk, Morton

Coronation Cup

This was a one-off, invitation-only knock-out tournament held in Glasgow in May 1953 to celebrate the forthcoming Coronation of Queen Elizabeth II at Westminster Abbey, London on 2 June (Her Majesty is actually Queen Elizabeth the *First* of Scotland as Elizabeth I had only reigned in England before the Union of the Crowns in 1603).

The competition involved four English and four Scottish clubs so technically it was an Anglo-Scottish Cup – it might have been a nice gesture to have included the likes of Cardiff City and Linfield or to have extended an invite to clubs from the Commonwealth, or perhaps that's being a wee bit too pedantic.

The teams invited were Aberdeen (1952/53 Scottish Cup runners-up), Celtic (1938 Empire Exhibition Trophy winners), Hibernian (1951/52 champions and

1952/53 runners-up), Rangers (1952/53 Scottish league and cup winners), Arsenal (1952/53 English champions), Manchester United (1951/52 English champions), Newcastle United (1951/52 and 1952/53 FA Cup winners), and Tottenham Hotspur (1951/52 English runners-up).

So there was no place for Motherwell (1952 Scottish Cup winners), Dundee (1951/52 and 1952/53 Scottish League Cup winners) or Preston North End (1952/53 English runners-up on goal average).

The tournament kicked off on Monday, 11 May with Celtic overcoming Arsenal 1-0 at Hampden in front of 59,000 and Bobby Collins hitting the winner. On the same day, over at Ibrox, Hibs and a Spurs side including future managerial greats Alf Ramsey and Bill Nicholson fought out a 1-1 draw. In a replay at Ibrox the following day, Hibernian triumphed 2-1 with both goals scored by Lawrie Reilly, the winner coming in the last minute of extra time. In the other two quarter-finals, Matt Busby's Manchester United defeated Bill Struth's Rangers 2-1 at Hampden Park while Newcastle United overwhelmed Aberdeen 4-0 at Ibrox.

On 16 May, goals from Neil Mochan and Bertie Peacock helped Celtic to a 2-1 victory over Manchester United at Hampden with 73,000 in attendance, and on the same day at Ibrox, Hibernian dished out a 4-0 masterclass to a Newcastle United side that featured future Lisbon Lion Ronnie Simpson and Geordie legend Jackie Milburn to set up an all-Scottish final. An incredible 117,060 turned up at Hampden on Wednesday, 20 May and saw Celtic win the trophy for keeps by defeating Hibs 2-0, Neil Mochan and Jimmy Walsh the scorers. The trophy was collected by the Celtic skipper Jock Stein, who like the aforementioned Ramsey and Nicholson went on to have a rather impressive managerial career himself.

Jimmy McGrory's Celtic were, debatably, the best of British and the following season the Parkhead club would win the league and cup double to be, undoubtedly, the best of Scottish.

Texaco Cup

The Texaco Cup took its name from its sponsor, the American petroleum company Texaco, and ran for five seasons – 1970/71 to 1974/75. Participants were clubs who had not qualified for European competitions and for the first two seasons consisted of sides from Scotland, England, Northern Ireland and the Republic of Ireland; thereafter it was a Scotland/England affair – which still offered up the opportunity to take on, and occasionally beat, some top English clubs in a competitive environment.

For the first four seasons it was a straightforward knock-out competition involving 16 clubs with ties being two-legged. In 1974/75 16 English clubs played in four groups of four with the group winners joining four Scottish teams in the quarter-finals. When

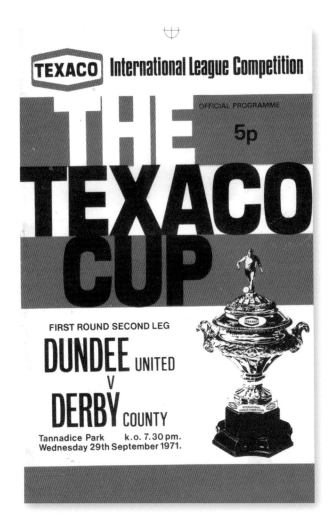

Texaco withdrew its sponsorship, the tournament was succeeded by the Anglo-Scottish Cup.

A total of 14 clubs represented Scotland across the seasons with Hearts appearing in all five tournaments.

In 1970/71 the first round saw six Scottish clubs pitted against six from England while the four Irish clubs faced one another. Four Scottish clubs progressed to the last eight – Airdrie, Hearts, Morton and Motherwell at the expense of Nottingham Forest, Burnley, West Bromwich Albion and Stoke City respectively – while Dundee and Dunfermline Athletic lost out to Wolverhampton Wanderers and Tottenham Hotspur. As an aside, the following season saw Wolves beaten by Spurs in the first UEFA Cup Final.

In the quarter-finals Hearts defeated Airdrie 7-3 on aggregate while Motherwell claimed the scalp of Spurs by beating them 5-4. Wolves prevented three out of three, however, by winning 3-0 at Cappielow, although Morton did themselves proud with a 2-1 victory at Molineux. In the last four, Derry City lost to Wolves and in the all-Scottish semi-final Hearts edged Motherwell 3-2 on aggregate.

Tynecastle hosted the first leg of the final on 14 April 1971 – 'Tiny' Wharton was the referee – and a crowd of 26,000 saw Donald Ford give Hearts the lead after only seven minutes, but Wolves came storming back with three goals – including two from Glaswegian Hugh Curran. In the second leg, George Fleming scored for the Jambos after 25 minutes but the Edinburgh side couldn't get that crucial second goal so Wolves won 3-2 on aggregate to become the competition's first winners.

The 1971/72 competition had to rely on Ian McMillan's Airdrie, who defeated Manchester City 4-2 on aggregate, for preventing Scottish clubs from being on the receiving end of a 6-0 first-round whitewash at the hands of their English opponents. Falkirk lost to Coventry City, Dundee United to Derby County, Hearts to Newcastle United, Morton to Huddersfield Town, and Motherwell to Stoke City.

In the quarter-finals Airdrie did the business again with an impressive 7-2 aggregate win over Huddersfield Town, winning 2-1 in Yorkshire and 5-1 at Broomfield. In the semis it was across the water to Northern Ireland for the Diamonds and another comfortable victory, 3-0 against Ballymena, before winning 4-3 back in Airdrie.

The first leg of the final took place at Broomfield on 26 January 1972 where 16,000 witnessed a goalless draw, with Archie Gemmill prominent for the visitors from Derby. The return match at the Baseball Ground, which was not noted for its immaculate playing surface, didn't take place until 26 April as torrential rain caused a late postponement on 8 March. The Rams, minus Gemmill and John O'Hare who were on international duty against Peru, won 2-1 in front of 25,102. Derby took the lead in the 40th minute when Alan Hinton converted a penalty after Kevin Hector had been pulled down by goalkeeper Roddy McKenzie. Derby's own stopper, Colin Boulton, then went unpunished by referee Jack Taylor after punching Airdrie's Drew Jarvie while in the penalty box. Roger Davies headed the second goal in the 50th minute with Airdrie skipper Derek Whiteford netting for the visitors 13 minutes from time. So the cup went to Brian Clough's Derby who would finish the season as English champions. Airdrie, incidentally, would finish in 15th place in the old Scottish First Division and narrowly avoided relegation.

Irish sides then withdrew for political reasons so in 1972/73 the first round comprised nine English sides and seven from Scotland – only two of whom made it to the last eight. Motherwell disposed of Coventry City 4-3 on aggregate while Hearts beat Crystal Palace 1-0 home and away. Ayr United, Dundee, Dundee United, Kilmarnock and St Johnstone were slain by Newcastle United, Norwich City, Leicester City, Wolves and Ipswich Town respectively.

The quarter-final draw pitted the two Scots clubs against one another and the first leg at Tynecastle finished goalless. At Fir Park there were six goals – Hearts got the first two and then had Ian Sneddon sent off, followed by four goals for Motherwell. In the semi-finals Motherwell couldn't get past Norwich, however, losing 2-0 at Carrow Road before defeating the Canaries 3-2 at Fir Park with Jim McCabe grabbing a hat-trick and almost making it four near the end.

The final was an East Anglian derby in which Bobby Robson's Ipswich triumphed 4-2 on aggregate. A young George Burley was a Portman Road apprentice at the time.

The starting line-up for 1973/74 was again 9-7 in favour of the English teams but this time three Scottish clubs made it through to the last eight. Dundee United drew 0-0 at Bramall Lane against Sheffield United and won 2-0 at Tannadice; Hearts beat Everton 1-0 at Goodison Park before drawing 0-0 at Tynecastle; and Motherwell who, like the season previous, eliminated Coventry, winning 1-0

TEXACO
International
League
Competition

The
TEXACO
Cup

SECOND ROUND
FIRST LEG

NORWICH C.
v
MOTHERWELL

Tuesday October 23rd.
Kick Off 7:30pm.

Official Programme 7p.

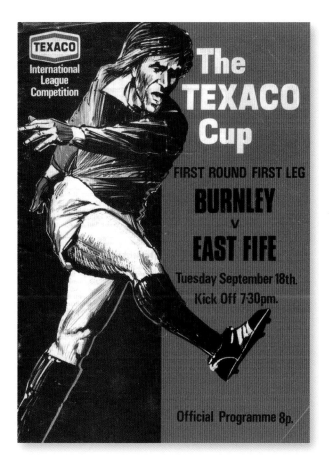

at Highfield Road and 3-2 at Fir Park. The fallen were Ayr, East Fife, Morton and St Johnstone who were seen off by Leicester, Burnley, Newcastle and Norwich respectively.

Burnley now smelled Caledonian blood and in the quarter-finals Hearts were ripped asunder, 8-0 on aggregate – on the back of them beating East Fife 10-2 across the two legs of the previous round. Motherwell were also beaten 3-0 by Norwich. On the plus side, Dundee United overcame Leicester 2-1 on aggregate. In the semi-final first leg, United beat their Newcastle namesakes 2-0 at Tannadice with Frank Kopel and Archie Knox the scorers and things looked good. At St James' Park, however, the Tangerine dream ended with a 4-1 reverse, after extra time – Andy Gray netting the visitors' goal. In a one-game final at St James' Park a crowd of just under 35,000 saw the Magpies win 2-1 after extra

time, the goals coming from Malcolm Macdonald and Scotland's Bobby Moncur. That success may have helped soothe some of the pain of local rivals Sunderland lifting the FA Cup 12 months previous and Newcastle failing to emulate that feat, against Liverpool at Wembley, just ten days after their Texaco triumph.

The 1974/75 season saw the format of the competition change to the extent that the English Football League had 16 participants with four Scottish entrants coming in at the quarter-final stage. Jock Wallace's Rangers entered the fray and hopes of breaking the English stranglehold were high with Aberdeen, Hearts and Ayr United completing the 'Tartan Fab Four'.

Life, of course, is full of disappointments and the 1974/75 Texaco Cup was a big one. I was at Ibrox the evening Lawrie McMenemy's recently relegated Southampton came to town and won 3-1 with two of the goals being provided by Peter Osgood – Colin 'Bomber' Jackson scored for Rangers. At least my English 'anti-hero' Mick Channon didn't score. Down at The Dell, a stadium I regret never visiting, Southampton won 2-0 and went through 5-1 on aggregate. Ayr fared slightly better with a 3-0 aggregate deficit against Birmingham City and Hearts kept it to 2-1 against Oldham Athletic. Against the holders Newcastle, Aberdeen drew 1-1 at Pittodrie with Willie Young opening the scoring and Macdonald equalising before losing 3-2 at St James' Park despite leading twice, with Supermac hitting a double for the Magpies.

Newcastle would retain the cup by defeating Southampton in the final, 3-1 on aggregate. The Texaco Cup still remains Newcastle United's most recent trophy success, excluding second-tier league championships.

In conclusion, what else can I say about the Texaco Cup era other than that it began against the backdrop of the break-up of The Beatles, continued throughout the Glam-Rock years and ended with the Bay City Rollers in their pomp. You could say that tartan 'triumphed' in the end so to speak.

Anglo-Scottish Cup

This was a reincarnation of the Texaco Cup but for
the English and Scottish leagues only. There were
six such tournaments, running from 1975/76 until
1980/81, by which time the English participants
were largely from the lower leagues. Public interest
waned and the Scottish clubs withdrew but not
before we endured some embarrassing defeats.
Thank goodness for St Mirren who reached two
finals, winning the second one – actually, they
romped the second one. Overall, a total of 25
Scottish league sides took part, including, ironically,
Berwick Rangers. English teams taking part
included Chelsea (three times), Manchester City and

Newcastle United while Brian Clough's Nottingham Forest would win this tournament as a precursor to success in England and Europe. Partick Thistle had the most appearances with five.

The format involved 16 English clubs competing in four mini-leagues of four, with the four winners progressing to the quarter-finals. Bonus points were awarded to teams scoring three or more goals in a single match. Meanwhile, eight Scottish clubs played a two-legged knock-out round with the aggregate winners of each tie also progressing to the quarter-finals. The overall competition then progressed on a two-legged knock-out basis, including the final, with Scottish clubs being drawn against their English counterparts at the last-eight stage.

———————

In the Scottish half of the draw for 1975/76, Aberdeen overcame St Johnstone 2-0, Ayr United beat Falkirk 4-3, Hearts beat Queen of the South 6-3 and Motherwell defeated Dundee 2-1. In the quarter-finals there was just the one solitary success for Scotland, though, when Motherwell bested Blackburn Rovers 2-1. Ayr lost 2-0 to Mansfield Town, Fulham edged Hearts 5-4 and Aberdeen crashed out 7-2 to Middlesbrough. 'Oh dear, oh dear!' as the legendary BBC Radio Scotland commentator David Francey was wont to say.

In the semi-finals, Motherwell did the difficult bit by gaining a 1-1 draw against Fulham in the first leg at Craven Cottage – a Willie Pettigrew equaliser inspiring the *Glasgow Evening Times* headline of 'Motherwell are all set for the final'. You know what's coming – in the return at Fir Park the Steelmen lost 3-2 to go out 4-3 on aggregate. 'Well are hit by the Shakes' said the *Evening Times* on 5 November. In the final, Middlesbrough would lift the trophy by winning 1-0 on aggregate with ex-Celt and Lisbon Lion Bobby Murdoch getting his hands on yet another winners' medal. A young Graeme Souness was waiting in the wings.

The 1976/77 'Eightsome Reel' went like this – Ayr United defeated Clydebank 1-0 on aggregate, Aberdeen edged past Dundee United 3-2, Kilmarnock thumped Motherwell 5-1 and Partick Thistle bested Raith Rovers 5-2. In the quarter-finals it was Scotland 2 England 2 as Partick beat Bolton Wanderers 1-0 (Alan Hansen scored it) and Ayr were awarded a semi-final place after Newcastle were disqualified for fielding a weakened team in the first leg – which the Honest Men won 3-0. Ironically, in the match programme I recognised nine of the 11 Magpie names listed – which included Glasgow-born Tommy Craig. Of the Ayr group, goalkeeper Hugh Sproat and defender Joe Filippi were the most familiar. As for the two Scottish reverses, Aberdeen lost 1-0 home and away to Orient while Kilmarnock went out 4-3 to Nottingham Forest.

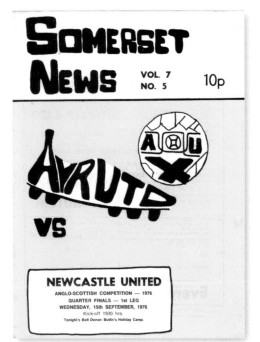

In the last four there was no Scottish joy as Orient overcame Partick Thistle 4-2 with Laurie Cunningham grabbing one of the Orient goals and Forest overpowered Ayr 4-1. Forest would win the cup in December 1976 by defeating Orient 5-1 on aggregate with winners' medals going to the three Scottish Johns – McGovern, O'Hare and Robertson. Come May, Forest would also win promotion to the First Division.

––––––––––

At the end of 1977/78 Scotland travelled to the World Cup finals in Argentina while England stayed at home – like it was in 1974. Perhaps that was the inspiration for a third consecutive English triumph in the Anglo-Scottish Cup.

Let's start with the basics, however – Hibernian out-thought Ayr United 4-3, Partick Thistle cruised past Clydebank 4-1, St Mirren sorted Stirling Albion 7-1 while Motherwell gave Alloa Athletic a damn

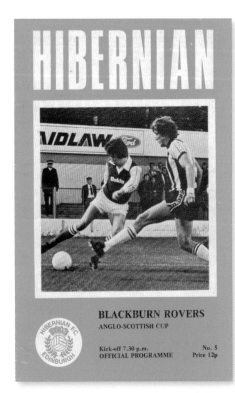

good seeing to with an 11-1 aggregate triumph.

In the last eight St Mirren defeated Fulham 6-4 and Hibernian, with a squad including Erich Schaedler, Ally Brazil, John Blackley and Tony Higgins, beat Blackburn home and away to win 3-1 on aggregate. Bertie Auld's Partick somehow contrived to throw away a 2-0 first-leg lead against Norman Hunter's Bristol City to lose 3-2 on aggregate while Notts County edged Motherwell 2-1.

In the semis, Alex Ferguson's St Mirren made it to the final by beating Notts County 2-0 at Love Street to win 2-1 on aggregate, but Bristol City, then a top-flight club, eliminated Hibernian 6-4. In the final, the Paisley Saints slipped up at home in the first leg, conceding a goal in the first minute and then going 2-0 behind after 73 minutes thanks to a goal from former Scotland international Peter Cormack. Billy Abercromby pulled one back for the home side three minutes from time. At Ashton Gate, Bobby Reid put St Mirren in front after 68 minutes, but the Robins equalised only four minutes later and 1-1 it finished, 3-2 on aggregate to City and the trophy remained in England.

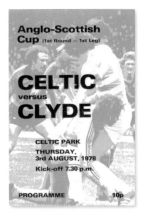

In 1978/79 the former champions of Europe, Celtic, with Billy McNeill having replaced Jock Stein as manager, won the East End derby against Clyde 8-2 on aggregate. West of Scotland clubs made it a clean sweep early on when Partick Thistle defeated Hearts 3-1, Morton beat Raith Rovers 6-2 and St Mirren ousted Motherwell 3-1.

In the last eight St Mirren got some revenge by eliminating holders Bristol City 3-2 while Renfrewshire friends Morton blew a 3-0 first-leg lead to lose 4-3 against Oldham Athletic. Partick

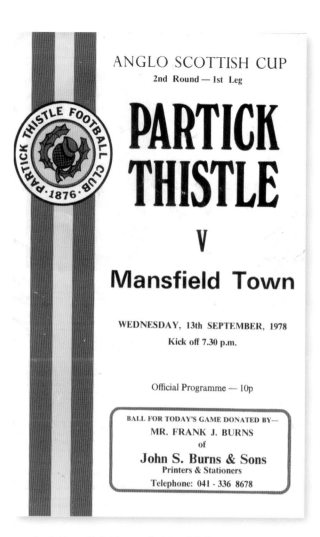

against Mansfield Town finished 3-3 on aggregate but the Nottinghamshire club won 3-1 on penalties. Celtic kind of let the side down on and off the pitch – losing away then at home to Second Division Burnley to go out 3-1 on aggregate. At Parkhead the Celtic team included Danny McGrain making his competitive comeback after being out for a year through injury, plus Alfie Conn and veteran Bobby Lennox, while the Welsh Wizard Leighton James starred for the visitors.

The Oldham Athletic against St Mirren semi would produce two 1-1 draws with Billy Stark getting both of the Saints' goals, before the Latics progressed to the final 4-2 on penalties. Celtic's Lancashire conquerors Burnley would lift the cup with Glasgow-born defender Jim Thomson collecting a winners' medal.

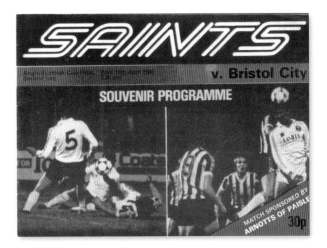

The 1979/80 competition was club football's equivalent of Mexico 1970 with St Mirren replacing Brazil as the near-perfect exponents of the Beautiful Game. Okay, so I may have stretched it a wee bit there but a Scottish success story is one to be cherished.

The Pride of Paisley began with a 3-3 home draw with Hibernian before winning 1-0 at Easter Road while the Greenock Galacticos overwhelmed Berwick Rangers 8-1 on aggregate (I've half a mind to count that as a victory over an English club). Partick Thistle beat Dunfermline 2-1 while Dundee needed penalties to overcome Kilmarnock after it had finished 4-4 on aggregate.

In the quarters, Dundee lost home and away to Sheffield United and were beaten 3-1 on aggregate, and Bristol City managed a 1-1 draw at Fortress Firhill before winning 2-0 at Ashton Gate. Morton beat Preston North End home and away to go through 5-1 on aggregate while the 1959 Scottish Cup winners St Mirren defeated the 1958 FA Cup winners Bolton Wanderers 5-4.

St Mirren then avenged Dundee's elimination by beating the Blades 4-0 on aggregate, but Morton narrowly failed to make it a dream 'Renfrewshire Classico' final when they drew 2-2 away to Bristol City before slipping up 1-0 at Cappielow.

In the final, old adversaries Bristol City – with Paisley's Prodigal Son Tony Fitzpatrick now in their ranks – were smited 2-0 at Ashton Gate with Billy 'Jairzinho' Stark getting both the goals and 3-1 at Love Street thanks to a double from Doug 'Pelé' Somner and one for Alan 'Rivellino' Logan. And so it came to pass that Jimmy 'Carlos Alberto' Bone lifted the Anglo-Scottish Cup in triumph – and God was pleased.

————

In 1980/81, holders St Mirren went off to Europe but the Scottish representation was bolstered by the inclusion of Rangers – at least, that was the theory. The town of Falkirk had two representatives, although both lost out early with the Brockville Bairns going out 7-3 on aggregate to Greenock Morton, and East Stirlingshire losing 6-1 to Kilmarnock. Diamonds trumped Hearts 6-3 while in the 'Govan-Partick Subway Classico' the Gers beat the Jags 5-4.

In the quarter-finals, only Kilmarnock did Scotland proud when after losing the first leg at Bloomfield Road 2-1 they powered to a 4-2 victory over Blackpool at Rugby Park, aided by an Archie Gemmill-style goal from Gordon Cramond. Meanwhile, Airdrie lost 4-2 at home and 1-0 away to Fourth Division Bury and Morton drew 1-1 at home with Notts County after losing 2-0 at Meadow Lane.

John Greig's Rangers should have swept past Third Division Chesterfield, conquerors of Grimsby Town, Hull City and Sheffield United, but could only draw 1-1 with the Derbyshire club at Ibrox with a Gordon Dalziel equaliser before crashing 3-0 at Saltergate – two goals from former Ibrox man Phil Bonnyman while Rangers' Colin McAdam morphed into Don Masson and missed a penalty. Was lack of motivation a problem or excuse for Rangers? Four days later they managed to beat Celtic 3-0 in a league match. Whatever the reason, the Chesterfield result doesn't sit too well with the title of this book.

In the semis the black and white stripes of Notts County beat the blue and white stripes of Kilmarnock both home and away for a 7-3 aggregate, but in the final it was the Spireites of Chesterfield who lifted the trophy – quite possibly as a result of gaining super-human powers following their earlier victory over the mighty Glasgow Rangers.

Chesterfield may no longer be in England's Football League but they still retain (and display) the Anglo-Scottish Cup trophy. Everyone loves a 'giantkiller' – I just wish their CV didn't include one of *our* giants.

Summer Cup

The origins of the Summer Cup are in a wartime competition which was open to teams in the top flight of the interim Scottish Southern League. It ran from 1940 to 1944 with the winners being Hibernian, Rangers, St Mirren, Motherwell and then Partick Thistle.

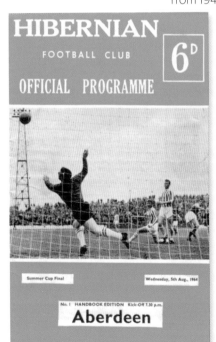

The competition was reintroduced for two summers in the early 1960s with the intention of assisting Division One clubs with their escalating running costs, but both Celtic and Rangers declined to take part. The format was four groups of four playing each other home and away with only the group winners progressing to the semi-finals stage, with the semis and the final being played on a home and away/ aggregate score basis.

In the 1964 competition Partick Thistle topped a group which included Morton, St Mirren and Third Lanark to progress to the semi-finals, while Aberdeen finished ahead of Dundee, Dundee United and St Johnstone in their mini-league.

In the semi-finals Thistle defeated Aberdeen 1-0 in the first leg at Firhill on 23 May, but by the time of the second leg four days later typhoid had taken a firm grip in the Granite City and after much deliberation the decision was taken for the Jags to travel to Aberdeen as late as possible and then depart straight after the final whistle. Thistle 'got out of Dodge' on the back of a 3-1 defeat but with a 3-2 aggregate result in their favour. Apparently it took a high-profile visit to the city by the Queen in July 1964 to help restore confidence that Aberdeen was safe once more.

Jock Stein's Hibernian headed their group, which featured Hearts, Dunfermline Athletic and Falkirk, before overcoming Kilmarnock 6-4 on aggregate in the semi-finals. Earlier, Kilmarnock had topped Airdrie, Motherwell and Queen of the South. The delayed final commenced in August and required three matches to settle things with 20,000 seeing Aberdeen win 3-2 at Pittodrie and 28,000 witnessing a 2-1 victory for the Hibees at Easter Road. The third match was played at Pittodrie on 2 September 1964, two days before the Forth Road Bridge was officially opened to the public, and Hibs won 3-1. Willie Hamilton, Jim Scott and Peter Cormack scored for the Edinburgh club while the Aberdeen goal came from Ernie Winchester.

In May 1965 the four group winners were Dundee United (ahead of Aberdeen, Dundee and St Johnstone), Hibernian (beating Dunfermline, Falkirk and Hearts), Motherwell (in front of Airdrie, Kilmarnock and Third Lanark) and Partick Thistle (coming out on top against Clyde, Morton and St Mirren). In the semi-finals, Dundee United defeated Partick Thistle 3-0 on aggregate while Motherwell beat Hibernian 6-4. Hibs had won the first leg 2-0 at Easter Road but crashed 6-2 in the return match.

In the final, Motherwell triumphed 3-2 on aggregate against Dundee United. At Fir Park it was 3-1 for the Steelmen with Joe McBride plus a Pat Delaney double scoring and Finn Døssing replying for United. At Tannadice, the home side again came out on top but only by a solitary goal scored by another Danish delight named Mogens Berg. So the cup went to Lanarkshire while in the background there was 'Ticket to Ride' (The Beatles), 'King of the Road' (Roger Miller) and 'Subterranean Homesick Blues' (Bob Dylan).

Apparently the Scottish Football League were keen to continue with the competition but when only 11 clubs confirmed their interest in participating in a 1966 tournament they said something along the lines of 'bugger this for a game of soldiers', although it might not be minuted in those words. That was a pity because the world could have done with a half-decent football tournament in the summer of 1966. In May and June the following year, Aberdeen, Dundee United and Hibernian did a summer 'moonlight' across the pond to become Washington Whips, Dallas Tornado and Toronto City respectively in a couple of North American soccer leagues, with the Whips winning the Eastern Division.

Anyway, back in the old world, the Summer Cup trophy was 'gifted' to Hibernian and remains on permanent display in Easter Road. Sunshine on Leith, indeed.

Drybrough Cup
This was a short-lived knock-out tournament running for a week during the pre-seasons of 1971 to 1974, and then again in 1979 and 1980. It involved eight teams – the four highest-scoring teams from Divisions One and Two initially – and was the first tournament in Scotland to bear a sponsor's name. Drybrough & Co. was an Edinburgh-based brewery which operated from 1895 to 1987 and whose delicacies included Keg Heavy and India Pale Ale. Over the six competitions that were played, a total of 25 clubs participated with notable absentees being Hearts and Motherwell. Celtic were the only ever-present side.

Jimmy Bonthrone's Aberdeen won the inaugural competition by overcoming East Fife 3-0 and Airdrie 4-1 – both away from home – before defeating Jock Stein's Celtic 2-1 in the final at Pittodrie. Davie 'The Brush' Robb had given the Dons a first-half lead before John 'Yogi' Hughes equalised for Celtic in the 58th minute. Five minutes later, however, Aberdeen were awarded a penalty which was slotted home by Joe 'The Barrel' Harper.

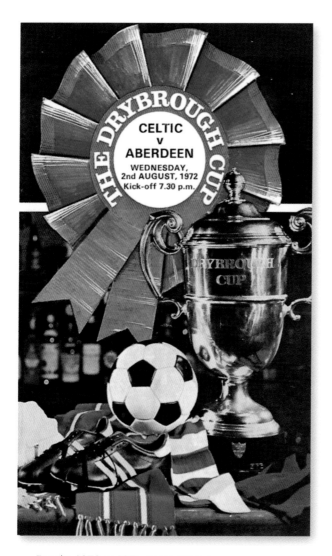

For the 1972 to 1974 competitions an experimental version of the offside rule was trialled whereby it only applied within the final 18 yards with a solid white line being extended across the pitch from the penalty box to the touchlines. It was a tad confusing at times.

In 1972 Eddie Turnbull's Hibernian won a goalfest of a final 5-3 against Celtic – it had been 3-3 after 90 minutes – at Hampden Park, which would host all future Drybrough Cup finals. On their way to the final Hibs had disposed of Montrose 4-0, and Rangers 2-1, both at Easter Road. Hibs' five cup final goals consisted of braces

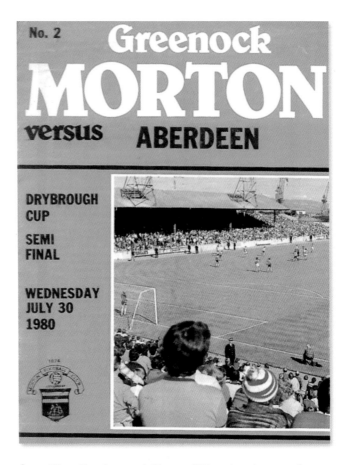

No. 2

Greenock

MORTON

versus ABERDEEN

DRYBROUGH
CUP

SEMI
FINAL

WEDNESDAY
JULY 30
1980

from Alan Gordon and Jimmy O'Rourke plus one from Arthur Duncan. Celtic's Jimmy Johnstone also netted a pair while skipper Billy McNeill scored the other. It was some sort of revenge for the 6-1 doing Hibs received from Celtic in the Scottish Cup Final three months previous.

In 1973, Celtic lost their third successive Drybrough Cup Final when Hibs retained the trophy thanks to a solitary goal from Gordon one minute from the end of extra time. This time Hibs' route to the final was two home victories, both 2-1, over St Mirren and Rangers.

The following year it was fourth time lucky for Stein's Celtic who triumphed 4-2 at Airdrie and 2-1 at Dundee then edged out Rangers 4-2 on penalties after the final had finished 1-1 after 90 minutes and 2-2 after extra time. Twice Celtic had taken the lead, through Steve Murray and Paul Wilson, and twice they had been pegged back via Ally Scott then a Pat McCluskey own goal. Denis Connaghan was the Celtic hero with two saves in the penalty shoot-out while Johnstone netted the decisive spot-kick. It was an excellent game of football, although it nearly didn't go ahead due to the threat of strike action from the players' union in a dispute over the distribution of the TV fee.

The competition then ceased until a mini revival occurred in 1979 when Rangers, with John Greig as manager, became the fourth club to win the tournament with a 3-1 victory over Celtic, who were in their fifth successive final. John MacDonald, Sandy Jardine and Davie Cooper scored for the Ibrox club while Bobby Lennox got the Celts' late consolation. Rangers had defeated Berwick Rangers 1-0 at home and Kilmarnock 2-0 at Rugby Park on their way to the final which is chiefly remembered for Cooper's 'wondergoal' in which he played 'keepy-uppy' with the ball, lifting it over several Celtic defenders before smashing it past Peter Latchford. Indeed, it was just like watching Brazil.

And so to the final final, in 1980, where a disappointingly small crowd of under 10,000 saw Alex Ferguson's Aberdeen defeat his former club St Mirren 2-1. Their earlier victories had been 4-1 at home to Airdrie and 4-2 away to Greenock Morton to help them get to the final. A Dougie Somner penalty in the 68th minute had given the Paisley side the lead but Drew Jarvie equalised six minutes later. Seven minutes from time Steve Cowan hit the winner as well as the last goal in the history of the Drybrough Cup. The tournament (like the sponsor's beers) has long since gone – but they were both a bit tasty while they lasted.

Incidentally, in England from 1970 to 1973, there was a sister competition entitled the Watney Mann Invitation Cup with Scotland's Dave Mackay skippering Derby County to glory in the inaugural final at the Baseball Ground against a Manchester United side which included Denis Law.

Greatest Rangers Team

Davie Cooper
Appearances: 540 Goals: 75

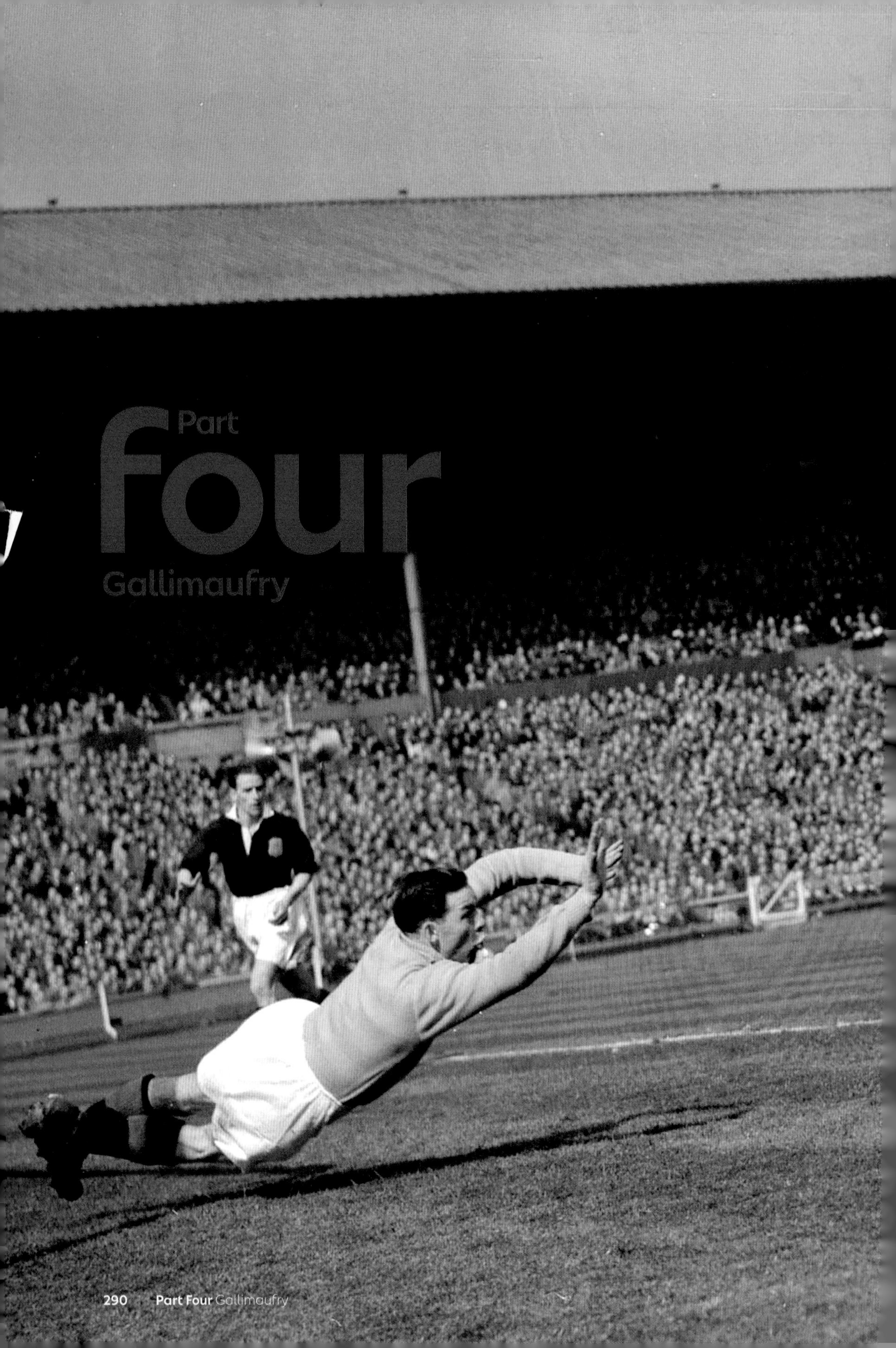

Part four

Gallimaufry

British Champions

Back in the day, the annual British Home Championship really mattered. Being the best of British and sticking it to England were important sporting achievements in the mindset of the Scottish football supporter. By comparison, the World Cup and European Championships were mere sideshows.

The oldest international football tournament commenced in 1883/84 and would come to an end exactly 100 years later. England, Ireland (later Northern Ireland), Scotland and Wales were the 'Victorian Fab Four'. Scotland were British champions on no fewer than 41 occasions, which included 17 shared titles, and there were 11 clean sweeps – or 'triple crowns' if you are so inclined.

After the Second World War, Scotland had to wait until 1948/49 to become outright British champions for the first time since 1935/36. Seeing as back then we didn't bother with competing in lesser tournaments such as the World Cup, 13 years was a long time to wait for this success – not that we have had much success when we *have* taken part in the World Cup.

For the record, the Scotland team that defeated England 3-1 at Wembley in April 1949 to clinch the British Championship with a clean sweep of victories comprised of ten home-based Scots – the line-up being Jimmy Cowan (Morton), George Young (Rangers), Sam Cox (Rangers), Bobby Evans (Celtic), Willie Woodburn (Rangers), George Aitken (East Fife), Willie Waddell (Rangers), Jimmy Mason (Third Lanark), Billy Houliston (Queen of the South), Billy Steel (Derby County) and Lawrie Reilly (Hibernian). The England side put to the sword included the likes of Billy Wright, Stanley Matthews, Stan Mortensen and Tom Finney.

Other outright title wins would follow in 1950/51, 1961/62, 1962/63, 1966/67, 1975/76 and 1976/77 with 1950/51, 1961/62, 1962/63 and 1975/76 being clean sweeps. The 1951 clean sweep clincher at Wembley – this time a 3-2 victory for Scotland – again saw the visitors win the game with ten home Scots in the line-up. The changes to the magnificent XI of two years previous saw Aitken, Mason and Houliston replaced by Willie Redpath (Motherwell), Bobby Johnstone (Hibernian) and Billy Liddell (Liverpool) respectively while Billy Steel was now with Dundee.

George Aitken made his international debut against England in 1949 and went on to win a total of eight Scotland caps – the first five with East Fife (a club record) then three with Sunderland. The wing-half was a member of the East Fife teams that won the League Cup in 1947 and 1949.

Jimmy Mason was an inside-forward who netted in the victory over England in April 1949 as well as in the 3-2 win over Northern Ireland five months previous. Mason would be capped seven times for his country and score four goals, all while with the Hi Hi for whom he played over 200 league games.

Although Billy Houliston won but three caps he is the only Queen of the South player to have won full international honours. The centre-forward netted twice for Scotland and vital goals they were too as along with Jimmy Mason's strike they helped Scotland come back from 2-0 down to defeat Northern Ireland 3-2 in front of 93,182 at Hampden in November 1948. Houliston scored 60 goals in the course of his 120 league games with the Dumfries club.

Left-half Willie Redpath won all his nine Scotland caps while at Motherwell and he was a key player in the Fir Park side's Scottish Cup-winning run of 1952, scoring in both the semi-final against Hearts and the final versus Dundee. In the match programme for the 1951 game against England at Wembley his pen picture advises, 'He is rated one of the finest ball players in Scotland and is much in demand as an exhibition player and a ball juggler at boys' clubs during the winter.'

The 1962 title-clinching side beat the Auld Enemy 2-0 at Hampden with the Rangers duo of Davie Wilson and Eric Caldow making the scoresheet while the likes of Jimmy Greaves and Bobby Charlton did not. The Old Firm provided six of the seven home Scots in the winning line-up with the newly crowned Scottish champions Dundee being represented by defender Alex Hamilton.

Hamilton made his Scotland debut in front of 74,329 at Hampden in a 2-0 win over Wales in November 1961. Twenty-three more appearances would follow to make the right-back Dundee's most capped player. Hamilton helped his club win the league title in 1961/62 and as an added claim to fame, in 1964 he was also the frontman of a band known as Hammy and the Hamsters which comprised of team-mates such as future Scotland manager Craig Brown.

In 1962/63, Scotland defeated Wales 3-2 in Cardiff, Northern Ireland 5-1 at Hampden, then England 2-1 at Wembley – where the home-based Scots were still in the majority with six and included Dundee centre-half Ian Ure. Ure made 11 appearances for Scotland, eight of which came while at Dens Park including the aforementioned victories over the Welsh and Irish. He left Dundee, with whom he had picked up a league winners' medal in 1961/62, for Arsenal in August 1963 and as such just missed out on the 'Hamstermania' which subsequently swept through Tayside. Allegedly.

In 1966/67, as most supporters north of the border know, Scotland were crowned unofficial world champions (as well as official British champions) when Bobby Brown's XI defeated the real world champions, England, 3-2 at Wembley. Six home Scots were in the winning line-up, including Celtic goalkeeper Ronnie Simpson who made his international debut that day, aged 36. 'Faither', as he was fondly referred to at Celtic Park, would win only four more Scotland caps but a mere five weeks after the Wembley success came Celtic's Lisbon triumph and a European Cup winners' medal. Earlier in his career Ronnie, as a Queen's Park player, had represented Great Britain at the 1948 Olympic Games while in the 1950s he picked up two FA Cup winners' medals playing for Newcastle United. Simpson also served on the Pools Panel which adjudicated on results of postponed matches in England and Scotland in periods of exceptionally bad weather.

It's fair to say that 1976 was the Scottish 'Year of the Nutmeg' when Willie Ormond's side completed the clean sweep by defeating England 2-1 at Hampden with Kenny Dalglish's winning, mis-hit shot going through the legs of visiting goalkeeper Ray Clemence. Six of the players used against England were home Scots and included unsung hero Colin 'Bomber' Jackson. The Rangers centre-half, who made over 500 games for his club, won his eighth and final cap against England which followed on from appearances in the 3-1 victory over Wales and a 3-0 success against Northern Ireland. Indeed, Jackson was never on the losing side in a full international.

The four home Scots in Ally MacLeod's 1977 title-winning team were Alan Rough of Partick Thistle, Danny McGrain of Celtic, Rangers' Tom Forsyth and Celtic's Kenny Dalglish. Tom 'Jaws' Forsyth, who won the first of his 22 Scotland caps against Denmark in 1971 when he was a Motherwell player, appeared in all six British Home Championship matches of 1976 and 1977. His final three Scotland games came at the 1978 World Cup in Argentina. Tom made over 300 appearances for Rangers before injury forced the uncompromising but likeable defender to retire from the game in 1982.

Almost 40 years on from its demise, I still pine for the British Home Championship but then again I also still pine for the days of black football boots, Saturday evening 'pink' newspapers, television restricted to three or four channels and no smart(arse) phones. Derek Dougan (Northern Ireland), Terry Yorath (Wales), Norman Hunter (England), John Greig (Scotland): none of these British giants – these footballing Humphrey Bogarts – would have appeared on a 1970s version of *Strictly Come Dancing* or *The Masked Singer*. I like to think not, anyway.

Fives and Sixes

Exciting and entertaining football competitions are not of course restricted to 11-a-side matches. For decades, many clubs organised pre-season five- or six-a-side tournaments often as part of a sports day. Two notable nationwide examples of the shortened game were the *Daily Express* National Five-a-Sides at Wembley Arena, usually in November, from 1968 to 1986 and the Tennents' Sixes competition which took place in Scottish venues between 1984 and 1993.

Back in the early 1970s, television coverage of the annual *Daily Express* event was considered to be a rare treat. Four hundred miles away in Glasgow, me and my classmates viewed it in awe – a tournament in which Scottish clubs got to mix it with the English in that fabled land called Wembley. Gerrintaethem! – Oops, sorry about that.

Taking a look at the programme from the inaugural competition, there were words of welcome from the chairman of Beaverbrook Newspapers Ltd as well as from Alan Hardaker, secretary of England's Football League. FIFA president Sir Stanley Rous was listed as one of the 'Tournament Officials' – a tournament which had originally attracted 83 entrants from across England and Scotland.

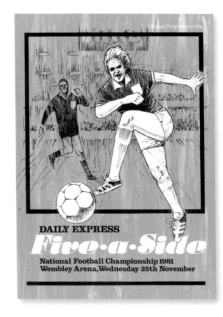

The 1968 finals had a straightforward knock-out format with only eight teams taking part, all of them regional winners and arguably all of them 'unfashionable'. For example, Greenock Morton represented Scotland having triumphed at Glasgow's Kelvin Hall in April of that year; Preston North End for the north-west of England; Peterborough United for the Midlands; and Charlton Athletic for London. To help supplement the action there was a demonstration of Olympic gymnastics as well as a schoolboys match.

Come 1971 and the big names were now competing – Arsenal, Chelsea, Manchester United, Spurs, Rangers and Celtic (with

COASTERS ARENA, FALKIRK

TENNENT'S SIXES

TENNENT'S SIXES

16/17 JANUARY 1984

SOUVENIR PROGRAMME £1.00

Danny McGrain and Paul Wilson listed) to name but six of the now 16 competitors. This time, the interval entertainment comprised a ladies football match which was considered something of a novelty item back in the days of rampant sexism.

Celtic were beaten finalists in 1973, losing 3-1 to Derby County. In 1981, however, the Celts, with a squad comprising Peter Latchford, Willie McStay, Charlie Nicholas, Danny Crainie, Willie Garner and John Weir, lifted the trophy after beating a Southampton side, which included Alan Ball and Kevin Keegan, 1-0 in the final. Celtic had disposed of Watford (with John Barnes listed), Manchester United (who featured Lou Macari, Bryan Robson and Ray Wilkins) and Ipswich Town (whose named squad included Terry Butcher and Alan Brazil).

NO OFFSIDE! NO THROW-INS!

Aberdeen, with Bryan Gunn in goal, represented Scotland in the 1985 competition and according to the tournament programme it was to be graced by the likes of Kenny Sansom and Graham Rix of Arsenal, Paul Gascoigne and Peter Beardsley from Newcastle United, Nottingham Forest's Garry Birtles, Southampton's Peter Shilton, and Ray Stewart and Frank McAvennie from West Ham United. All that talent under the one roof for one night of the year – it must have been like Christmas come early for those lucky enough to be able to attend these tournaments. The rest of us were just grateful for John Logie Baird.

The Tennents' Sixes was another indoor football tournament, contested over two days in January by senior Scottish clubs along with occasional English guests such as Manchester City in 1986. The number of entrants was either ten or 12 with a combined league/knock-out format and the tournament was sponsored by Tennent Caledonian Breweries and organised by the SFA.

The concept of indoor six-a-side football was born in the north-east of the United States where harsh weather drives sport indoors during the winter months. The inaugural tournament took place at the Coasters Arena, Falkirk, in 1984 followed by the Ingliston Exhibition Centre near Edinburgh in 1985. Glasgow's Scottish Exhibition and Conference Centre was host venue from 1986 onwards.

Only the first three of the ten Tennents' Sixes competitions took place within the timeframe of this book. In 1984 Rangers beat Dundee 6-4 with Davie Cooper, Bobby Williamson and Ally Dawson starring for the winners; 1985 saw Hearts beat Morton 4-1 thanks to their squad of 'Gorgie Galacticos' such as Henry Smith, Jimmy Bone, Willie Johnston, Craig Levein, John Robertson and Gary MacKay; and in 1986 Aberdeen beat St Mirren 3-0 with Ian Porteous as the Dons' top scorer.

It would be remiss of me, however, not to mention that Aberdeen were the only team to retain their title; that Rangers and Hearts also won the competition twice; that Celtic, Dundee, Hibernian and Partick Thistle were the other winners; and that after the 1993 competition Tennents withdrew their sponsorship, the tournament folded and the trophy has resided in Thistle's Maryhill 'Theatre of Screams' ever since.

These tournaments were warmly embraced by supporters of all sides and, for example, I understand that at Hearts' triumph in 1985 scores of freebie Panini stickers albums were converted into confetti resulting in the Ingliston Exhibition Centre being transformed into the Estadio Monumental of the 1978 World Cup Final in Argentina. All things considered, Walter Kidd and Daniel Passarella had a lot in common.

Lost (or Completely Re-jigged) Cathedrals

The Taylor Report, produced following the Hillsborough disaster of 1989, changed the design of British football stadia for the better but that doesn't prevent us from pining for now-demolished or dramatically altered 'football cathedrals' of yesteryear. Perhaps it is stretching it a bit to refer to the likes of the now-departed Brockville Park, Love Street and Muirton Park as cathedrals, so how about 'temples of earthbound gods' such as determined defender Stuart Kennedy, who made around 200 appearances for Falkirk between 1971 and 1976; mindful midfielder Iain Munro with over 200 appearances for St Mirren between 1969 to 1973 and 1977 to 1980; and silky striker Henry Hall after more than 100 goals for St Johnstone between 1968 and 1975.

Love Street, Paisley

Falkirk FC were founded in 1876 and Brockville Park, on Hope Street near the town centre, was their home from 1885 to 2003. Brockville comprised a large Main Stand, built in 1928, with non-symmetrical terracing and was hemmed in by housing, industry and a railway line to give it that traditional British look. Main Stand features included an entrance hall resplendent with coloured glass, polished wood and lino; a decorative gate at the tunnel which was designed by former player and manager John Prentice; and a press box with its own sash windows. Brockville has since been replaced with a Morrisons supermarket and an old turnstile is on display in the adjacent car park. No doubt, one day, Aldi will replace the Acropolis.

Brockville's record attendance of 23,100 came about in February 1953 with the visit of Celtic for a Scottish Cup tie, but the stadium never saw European action – Falkirk's Scottish Cup triumph in 1957 coming three years too early for participation in the Cup Winners' Cup while actual qualification didn't come until the 2009/10 Europa League. That said, promotion to the top flight was achieved while at Brockville in 1951/52, 1960/61, 1969/70 and 1985/86 and the ground also hosted greyhound racing in the 1930s and a Scotland victory in the European Under-23 Championship, 4-0 against Romania in 1975, en-route to the quarter-finals.

St Johnstone were founded in 1884 but it was 1924 before they moved into Muirton Park; indeed the official opening was on Christmas Day when the Saints defeated Queen's Park 2-1 in a Division One match. The ground's main feature was the then-traditional two-tier Main Stand, with seating and a standing enclosure, with its white and blue façade and a roof that was once distinguished by its large advertisement – 'Drybrough's beer for the discriminating man'. 'More discerning' might have been a better choice of words, but hey, I'm just being picky. Terracing curved round the other three sides with only the east side covered and the ice rink and town ends behind each goal totally exposed to the bracing Perthshire weather. The four traditional floodlight pylons were officially inaugurated in December 1964 with the visit of England's reigning FA Cup holders, West Ham United.

While Muirton Park was home, second-tier titles in 1959/60, 1962/63 and 1982/83, Willie Ormond as manager from 1967–'73 and Inter-Cities Fairs Cup football in 1969/70 all came to the Fair City, as did the hosting of the 1970 Scottish Cup semi-final between Aberdeen and Kilmarnock, Highland Games, hockey internationals, cattle sales, donkey racing and even re-enactments of the Battle of the Clans!

After almost 65 years, the last football match played at Muirton Park was St Johnstone against Ayr United in April 1989. The highest official attendance was 29,972 for St Johnstone against Dundee in February 1951. The replacement McDiarmid Park, which actually predated the Taylor report, has an all-seated capacity of 10,696 and while both comfortable and practical is also architecturally unimaginative and atmospherically soulless in my humble opinion.

St Mirren were founded in 1877 and in 1895 they moved into Love Street, Paisley – which, at the time, was right next door to a slaughterhouse but which eventually inspired the 1980s fanzine *Love Street Syndrome* as well as becoming home to the legendary/infamous club mascot 'Paisley Panda'.

The stadium featured a Main Stand from 1921 and for many a year, a covered North Bank terracing opposite, but by the time of its closure in 2009 Love Street was a collection of four different-sized and shaped grandstands. The Main Stand was only 60 yards long but for a while its black-and-white-striped façade was like a large-sized tribute to the cover of the classic 1978 Blondie album *Parallel Lines*. One wonders if the track 'Heart of Glass' was some sort of subliminal dedication to Saints striker/disco diva Frank McAvennie. Anyway, to the right of the stand was a section of terracing known as Cairter's Corner – a favourite gathering spot for Paisley's answer to Kirk Douglas and Burt Lancaster (the so-called 'Tough Guys').

St Mirren enjoyed four European campaigns at Love Street in the 1980s and twice brought the Scottish Cup back to the stadium's trophy room, in 1959 and 1987. Second-tier titles were also celebrated in 1967/68 and 1976/77.

Love Street hosted St Mirren's record victory in January 1960 – a 15-0 thrashing of Glasgow University in a Scottish Cup tie – while the record crowd of 47,438 came against Celtic in a League Cup tie in August 1949. The Saints' final game at the stadium was against Motherwell in January 2009.

Love Street hosted several Scotland under-23, under-21 and schoolboy internationals as well as a full international against Wales in 1923, plus it was a venue for the 1970 European Under-18 Championship which Scotland hosted. In 1975 and 1976, Love Street was also home to the Paisley Lions speedway team while prior to that there was athletics, cycling, greyhound racing and rugby union matches.

Also lost are Broomfield Park, the home to Airdrie from 1892 to 1994, which boasted an attractive, standalone pavilion complete with three pointed gables and a flagpole; Boghead Park, Dumbarton's ground from 1879–2000; Bayview, home of East Fife from 1903–'98 with its very low press box resembling a machine gun post; Hamilton Academical's Douglas Park which was used from 1888–1994 and then part of the Main Stand was sold to Auchinleck Talbot; Annfield Park, home of Stirling Albion from 1945–'93 with the adjacent Listed Building of Annfield House once providing changing rooms and club offices and Shawfield Stadium, Clyde's ground from 1898–1986, now used purely for greyhound racing.

And let's not forget Cathkin Park, formerly known as the 'Second Hampden Park', which was home to Third Lanark from 1903 until their demise in 1967. Today the site is a leafy, landscaped, partially hidden, open access ground, but the stadium's original basic outline including the perimeter wall plus some of the terracing and crush barriers still survives. Well worth a visit, it's like discovering the remains of a Scottish Colosseum within the confines of a Scottish Machu Picchu. Sort of.

Most Scottish clubs have chosen to stay put rather than relocate but nevertheless a considerable percentage have rebuilt their existing homes. By and large, perimeter tracks became passé, so, for example, there's no more cycling or athletics at

Cathkin Park, Glasgow

Ibrox – 1970 Commonwealth Games 10,000m gold medallist Lachie Stewart was one of many well-known athletes to race at the home of Rangers. There's no room now for greyhound racing at East End Park and Firhill, which was popular at both these venues in the 1940s and '50s. The 'dugs' was also a feature at both Dundee clubs in the 1930s. Gone as well is the short-lived pony trotting at Motherwell – given time I'm sure that could have evolved into something attractive to all *Ben-Hur* wannabes.

The biggest disappearing acts were of course the large terraces, many of which are still fondly remembered as being home to some of the loudest and most fanatical supporters such as the intimidating Jungle at Parkhead, the cavernous Beach End at Pittodrie, the Wheatfield Street Shed home of the Gorgie Boys at Tynecastle, and the once massive East Terrace at Easter Road – aka the Leith San Siro.

Once upon a time our stadia had soul, which often outweighed any sanitary shortcomings. However, it has to be conceded that our grounds are now safer, saner and more fan-friendly than ever before – but as some sage once said, 'Only Val Doonican sits down to sing.' Chants of 'Gerrintaethem!' are still much more effective when delivered while on our feet, not our arses.

Player of the Year Awards in Scotland

Season	Football Writers'	SPFA Winners	SPFA Young Player
1964/65	Billy McNeill (Celtic)	–	–
1965/66	John Greig (Rangers)	–	–
1966/67	Ronnie Simpson (Celtic)	–	–
1967/68	Gordon Wallace (Raith)	–	–
1968/69	Bobby Murdoch (Celtic)	–	–
1969/70	Pat Stanton (Hibernian)	–	–
1970/71	Martin Buchan (Aberdeen)	–	–
1971/72	Dave Smith (Rangers)	–	–
1972/73	George Connelly (Celtic)	–	–
1973/74	Scotland World Cup Squad	–	–
1974/75	Sandy Jardine (Rangers)	–	–
1975/76	John Greig (Rangers)	–	–
1976/77	Danny McGrain (Celtic)	–	–
1977/78	Derek Johnstone (Rangers)	Derek Johnstone (Rangers)	Graeme Payne (Dundee Utd)
1978/79	Andy Ritchie (Morton)	Paul Hegarty (Dundee Utd)	Ray Stewart (Dundee Utd)
1979/80	Gordon Strachan (Aberdeen)	Davie Provan (Celtic)	John MacDonald (Rangers)
1980/81	Alan Rough (Partick Thistle)	Mark McGhee (Aberdeen)	Charlie Nicholas (Celtic)
1981/82	Paul Sturrock (Dundee Utd)	Sandy Clark (Airdrie)	Frank McAvennie (St Mirren)
1982/83	Charlie Nicholas (Celtic)	Charlie Nicholas (Celtic)	Paul McStay (Celtic)
1983/84	Willie Miller (Aberdeen)	Willie Miller (Aberdeen)	John Robertson (Hearts)
1984/85	Hamish McAlpine (Dundee Utd)	Jim Duffy (Morton)	Craig Levein (Hearts)
1985/86	Sandy Jardine (Hearts)	Richard Gough (Dundee Utd)	Craig Levein (Hearts)

Observations, hindsight and argument-starters

For this particular period the press and the players agreed with one another on three out of nine occasions – Derek Johnstone in 1978, Charlie Nicholas in '83 and Willie Miller in '84.

John Greig (Rangers) and Sandy Jardine (Rangers and Hearts) were both twice winners of the football writers' award.

In 1964/65 Kilmarnock were crowned Scottish champions for the first (and to date only) time, yet the writers' award went to Billy McNeill, who scored the winning goal in the Scottish Cup Final for Celtic – who had finished in eighth place having conceded 57 goals. Surely 1965/66 or 1966/67 was Big Billy's season?

Gordon Wallace became the first non-Old Firm player to win the award, in 1967/68 – his goals had helped Raith Rovers narrowly avoid relegation and finish 16th in an 18-team Division One. Somewhat surprisingly though, the prolific Wallace was never capped for his country, but he went on to grab a League Cup winners' medal with Dundee in 1973. He returned to Stark's Park in 1978 to manage Raith.

In 1974 the award went to the Scotland squad in recognition of reaching the World Cup finals for the first time since 1958. Surely the Scotland squad could have been given a separate, special prize, with the player of the year honour going to someone like Davie Hay or Jimmy Johnstone, both of Celtic.

In 1978/79 the scribes' winner was Andy Ritchie, the Premier Division's top goalscorer that season. Ritchie was a somewhat rotund striker revered by Morton fans as 'The Idle Idol'. Some saw him as 'the epitome of the Scottish footballer – a fat, lazy bastard but with great ball skill'. A cult hero indeed whom I would liked to have seen play for his country, but apparently Scotland boss Jock Stein was not a fan.

In 1984/85 another cult hero won the writers' trophy – the somewhat eccentric Dundee United goalkeeper (and occasional penalty taker) Hamish McAlpine, who also had a penchant for leaving his 18-yard box to take on opponents.

Rex Kingsley Awards

Between 1951 and 1964 there was the prestigious Rex Kingsley Scottish Footballer of the Year award. Kingsley was a respected journalist with the *Sunday Mail* newspaper, as well as a former actor and radio sports announcer, and his winners included several players from the so-called lesser lights:

Year	Winner
1951	Gordon Smith (Hibernian)
1952	Willie Thornton (Rangers)
1953	Bobby Evans (Celtic)
1954	Jimmy McGowan (Partick Thistle)
1955	George Young (Rangers)
1956	Willie McNaught (Raith Rovers)
1957	Alex Parker (Falkirk)
1958	Dave Mackay (Hearts)
1959	Harry Haddock (Clyde)
1960	Willie Toner (Kilmarnock)
1961	John Cumming (Hearts)
1962	Ian Ure (Dundee)
1964	Charlie Aitken (Motherwell)

Further debate

And just to keep the arguments going, and following some extensive research (a few emails and a couple of sessions in our local hostelry), here's some more retrospective/alternative suggestions of our own.

1948/49 Jock Shaw (Rangers)
Skippered his club to Scottish football's first Treble.

1959/60 Gordon Smith (Hearts)
Declared unfit by Hibernian at 34 and freed. Smith pays for surgery to cure the ankle injury, promptly signs for Hearts and then wins the league and League Cup in his first season with the Tynecastle outfit. Plays 38 competitive games and scores 13 goals. A crowd of 13,000 turned up to see him make his debut for Hearts' reserves.

1961/62 Alan Gilzean (Dundee)
Perhaps the high-scoring striker should have shared Kingsley's award with team-mate Ian Ure.

1962/63 Eric Caldow (Rangers)
Double winner with his club and skippered Scotland to a second successive clean sweep in the British Home Championship.

1963/64 Jim Baxter (Rangers)
Helped his club to Scottish football's second Treble and was part of Rest of the World squad against England in FA centenary match at Wembley in October 1963.

And finally, a quick mention for the managers' awards. The Scottish Football Writers' Association Manager of the Year honour was first given for 1986/87 when Dundee United's Jim McLean was the recipient. The Professional Footballers' Association Manager of the Year didn't appear until 2006/07 and we still await the introduction of any significant awards for much-loved match officials and administrators. Yes, really.

HEARTS
CENTRE HALF
ALAN ANDERSON

Quizball

Quizball was a short-lived BBC TV quiz show running from 1966 to 1971, dedicated to stars of the Beautiful Game (sort of) in which the competing teams represented English and Scottish football clubs and usually comprised three players and one celebrity guest supporter. It has been described as a studio-bound version of the Anglo-Scottish Cup and 'goals' could be scored in four ways – from Route 4 (correctly answering four relatively easy questions) to Route 1 (one extremely difficult question). So a tiki-taka approach got you nowhere. Quizmasters included David Vine and Stuart Hall.

In 1966 16 teams took part with Arsenal, featuring former Dens Park hero Ian Ure, defeating Dunfermline Athletic 7-3 in the final with all the Pars' goals coming from guest star Gordon Jackson, who appeared in *The Great Escape*. I can't help but wonder if Ure wished Jackson 'good luck' beforehand.

A year later Hearts lost in the second round to the defending champions with Ure scoring all five for the Gunners. Arsenal would, however, lose to the eventual winners West Bromwich Albion, who beat Nottingham Forest in the final.

The competition returned in 1969 and was won by a Glasgow Celtic team which comprised Lisbon Lions Jim Craig, Billy McNeill and Willie Wallace plus actor John Cairney whose brother Jim was a professional footballer with York City. John would also go on to write several excellent football books including *The Sevenpenny Gate: A Lifelong Love Affair with Celtic FC*. Celtic beat Hearts, who included Jim Cruickshank, Alan Anderson and Donald Ford, in an all-Scottish Final. In an earlier round, actor John Laurie – Private Frazer in *Dad's Army* – helped ensure Dundee were 'doomed' to defeat.

The first edition of 1970, featuring league- and cup-winning sides, saw Celtic retain the trophy by beating Everton 7-5 in the final. In the semi-finals the Goodison Park outfit defeated a Falkirk side who had won the Scottish Second Division title in 1969/70 and included Alex Ferguson.

Jon Pertwee, Gallifrey &
Dunfermline Athletic.

The year's second edition saw Derby County, including Scotland international John O'Hare, beat Crystal Palace 4-2 in the final.

In 1971 Dunfermline Athletic initially had comedian Jimmy Logan as their guest but by the time the Fife club defeated Leicester City, including Nicholas Parsons, in the final he had been replaced by the third Doctor, Jon Pertwee. John Cushley (ex-Celtic and West Ham), defender Jim Fraser and manager Alex Wright were Pertwee's three time-travelling companions.

Other sporting quiz shows such as *A Question of Sport* and *They Think It's All Over* have enjoyed a much greater longevity, although they lacked the partisanship of a 'club contest'. As a (mercifully) brief footnote, between 1995 and 1997 Scottish Television produced *A Game of Two Halves* – a quiz show which looked at the funny side of Scottish football (allegedly) and regularly involved comedians/comedy actors Tony Roper and Fred MacAulay. Unfortunately, His Majesty the King, Denis Law, was also talked into appearing as a team captain, but thankfully the show wasn't networked.

Seaside Success Stories

It's a bit misleading to suggest that all of Scotland's best footballers have come from our large cities or former industrial heartlands that were once linked to the likes of coal mining or steel making. A fair number of our soccer stars have hailed from our once vibrant seaside resorts and fishing towns, so credit where credit is due as the following examples – all of whom were Scotland internationals throughout the Golden Years – serve to illustrate. It's perhaps also worth pointing out that none other than Cristiano Ronaldo is a 'Happy Sandboy' (sort of) from Funchal on the holiday island of Madeira.

Back home, and doon the watter from Glasgow you'll find Ayrshire. Never mind Rabbie Burns, this fine county has also given us footballers from holiday towns, such as Bobby Ferguson (Ardrossan), Peter McCloy (Girvan), Roy Aitken and Steve Nicol (Irvine) and Bobby Lennox (Saltcoats).

Ferguson helped Kilmarnock become Scottish champions in 1964/65 and kept goal during Killie's run to the semi-finals of the 1966/67 Inter-Cities Fairs Cup before heading south to West Ham United and ultimately the warmer climes of Australia.

McCloy, also affectionately known as the 'Girvan Lighthouse', kept goal for Rangers in over 500 matches across a 16-year period from 1970. Big 'Gas Meter' helped the Ibrox side win two league titles, four Scottish Cups and four League Cups plus the European Cup Winners' Cup in 1972.

Aitken, 'The Bear', was a tough midfielder who made over 600 appearances for Celtic between 1975 and 1990, winning six league titles, five Scottish Cups and one League Cup. He also featured for Scotland at the 1986 and 1990 World Cups and won 57 caps in total.

Nicol was a defender who started his professional career at Ayr United and made almost 100 appearances for the Honest Men between 1979 and 1981. His career then went south – to Liverpool, where he won a glittering array of domestic and European honours. He also represented Scotland at the 1986 World Cup finals.

Dunoon Pier

Lennox played around 600 matches for Celtic and the winger's winners' medals collection is second to none – 11 league titles, eight Scottish Cups and five League Cups plus the European Cup in 1967. A genuine legend who was honoured with a statue in his home town in 2018.

Across the Firth of Clyde from Ayrshire is Argyllshire and the town of Dunoon, a once popular holiday destination for steamships from Glasgow and during the Cold War it was a garrison town to the United States Navy. As for football, Dunoon was the birthplace of Stewart Houston whose youth career was spent at Port Glasgow Rangers before joining Tommy Docherty's Chelsea in 1967 and then Manchester United under Docherty in 1973.

From Dunoon, a ferry will transport you back across the water to Inverclyde's erstwhile seaside resort of Gourock which boasts one of the three remaining outdoor swimming pools in Scotland –

CELTIC

BOBBY LENNOX

originally built in 1909, the same year the Scottish Cup was withheld due to a riot at the drawn final replay between Celtic and Rangers. A Scottish Cup winner, however, in 1980 and 1985, was Celtic winger Davie Provan who was born in Gourock in May 1956. Davie scored in the '85 final and also collected four Premier Division and one League Cup winners' medals.

East of Eden (aka Edinburgh) we discover Musselburgh, the home to the Silver Arrow, an annual competition for the Royal Company of Archers, and whose most famous footballing son is inside-forward John White. White turned out for Alloa Athletic before moving on to Falkirk where he won his first four Scotland caps. In 1959 he transferred to Tottenham Hotspur where he would win domestic and European honours before his life was tragically cut short in 1964.

Right next door to Musselburgh is Prestonpans, the scene of a famous Jacobite victory in 1745 as well as the birthplace of Alfie Conn, who as part of Hearts' 'Terrible Trio' helped the Edinburgh club to success in the 1954/55 League Cup and the 1956 Scottish Cup. Conn scored over 221 goals in 408 games for the Jambos.

Also from Prestonpans were goalkeeper Eddie Connachan, who played over 170 games for Dunfermline Athletic and produced heroics in the 1961 Scottish Cup Final, and Eddie Colquhoun, winner of nine Scotland caps between 1971 and 1973 and who starred at Bury, WBA and Sheffield United as well as Edinburgh Norton.

'Across the magnificent, 1890, steel cantilever Forth Rail Bridge is the Kingdom of Fife and the birthplaces of Andy Penman (Rosyth), Charlie Cooke (St Monans) and Alfie Conn Junior (Kirkcaldy).

The Rosyth Royal Naval Dockyard was still in operation when Andy Penman starred for Dundee from 1959–'67, winning the league in 1962, Rangers from 1967–'73 and Arbroath from 1973–'76.

The picturesque village of St Monans gave us the classy winger Charlie Cooke, who played for Aberdeen and Dundee before heading for Chelsea in the swinging 1960s where he went on to help the Pensioners lift the 1970 FA Cup and the 1971 European Cup Winners' Cup.

'Terrible Trio' star Alfie Conn's son, also Alfie, has that rare distinction of having been a success at both Rangers (winning the 1972 European Cup Winners' Cup and 1973 Scottish Cup) and Celtic (1977 league and cup winner, plus the 1979 league title), while being popular at White Hart Lane in between. Alfie is also fondly remembered for his long, curly locks which gave him a distinctive 'McEwan's laughing cavalier' look.

Over the rebuilt Tay Rail Bridge, a lengthy pier-and-lattice-girder construction from 1887, to Angus, just outside Dundee is Broughty Ferry – a prosperous former fishing and whaling village and birthplace of Davie 'The Brush' Robb. The striker scored 99 goals in 345 games for Aberdeen, winning the Scottish Cup in 1970 and League Cup in 1976.

Close by is golf's Open Championship town of Carnoustie which also gave us goalkeeper Fred Martin, who admittedly was seven over par against both Uruguay at the 1954 World Cup finals and England at Wembley in 1955. That said, he spent 14 years at Aberdeen where he helped the Dons to win the 1954/55 championship and the 1955/56 League Cup.

Completing this particular Angus trinity is the town of Arbroath, famous for its Declaration of Scottish Independence in 1320, the fish delicacy known as the Smokie, and the oldest miniature railway in Scotland dating from 1935 and sadly closed in late 2020. Equally as important, Arbroath was also the birthplace of Bill Brown, who made his international debut at the 1958 World Cup and played over 250 games for Dundee, helping them to lift the 1951/52 League Cup. Brown was also central to Spurs' domestic and European successes of the early 1960s.

About 600 miles north of Bournemouth lies Inverness – the cultural capital of the Highlands, one-time home to Macbeth and the birthplace of prolific goalscorer Ted MacDougall. He won seven

KERR'S MINIATURE RAILWAY, ARBROATH

caps for Scotland and played around 600 games for English league clubs, over 200 of which were with the Cherries where he netted nine in an 11-0 trouncing of Margate in an FA Cup tie in 1971.

About 45 miles east of Inverness, along the Moray coast, the town of Lossiemouth pitches in with RAF Tornado and Typhoon jets plus Stewart Imlach who was born there in 1932, eight years prior to the arrival of Handley Page Hampden aircraft – how's that for a contrived football connection? Anyway, Lossie boy Imlach played for his local Highland League side, Scotland at the 1958 World Cup finals and Nottingham Forest, where he collected an FA Cup winners' medal in 1959.

The most notable seaside success at team level has come via Aberdeen but as that is a sizeable city we'll let that one slide and so instead head back south to the Angus towns of Montrose, which overlooks a two-miles-square tidal lagoon, the largest inland saltwater basin in the UK, and Arbroath.

Montrose FC, aka the Gable Endies, were founded in 1879 but had to wait until 1984/85 before they won their first championship – the third-tier Second Division. In 1975/76 the Links Park club reached the semi-finals of the League Cup where they lost to eventual winners Rangers. Earlier, Montrose had eliminated East Fife, Raith Rovers, St Mirren and Hibernian.

Forfarshire, the anglicised name for Angus, gave its moniker to a cup competition in 1883/84 involving clubs from Dundee and Perth, as well as Angus. Montrose were Forfarshire Cup winners in 1951/52, 1961/62 and 1972/73.

Arbroath FC – aka the Red Lichties after the red light which used to guide the fishing boats safely back to harbour – were founded in 1878 and have enjoyed several seasons in the top flight having finished runners-up in the second tier in 1958/59, 1967/68 and 1971/72. The Gayfield Park club also reached the semi-finals of the Scottish Cup in 1946/47 and the last four of the League Cup in 1959/60. Arbroath were the inaugural winners of the Forfarshire Cup and during the Golden Years lifted the trophy in 1957/58. The club's best-loved manager is the legendary Albert Henderson, a League Cup-winning half-back with Dundee in 1952 whose reign as boss extended from September 1962 (pre-Beatles) to January 1980 (ie post-punk).

Scotland's coastal football kings, however, are arguably East Fife, located in the town of Methil – once Scotland's greatest coal port. The Fifers have won the Scottish League Cup in 1947/48, 1949/50 and 1953/54, defeating Falkirk, Dunfermline Athletic and Partick Thistle in the finals respectively. A Scottish Cup Final was reached in 1950 but lost to Rangers. Third place in the top flight was achieved in 1951/52 and 1952/53 while fourth place was reached in 1948/49 and 1949/50 – where was the Inter-Cities Fairs Cup when you needed it?

Notable players include Henry Morris, who hit over 100 goals for the Fifers plus a hat-trick in a World Cup qualifying win against Northern Ireland in 1949 on his only Scotland appearance, and

Charlie 'Cannonball' Fleming, another scorer of over 100 goals for the Methil club plus a brace in a World Cup qualifying win against Northern Ireland in 1953 – his only Scotland cap.

Raith Rovers were founded in 1883 and hail from the Fife town of Kirkcaldy – famous for its linoleum production and as the birthplace of political economist and moral philosopher Adam Smith (1723) and former world darts champion Jocky Wilson (1950). Rovers' two major trophies have come as recently as the 1994 League Cup and 2014 Challenge Cup, but back in the Golden Years they managed to reach the 1948/49 League Cup Final where they lost to Rangers. Promotions to the top flight were also achieved in 1948/49 and 1966/67 with elevations to the second tier in 1975/76 and 1977/78.

Returning to the west of Scotland we find Ayr United, who were founded in 1910 and who are nicknamed the Honest Men – from a line from the Robert Burns poem 'Tam o' Shanter'. The county town of Ayr is also well known for its racecourse which is home to the Scottish Grand National, the adjacent former Butlin's holiday camp and ebullient Ally MacLeod who managed United from 1966–'75, briefly again in 1978 and then from 1985–'90. The Honest Men were second-tier champions in 1958/59 and 1965/66 and runners-up in 1955/56 and 1968/69. Ally's Ayr also reached the Scottish Cup semi-final in the SFA centenary year of 1973 where they lost to the eventual winners Rangers.

Notable United players include John 'Spud' Murphy, a full-back who spent his entire senior career at the club and made over 450 league appearances between 1963 and 1978, winger Johnny Doyle, with around 200 appearances and remains the last Ayr player to be capped for Scotland, in a European Championship qualifier against Romania in 1975, and Brian McLaughlin, who in 1978/79 won what was only the second SPFA First Division Player of the Year award.

Stranraer FC are arguably a sea-loch club, but as they were founded in 1870 they are also the third-oldest club in Scotland behind Queen's Park and

Kilmarnock. A century later, the port, which provides the main sea link between Scotland and Northern Ireland, entered the record books with the first hotel in the world to have an indoor curling rink. On the football front, the Blues have always been a lower-tier club, but between 1948/49 and 1982/83 Stranraer reserves enjoyed their own unique golden years when they won the South of Scotland League on no fewer than 15 occasions.

And finally, let's head into north-east England and across the magnificent Royal Border Bridge – 659 metres long, with 28 arches, stone-built and Grade I-listed – to Shielfield Park, Tweedmouth, home to Berwick Rangers. Founded in 1884, the Wee Rangers' greatest claim to fame is arguably when they stuck it to Glasgow Rangers in the first round of the 1967 Scottish Cup – which was probably some sort of revenge for losing to the Ibrox outfit in the semi-finals of the 1963/64 League Cup. More tangible success has come in the shape of winning the 1978/79 third-tier championship. The market town of Berwick is only 56 miles from Edinburgh and 102 miles from Glasgow, so who knows, perhaps with the right kind of investment, the Borderers could have become the Scottish league's Cardiff City.

————————

And so to echo the sentiments of Bill Nash, Kris Kristofferson, Perry Como and, er, other followers of Scottish football, please raise a glass 'for the good times'.

Bibliography

Glasgow Herald, *Evening Times* and *Daily Record* newspaper archives

Bell, B. – *Still Seeing Red: A History of Third Lanark A.C.* (Glasgow, Glasgow City Libraries and Archives, 1996)

Cairney, J. – *A Scottish Football Hall of Fame* (Edinburgh, Mainstream Publishing, 1998)

Inglis, S. – *Football Grounds of Great Britain* (Glasgow, William Collins Sons and Co Ltd, 1989)

Reid, R. et al – *Partick Thistle Football Club: 1876–2002 The Official History* (Harefield, Yore Publications, 2002)

Greig, J. (with Black, J.) – *John Greig: My Story* (London, Headline Book Publishing, 2005)

Hayes, D.P. – *Scotland! Scotland!: A Complete Who's Who of Scotland Players Since 1946* (Edinburgh, Mercat Press Ltd., 2006)

Gaffney, C.T. – *Temples of the Earthbound Gods* (Austin, University of Texas Press, 2008)

Grant, M. and Robertson, R. – *The Management: Scotland's Great Football Bosses* (Edinburgh, Birlinn Ltd, 2010)

Keevins, H. and McCarra, K. – *100 Cups: The Story of the Scottish Cup* (Edinburgh, Mainstream Publishing, 1985)

Paterson, J. and Scott, D. – *Black and White Magic: 1959–1970 The Halcyon Days of Dunfermline Athletic Football Club* (Dunfermline, Paterson and Scott, 1984)

Rafferty, J. – *One Hundred Years of Scottish Football* (London, Pan Books, 1973)

Robertson, F.H.C. – *The Men with the Educated Feet: A Statistical History of Queen's Park* (Glasgow, Queen's Park Supportes' Association, 1984)

Rollin, J. – *The Guinness Football Fact Book Second Edition* (Enfield, Guinness Publishing, 1993)

Ross, D. – *The Roar of the Crowd* (Glendaruel, Argyll Publishing, 2005)

Taylor, H. – *Great Masters of Scottish Football* (London, Sportsman Book Club, 1968)

Taylor, H. – *The Scottish Football Book 1955–56* (London, Stanley Paul and Co Ltd, 1956)

Turner, S. – *If Only: An Alternative History of the Beautiful Game* (Worthing, Pitch Publishing, 2017)

Sandler, S. and Brogan, J. – *The Wee Red Book: 2018–2019* (Newsquest Limited, 2018)

Scragg, S. – *A Tournament Frozen in Time: The Wonderful Randomness of the European Cup Winners' Cup* (Worthing, Pitch Publishing, 2019)

Scragg, S. – *Where the Cool Kids Hung Out: The Chic Years of the UEFA Cup* (Worthing, Pitch Publishing, 2020)

Watson, M. – *Rags to Riches: The Official History of Dundee United* (Dundee, David Winter and Son Ltd, 1985)

The Association of Football Statisticians – *Scottish Football League Cup: 1940–1984*

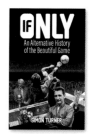

Several club websites were particularly useful including:

www.afc.co.uk (Aberdeen)
www.thecelticwiki.com (Celtic)
www.arabarchive.co.uk (Dundee United)
dafc.co.uk (Dunfermline Athletic)
hibshistoricaltrust.org.uk (Hibernian)
www.perthstjohnstonefc.co.uk (St Johnstone)

Acknowledgements

Several knowledgeable individual supporters also helped us out so special thanks go to Neil Wylie (Celtic), Scott Cockburn (Hearts) and Brian Johnson (Hibernian).

And finally, a big, big thank you to all at Pitch Publishing who made our 'Scottish hat-trick' possible.

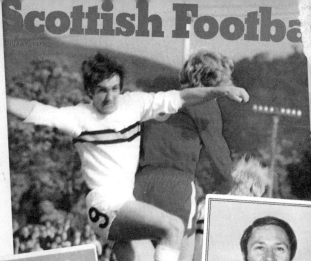

FOOTBALL SCOT

WEDNESDAY, AUGUST 25, 1971. No. 61

Scotland's OWN Football Magazine

is Ibrox
uble act
ks a
nner
Page 14

Scotland boss—
Our tip
for the job
Page 6

New Morton star nearly
went to Spurs—
Page 10

Scottish Footba

IN COLOUR—Alan Anderson and John Whitef

WILLIE RENTON
DUNFERMLINE
LEFT HALF

NEIL MARTIN
INSIDE FORWARD
QUEEN OF THE SOUTH F.C.

DOUG COWIE

DUNDEE & SCOTLAND

JIM FALLON
CLYDEBANK
DEFENDER

NAL STADIUM · LONDON N.5.

THE RANGERS
GLASGOW

Rangers
(GLASGOW)

European Champion Club's Cup
PRELIMINARY ROUND THIRD MATCH

Wednesday, 4th November, 1964
KICK-OFF 7.30 P.M.

Red Star
(BELGRADE)

FICIAL PROGRAMME   ONE SHILLING

FOOTBALL SCOT

Scotland's OWN Footba

WEEK BEGINNING WED., AUG

No. 58

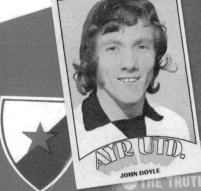

AYR UTD.
JOHN DOYLE

TONE'S SECRET FOR EUROPE SUCC
THE TRUTH ABOUT THOSE SOCCER SPRINTERS
JUNIOR PREVIEW – KEEP YOUR EYES ON ST.